Fundamentals of Managing Risk and Insurance

Charles Andoh

Fundamentals of Managing Risk and Insurance

A Focus on Frontier Markets

Springer

Charles Andoh
Department of Finance
University of Ghana Business School
Accra, Ghana

ISBN 978-981-95-4580-3 ISBN 978-981-95-4581-0 (eBook)
https://doi.org/10.1007/978-981-95-4581-0

This Springer imprint is published by the registered company Springer Nature Singapore Pte Ltd.
The registered company address is: 152 Beach Road, #21-01/04 Gateway East, Singapore 189721, Singapore

To my family: Patience, Abena, Janice, Abba and Brachah

Preface

A cursory look at the literature depicts a paucity of work that explains what insurers do to a person with little or no knowledge of insurance. This book fills this gap by explaining the basic concepts of risk and insurance in non-technical terms. It is intended to be used as a textbook for undergraduate students in economics, business schools or students enrolled in insurance, finance and financial planning programmes. The book can be used as a supplement to core reading by students studying finance, insurance, risk management or any related field. It can also be used by individuals, businesses and organisations that need a basic knowledge of risk, insurance and the methods for its management.

Every purchaser of an insurance product needs a basic knowledge of insurance: the benefits of the product purchased, the principles that govern the insurance product that has been purchased, the implicit benefits of insurance policies, the regulations that govern insurance contract between the purchaser and the insurance company. Also, when a loss occurs, and the payment of a claim is delayed, the insured only interacts with the insurer. However, there are other third parties who are indirectly implicated when a covered loss occurs. For example, a report from a medical officer may be needed by the insurer for a decision to be made. If the report does not arrive, the insurer cannot proceed with the disbursement of benefits.

Chapter 1 deals with the basic concepts of risk, the need to understand the risk concept and the methods for managing risk exposures. Any loss that occurs has an indirect loss. Even for covered losses, indirect loss does occur. The time between when a claim is reported and when an insurer honours his or her side of the contract, could lead to losses that must be carefully managed. The chapter discusses certain risk management techniques that will assist mitigate losses that can occur and the resulting indirect losses without having to employ insurance at all.

Chapter 2 discusses the features of risk for which an insurer can provide cover for, and the benefits of insurance. It also examines the principles under which insurance business operates. The chapter further highlights the point that the insurance market can be risky for insurance companies because of the presence of fraudsters who are ever ready to take advantage of insurers. Methods adopted by insurers to mitigate the effects of fraud are also discussed.

Chapter 3 focuses on forms of insurance products traded on the insurance market space and their benefits. The list has been divided into non-life and life insurance products. The non-life insurance products cover any insurable loss other than life of a person. The premium paid for non-life insurance products is usually on a one-time basis. The chapter also presents a brief discussion on bonds which are not insurance products but a contract between three parties: the principal, the contractor and the guarantee.

Chapter 4 deals with the risk exposures inherent in the home and discusses risk mitigating measures including insurance that provide solutions. Defiant behaviour that confronts every society is discussed and the role of insurance in minimising its impact on society is provided. The chapter ends with festivities and examines the inherent risk in these celebrations and suggests methods for its management.

The extractive sector provides jobs for people and revenue for governments. In Chapter 5, some risk exposures in the petroleum, mining, timber and the rubber industries are discussed including methods for managing the risk exposures identified. The chapter ends with the area of construction which strictly speaking does not belong to the extractive sector but uses raw materials (aggregates) used for the sector.

People, goods and services must necessarily move around, and it is the transport sector that is responsible for this function. Chapter 6 deals with this sector which comprises road, water, air, rail and other means of conveying people. The major threats posed by these sectors are discussed and methods for managing the identified risks and financing losses that might arise.

Chapter 7 discusses other industries where there is considerable risk exposure and where the acquisition of insurance can provide some solutions. These industries include fishing, alcohol, hawking, drug peddling and the scrap metal sectors. The threats posed by these sectors are discussed along with loss control and loss finance measures. The role of insurance in combating drug peddling is also examined.

Chapter 8 focuses on the insurance market and the competitive nature of the environment in which insurers operate. One of the desirable requirements of a perfect competitive market is that sellers (insurers) and buyers (policyholders) should have the freedom of entry and exit into and from the market. The chapter discusses the imperfections on the market that make this desirability an impossible task. The factors limiting the patronage of insurance products are considered along with the methods for marketing insurance products. The practice where some insurers sell their products below the market rate premium (called underpricing), the reasons triggering this practice, its effects and how it can be curbed are also discussed.

The existence of imperfections on the insurance market calls for the need for the market to be regulated. Chapter 9 centres on insurance regulation and the reasons underlying insurance regulation. It also discusses the bodies responsible for regulating the insurance market, the need for making certain products compulsory, the need for motivating the regulator and methods that can be implemented to regulate the regulator.

Chapter 10 focuses on premium and the management of claims. Proper management of premiums collected will ensure that the promised benefits by the insurer will be paid. This chapter discusses the areas that the premium collected by insurers can be invested for both non-life and life insurance products. The value of any insurance cover is judged by the way claims are handled. The reasons for the delay of payment of claims not only on the part of policyholders and insurers but also intermediaries who are no signatories to the contract between the insurer and the insured are considered. The reasons that slow down the work of intermediaries and which affects speedy payment of claims, the liability determination process and the practical steps that can be implemented by insurers to minimise delay in the payment of claims are also examined.

How to Use the Book

The book can be used as a semester course in introduction to insurance, introduction to risk management or risk management and insurance. Aspects can also be embedded in a course on counselling for students studying counselling as a major or as a course for students studying financial planning or personal financial management programmes.

Chapter 1 that provides the basic concepts in risk must be treated followed by the basic insurance concepts in Chap. 2. Chapter 3, which introduces the forms of insurance products typically available on the insurance market should also be treated. Chapter 4 through to Chap. 7 are the applications of the first three chapters in the home, the extractive industry, the transportation industry and other industries such as fishing, alcohol, waste management and the scrap sector. These can be selected depending on the problems that pertains in the jurisdiction the course is delivered. They can also be selected based on the title of the course being delivered. Chapter 8 discusses insurance markets and competition which is a specialised topic for insurance students or marketing students enrolled in risk management and insurance programmes. Aside mainstream insurance students who need to worry about insurance regulation, the content of Chap. 9, should appeal to students studying law who have chosen risk management and insurance as an elective course. Chapter 10 discusses premium and claim management. The first part on premium management should be ideal for finance students who have intention of working in the insurance sector. The remaining part of this chapter should appeal to all categories of students enrolled in a risk management and insurance course.

In an Introduction to Insurance course, after the treatment of the first three chapters, Chapter 4 can be elected as an application of the things learnt in the first three chapters. This should then be followed with Chaps. 8–10.

In an Introduction to Risk Management course, after the treatment of the first three chapters, Chaps. 4 and 6 can be elected as applications of concepts learnt in the first three chapters. Chapters 9 and 10 can then be treated.

As a Risk Management and Insurance course, after the treatment of chapters 1–3, Chapters 4–7 can be treated. Then Chaps. 9 and 10 follow.

If the course is embedded in counselling course, after the delivery of the first three chapters, Chapter 4 must be taught which conveys the risk exposures in the home and the methods that exist for its management. Aspects of Chapter 7 on drugs dealing with how insurance is available in its management should also be treated. The second part of Chapter 10 that deals with claim management can be taught if time permits.

I will be most grateful to receive your comments on any aspect of the book.

Legon, Accra, Ghana Charles Andoh

Acknowledgements

Many people have contributed in diverse ways in coming up with this book. First and foremost, my students for nearly two decades from whose class interactions was the motivation for writing this book. The book has evolved mostly as the fruit of their hard work. I received valuable inputs from Michael Kofi Andoh, Margaret Momo Laryea, Isaac Akomea-Frimpong and Ernest Amartey-Vondee who read the earlier draft of the book. Several of my National Service Personnel assistants namely, Sefakor Agbesi, Yasmine Baryeh, Chantelle Affum and Gifty Mbeah-Baiden contributed in diverse ways.

John Stuart and Gordon Senanau Adika performed fantastic jobs with editing the book and providing numerous suggestions to improve the content of the book.

I am most grateful to them all.

Contents

Definition of Terms

Admitted assets	the assets of an insurer that are easily converted into cash.
Adverse selection	the effect of insurance on the insured's incentive to reduce losses.
Agent	a person employed by an insurance company to assist with the sale of insurance products.
Annuity	a contract between an insurer and an annuitant (the person whose life the contract depends) that continues for the annuitant's entire life.
Appraiser	a person who determines the value of property, assets or damages for insurance purposes.
Asymmetric information	arises when one party to a transaction has superior information than the other.
Bancassurance	a term used to describe the collaboration between banks and insurance companies to distribute insurance products.
Bankruptcy law	a system of rules that governs situations where individuals, businesses or organisations have large amount of debt and are seeking a way to address it.
Benefit	the proceeds that accrue from an insurance policy.
Cascading failures	exist when the failure of one financial institution is the cause of failure of others.
Claim	tangible result of insuring.
Conditions	are provisions embedded in an insurance contract that qualify or place limitations on the insurer's promise to perform a certain act.
Contract	(see insurance contract)
Cover	the financial value of an insurance policy.
Covered loss	financial losses that an insurer will provide reimbursement within the terms of the insurance contract.

Debt instruments	a fixed-income security that legally mandates the debtor to provide lender interest and principal.
Defiant behaviour	a type of behaviour exhibited by children and young people that is not accepted by society.
Dividend policy	the annual gain from operations distributed in the form of dividends to policyholders in life insurance products.
Drug cartels	an organisation that promotes, controls and involves itself with the dissemination of illegal drugs.
Drug peddler	a person who sells illegal or unapproved drugs to people.
Economic loss	a financial loss experienced by a policyholder either directly and/or consequential.
Excess loss	a technique for sharing losses where the insurer only pays the surplus loss of the other insurer's policy's limit at the time of the loss.
Expected loss	the expected value of a loss distribution.
Experience rating	the modification of an insurance class rate based on the previous loss history of the insured.
Exposure	situation or circumstance in which a loss is possible, regardless of whether a loss occurs or not.
Express conditions	conditions that are explicitly stated in an insurance contract.
Express warranty	an explicit statement (promise) that a product or service will perform according to some standard.
Facultative reinsurance	reinsurance effected item by item and accepted or declined by the reinsuring company after scrutiny.
Facultative treaty reinsurance	a type of reinsurance in which the terms are set but neither the ceding insurer nor the reinsurer is obligated to participate in any arrangement with respect to any business.
Financial return	the amount (money) made or lost on an investment over a period.
Hawker	a street vendor, officially unauthorised, sell goods (usually small items) in metropolitan areas in developing countries.
Homogeneous	of similar kind or characteristics.
Implied condition	conditions that must be fulfilled prior to the formation of an insurance contract.
Implied warranty	an implicit performance guarantee that usually accompanies the sale of any product or service.
Indemnity	restoring a person or an entity to the position held immediately before a loss.

Indemnity contract	a type of contract in which the policyholder cannot recover more than their economic loss.
Insurable interest	the stake or ownership that insured has in the good for which insurance is being sought.
Insurable risk	a type of risk that an insurer can provide cover to the requesting applicant
Insurance	the sharing or pooling of a risk among a large group of people.
Insurance contract	a legal document that represents the agreement between the insured and the insurer.
Insurance market	a market where insurance products are traded.
Internal risk reduction	a method of handling risk and loss exposures whereby individuals, households and firms devise their own means of reducing the frequency and/or severity of losses without employing external parties.
Judgement of proof	a person who does not have sufficient money or assets to meet a court judgement.
Liability insurance	typically covers damages to other people's property (e.g., their cars) as well as medical costs for injuries you are responsible for.
Loss adjuster	a person who investigates losses.
Loss avoidance	*an* extreme form of loss control that involves a complete exit from a risky activity.
Loss control	measures put in place by an entity to reduce the frequency and/or severity of loss occurrences.
Loss finance	the financial arrangements put in place to cater for possible losses that might arise.
Loss reduction	measures put in place to lessen the severity (magnitude) of a loss.
Market power	the ability of one or few providers to control the price of a product.
Material	an information which can alter the terms at which an insurer enters a contract with a prospective policyholder.
Mis-selling	misrepresentation of a service or product suitability.
Moral hazard	a situation whereby an insured entity or individual does not take the necessary precautions to prevent or mitigate losses, because that entity or person has insurance.
Non-insurance transfer	a method of risk transfer whereby an entity facing a risk exposure goes into contract with another entity to transfer the risk.
Nuisance suit	a frivolous lawsuit.

Particular risk	a type of risk that affects only a portion of the entire population.
Peril	the cause of possible loss; the event insured against.
Pre-existing condition	an undisclosed health condition that was present within a specified number of years before an insurance policy was issued and required medical attention.
Principle of indemnity	the insured should not make a profit from a loss.
Pro rata loss	a technique for sharing losses where the insurer shares the loss incurred with the policyholder and any third-party insurance in proportion to the amount of the coverage.
Proposer	a person or an organisation/business that possesses a risk exposure and is seeking protection from an insurance company.
Reinsurance	insurance for insurance companies. It is an insurance placed by an underwriter in another company to cut down the amount of the risk assumed under the original insurance.
Reserves	the amount (of money) the insurer needs to ensure that obligations under the contract can be met.
Residual market	is the collective supply of insurance products by insurance companies in a given market to people who cannot obtain insurance at the voluntary market.
Retention	an individual or firm retains all or part of a loss.
Retention limit	the amount of insurance retained by the ceding (primary) company.
Risk averse	a person who prefers a certain amount of wealth to a risky situation with the same expected wealth.
Risk load	extra amount that policyholders must pay to compensate investors for providing capital for running an insurance company.
Runs on a bank	creditors demanding their money at once, resulting in the collapse of a bank.
Securitisation of risk	means that an insurable risk is transferred to the capital markets through the creation of a financial instrument, such as futures contract.
Soft market	these are periods at the insurance market when insurance coverage is restricted, and the price of insurance products are high.
Surplus position	the difference between an insurer's assets and liabilities.

Surveyors	conduct risk assessment for insurance companies' clients.
Systematic risk	risk that remains after extensive diversification. This risk is also called the nondiversifiable risk.
Systemic risk	risk associated with the losses of a financial institution due to runs on a bank or cascading failures.
Terms of trade	the number of days to recover debt.
Terrorism	is the act of causing fear and panic.
Terrorist	a person who use unlawful violence and intimidation especially against civilians in pursuit of political objectives.
Tort	a legal wrong which one person or entity commits against another person or entity and for which the usual remedy is award of damages.
Tortfeasor	a person or entity that commits a wrongful act that courses another person or organisation to suffer financial loss.
Umpire	an unbiased third party that provides resolution to a dispute between an insurer and an insured about a claim after reviewing all documentations and make an objective decision about the value of property damage.
Underpricing	the deliberate act of charging below the market rate premium.
Underwriting	the process by which an insurance company decides whether to issue requested insurance, and if it decides to issue it, on what terms and conditions and at what price.
Underwriting cycles	phenomenon (mostly prevalent in many lines of property-liability and business insurance) where premiums exhibited a cycle around the fair premium.
Unearned reserve	the portion of premium received that have had no claim made on them yet.
Valued policy	a type of policy for which the insurer pays a stated sum irrespective of the actual economic loss.
Variance	variability around the expected loss.
Warranty	is a condition in an insurance contract which describes the obligation of the insured.

Chapter 1
Basic Risk Concepts

Abstract This chapter presents the foundational concepts of risk that all individuals should be familiar with, underscoring the importance of developing a comprehensive understanding of these concepts. It outlines the basic approaches to risk management, including loss control, loss financing, and internal risk-reduction mechanisms. The discussion subsequently focuses on internal and external risk management techniques as they apply to both enterprises and households. Furthermore, the chapter differentiates between direct and indirect losses, providing illustrative examples and emphasising the necessity of considering indirect losses whenever a loss event occurs. The chapter concludes by proposing a range of risk-mitigation strategies relevant to individuals and organisations.

Keywords Direct loss · Indirect loss · Internal risk reduction · Loss control · Loss finance · Risk

Introduction

Risk is embedded in every activity we undertake. Be it the games we play, the travelling we do, the investments we undertake, the decisions we take and even the food we eat.

In playing a game, there is the possibility of losing the game, getting injured or even, in rare cases, death. Travelling is an activity that clearly has risk embedded within it because of the possibility of an accident, injury and perhaps even worse death. Investing involves taking a risk by placing one's capital into a project with the objective of gaining financial return on it. Even though the investor hopes for a positive return, there is the possibility of a negative outcome. The uncertainty makes this activity risky. Eating also involves some risk because the food we eat may be contaminated and cause illness or contain something that could choke us. The decisions we take in every aspect of life involve some element of risk.

Risk is a word that has many meanings that depend upon the context in which it is used. This section discusses several of these meanings of risk.

C. Andoh, *Fundamentals of Managing Risk and Insurance*,
https://doi.org/10.1007/978-981-95-4581-0_1

A situation is riskier than another when the expected loss from one activity is greater than the other. For example, a young male driver is riskier than a middle-aged driver because he is more likely to be involved in an accident. Youthful exuberance and inexperience are likely to make the younger driver less risk-averse and more adventurous than a more careful and experienced middle-aged driver. In another example, if an airline promises that the likelihood of a fatal crash on their aircraft is one in a million trips every five years while another states that the possibility is two in a million trips every five years, the latter airline will be considered the riskier proposition. Also, if there are two investment opportunities, X and Y, and the expected worst-case loss from investment X is 200 and 700 from investment Y, then investment Y is riskier than investment X.

Another way of defining risk is as follows: a situation is riskier than another if the variance of one alternative is greater than the other provided that the expected loss is the same for both situations. If investments X and Y have the same expected loss and the variance of Y is 50 and that of X 25, then investment Y is said to be riskier than investment X. Thus, the outcome of investment X is more predictable than investment Y (i.e., there is less variability around the expected loss of investment X).

Risk can also be defined as the possibility that something bad happens resulting in financial loss. For example, thieves or armed robbers may break into someone's home or business taking valuables and resulting in financial loss. Terrorists can attack innocent lives and property resulting in financial loss. A consumer may sue a manufacturer for injuries sustained using a defective product. A motorist may sue someone who negligently damages his/her car. A severe financial loss occurs when a cargo ship fully laden with goods is lost at sea or attacked by pirates. All these events trigger financial loss and consequently are exposed to risk.

Understanding the Concept of Risk

Understanding the concept of risk is very important because it makes the individual, firm or organisation aware of the possible losses that can occur. With adequate knowledge of risk, one can find measures to minimise the potential impacts.

An individual or business exposed to risk can suffer huge losses. Many firms have gone out of business because of a lack of insight about their risk exposure. Some risks result in a loss of life. If an electrician takes the risk of using sub-standard materials in wiring a client's building, it may catch fire and consequently destroy property and potentially lead to loss of life. If a builder takes the risk of saving money by building a weak foundation, the building may collapse and kill inhabitants. If a driver takes the risk of speeding to get to a destination quickly, both the driver, other road users and pedestrians are at risk of injury or death from an accident. Therefore, understanding the concept of risk can allow a person or a business to take measures to prevent or minimise the possible losses that can occur through prudent risk management. For example, a person or a business can insure itself to mitigate the financial consequences of a loss.

In addition, understanding the concept of risk makes individuals or businesses conscious of the fact that a loss can occur in almost any activity. This knowledge often helps to avoid the shock and disbelief that comes about as and when a loss occurs. By understanding the concept of risk, one can forecast potential losses and not only find ways to minimise their impacts but also reduce the losses and their effects when they occur.

In a nutshell, understanding the concept of risk allows us to make better choices with regard to the activities we undertake (compare with Sweeting, 2011, section 1.2).

Methods of Handling Risk

Risk evaluation involves the process of measuring the frequency and severity of losses faced by a firm or an individual.

Organisations undertake critical evaluations of risk and decide on which control measures to use. These include loss control measures, loss finance measures or internal risk reduction.

Loss Control

Loss control measures are put in place by an entity to reduce the frequency and/or severity of loss occurrences. Three forms of loss control measures can be identified. These are loss prevention, loss reduction and loss avoidance.

Loss prevention is a form of loss control that involves putting in place measures to reduce the frequency of loss occurrences. For example, to manage the number of times losses occur in homes, individuals build fences, walls and/or install security systems around their homes to prevent burglars from entering their premises. Also, educating a child to the university level where he or she can subsequently find well remunerated employment and manage his or her own affairs decreases the possibility of the child engaging in deviant behaviour, thus reducing the potential costs to society. Similarly, communities form neighbourhood watchdog committees to deter and lower the occurrence of stealing/burglary in their area.

Loss reduction is putting in place measures to lessen the severity (magnitude) of a loss. For example, installing automatic water sprinklers in offices and homes reduces the severity of a loss should a building catch fire. Placing plywood over a broken window prevents water from entering and causing further damage and prevents intruders from making away with valuables. To minimise the possibility of legal action brought against a pharmaceutical company from consumers using the company's products, the company can ensure that its products are certified as being safe. Thus, loss reduction seeks to tolerate the loss by finding ways and means to reduce its severity or magnitude.

Some actions undertaken are both loss prevention and loss reduction measures. Police vests worn by police officers in their line of duty affect the frequency and severity of losses. The vest reduces the frequency of fatalities in the case of shooting exchanges. The vest at the same time lessens the severity of injury that might occur. With the seat belt, for example, in the event of an accident, it decreases the frequency of injury that may occur and potentially affect the magnitude of injury.

Loss avoidance is an extreme form of loss control that involves a complete exit from a risky activity. That is, loss avoidance seeks to remove the possibility of a loss. For example, a pharmaceutical company might cease production of a product to terminate any lawsuits brought against it by users of its product. Japan's biggest car maker, Toyota, recalled all 2006 models of its Corolla model because of faulty engineering that had been identified as the cause of accidents. Such recalls are extremely costly for a company but could help protect against potentially greater losses incurred by worldwide lawsuits from users of that model of car.

Loss Finance

On the other hand, loss finance involves making financial arrangements to cater for possible losses that might arise (i.e., a financial arrangement put in place to fund the cost of a loss that is likely or is bound to happen). With this measure, the firm or individual sets aside finance or makes available financial resources before the loss occurrence. For instance, to reduce the scourge of waste plastic bags in a city, a company might put in place rewards for people who gather the waste and bring the bags to a collection point for recycling. Loss finance can be through retention, insurance and non-insurance transfers. Under retention, the loss is retained and treated financially. With insurance, the entity pays a premium to cover the possible loss that can arise. Under non-insurance transfers, an entity facing a risk exposure goes into contract with another entity to transfer the risk.

The difference between loss control and loss finance measures is that whereas a loss finance measure is necessarily a pre-loss decision made by an individual or a firm to finance a possible loss that might arise, loss control measures can be undertaken both pre-loss and/or post-loss. For example, insurance is purchased prior to the loss occurrence to finance a possible loss that might arise, whereas an individual may cover a wounded hand with a bandage to reduce or prevent further loss of blood following a cut (post-loss). On the other hand, building a fence or wall around a home close to a road where there is heavy traffic prevents the possibility of a child from being hit by a car (a pre-loss decision). Also, most loss control measures are enacted by the person or entity directly affected, whereas loss finance measures are mostly instituted with external parties.

Internal Risk Reduction

Internal risk reduction is a method of handling risk and loss exposures whereby individuals, households and firms devise their own means of reducing the frequency and/or severity of losses without employing external parties. For example, a firm can diversify its areas of business or invest in information as an internal risk reduction mechanism, whereas for an individual, methods such as good personal hygiene, putting in place home security systems or driving carefully will reduce their exposure to risk.

Internal Risk Management Techniques for Businesses

Competent Staff

By employing qualified and competent staff, the risks of making decisions that may lead to large losses are reduced. Qualified financial analysts, accountants and insurers will take decisions that are unlikely to lead to large losses. Similarly, competent lawyers will ensure that liabilities to third parties are avoided wherever possible. When experts are employed, the likelihood that they will make mistakes in their day-to-day activities is also reduced.

Legal Requirements

Every firm is established through a legal jurisdiction. Thus, this legal environment imposes some legal obligations on the firm, along with the risk of being legally liable if those legal requirements are not satisfied. For example, the Ghanaian Companies code 1963 (Act 179) requires that no company shall operate beyond six months without a shareholder. If the company fails to meet this obligation, it becomes liable to a fine. Thus, for a firm to avoid the risk of legal liability, it must meet its legal requirements.

Workplace Safety

A business can reduce its loss exposure by ensuring safety at work. The business should have an effective health and safety policy that must be strictly followed and led by a qualified expert. Employees are the backbone of the business and as such it is important to ensure that safety measures such as warning signs to highlight dangerous areas or machines are provided. In addition, there should be good ventilation, the work environment should be clean and the floors kept dry. The business should fix smoke detectors to detect early signs of fire. For businesses in sectors such as construction and manufacturing, protective clothing, boots, helmets, goggles, nose and face masks all reduce the possibility of employee injury. A business should outline the safety measures that it expects its workers to abide by. For example, a company can provide directional signs on how a building can be evacuated in case of fire.

Training

Firms must provide training for new employees and re-training where necessary for existing employees. For a business to be continuously productive, the skills and expertise of its employees must be up to date with current trends in the industry in which the business works. To ensure this, new employees and existing ones must be given the requisite training to help them acquire the skills needed for a high level of productivity. Training on internal structures and the use of machines, especially heavy equipment that is used in the business, is also important in reducing the possibility of injury. Effective training helps to reduce the operational risks of businesses.

Security Systems

The firm can reduce its exposure to risk internally by putting in place proper security systems. The assets of a company are very important to both its productivity and on-going existence. These assets need to be protected against risks such as fire or burglary. Security guards can be employed to deter robbery. The firm can reduce its fire and burglary risks by respectively providing fire extinguishers and putting in place burglar alarms. Management must ensure that all electrical gadgets are switched off throughout the night to reduce the possibility of fire. The business can also build transparent walls in cases where the walling of the business premises is deemed necessary. Transparent walls are helpful because they enable people outside the premises to see and report unlawful acts. Closed-Circuit Television (CCTV) cameras can be fixed around and within the business premises. This will help keep track of people who enter the business area and identify suspicious activity.

Sometimes, businesses fall prey to the fraudulent schemes of certain individuals. To prevent this, the company can, for example, use identification cards for all employees or encode classified information so that it is available to only a select few employees. The human resources personnel should also thoroughly vet prospective employees to prevent recruiting people who have obtained false references. This will prevent the business from losing money through the leaking of important information and losing both time and money through hiring, training and managing unscrupulous individuals.

Terms of Trade

A business can also reduce its risk of insolvency by putting in place good terms of trade. These are the conditions by which the business extends credit to its clients. The terms of trade (i.e., the number of days to recover debt) must be sustainable so that the firm's debtors do not default, leading to the insolvency of the business.

Culture of Maintenance

Routine checks and maintenance should be done on a regular basis to identify faulty machines and equipment and carry out repairs on them. This helps prevent operational risk that is a result of failed internal systems. Such checks will identify exposed wires, leakages and wear and tear on the assets of the business.

Monitoring and Evaluation System

The business should have well-structured and effective monitoring and evaluation system. This is particularly necessary in the Accounting and Finance departments. Such a system will check for theft, misappropriation of funds and fraud. An internal audit committee can be established to evaluate the activities of workers and officials in these departments. The risk of insolvency can be reduced if such a system is in place and these activities are done regularly and effectively.

Human Resources Management

Businesses should have an effective human resources management system. Since businesses do not operate in isolation their human capital must be motivated and properly rewarded. Benefits, both monetary and nonmonetary, the offer of flexible hours and telecommuting are attractive to employees. Stress management should consider ways of bringing out the best in employees to increase productivity. This, when done well, leads to employee satisfaction, loyalty and commitment, protecting the company against the costs of high staff turnover.

Investment in Information

The business can also allocate part of its budget to invest in obtaining information. Most businesses have access to information through various media. However, a forward-looking business can pay for superior information obtained through market research. With such findings, the business can better make sales forecasts and plan effectively. This proactive step helps the company to adapt in times of economic difficulty. In addition, it helps the business to identify and take advantage of opportunities that could put it one step ahead of its competitors.

Technology

The business must ensure that it invests in effective and up-to-date technology to support the accuracy, speed and efficiency of its operations. The company should hire skilled personnel to manage the upkeep of their business systems. The company should also purchase good and modern computer equipment and regularly update and maintain it to enhance business activities.

Diversification

A business should, if possible, invest in diverse assets. This way, losses from one asset are likely to be offset by profits from another reducing the risk of large losses. For example, a company that buys and sells building materials might branch out into real estate. Therefore, when the building materials business is not thriving, it can still benefit from sales in the real estate business.

Promotion and Rewards

A business can reduce the risk of a worker being unhappy or unproductive in their job and moving to a competitor by rewarding and promoting hardworking employees. In addition, a 'no accident bonus' can be instituted by the business to induce employees to follow health and safety rules to minimise risk exposure. Businesses that implement measures to reduce the frequency and severity of loss reduce risk internally in their organisations.

Division of Labour

There should be a clear division of labour and specialisation in the business to reduce the level of mistakes and erroneous transactions. There should be departments within the business and each department should have a head that reports to the chief operations officer. This way, communication barriers in the organisation will be reduced.

External Risk Reduction Techniques for Businesses

Insurance

One way a business can decrease its risk exposure externally is through adequate insurance. Businesses can, for example, insure their employees and staff against injury in the workplace. They can also insure the business against losses caused by fire and theft. Most businesses own machines and other equipment that can cause harm to their users. With insurance, when a loss occurs, the insurer reinstates the business to its pre-loss financial position. In addition, insurers offer loss control services that businesses can tap to minimise their loss exposure.

A business can also buy insurance policies to protect against errors, omissions and misstatements arising from the actions of directors or managers. Without insurance, huge sums of money can be lost as compensation to third parties in the case of malpractice.

Non-insurance Transfers

The business can transfer its risk exposure to a third party by sub-contracting some operations of the firm to another that has the expertise to handle the risk exposure. This can also be done through disclaimer notices to consumers on the firm's products. For example, some hotels or shopping malls have disclaimer notices that state: 'all customers who park their cars in the car park do so at their own risk'. Thus, the risk exposure of the firm is shifted to its customers.

Hedging

Hedging is an investment to reduce the risks of adverse price movements in an asset. Businesses hedge because the marginal costs of a product can differ across different countries and so they shift cash flows to equalise marginal costs. Another reason for hedging is because marginal benefits can differ between countries, so businesses shift cash flows from low benefit states to high benefit states. For example, a firm that uses a lot of crude oil or petroleum in its operations might enter into an agreement with an oil producing company and agree on the price they want to pay for crude oil today and for a specific period in the future, irrespective of the changes in the price of crude oil in the future.

Educational Campaigns

A business can embark on an educational campaign on the use of its products. This will reduce the possibility of the company's products being used unsafely and consequently reduce its product liability exposure.

Legal Advisors

A business can employ the services of seasoned legal experts to defend the business against lawsuits brought against it and ensure that it is compliant with all relevant regulations.

Reducing the Risk of Liability Lawsuits

One way to reduce the risk of product liability lawsuits is to make the product safer for consumers by design changes, greater quality control in the manufacturing process or by providing warning labels or safety instructions to mitigate against the possibility that consumers will use the product dangerously. Also, the business can establish a specific department to be responsible for consumer feedback and service. Information collected can also be used to improve the product. In an extreme case, the manufacturer can stop production altogether.

The business can buy liability insurance to reduce the direct impact of the verdict of any lawsuit brought against it. Besides, the business can employ the services of a legal team to defend it especially in the case of a nuisance suit to serve as a deterrent to other consumers. An example is fraudulent or exaggerated compensation claims that are frequently brought against a business by consumers that use the firm product. The business must decide whether to incur greater cost in fighting these claims in the short run to deter others in the future. The business can also opt for out of court settlements with aggrieved individuals who may have been injured by a defective product.

The business should make regular checks on retailers to ensure that all expired products are removed from their shelves to reduce product liability risk. In extreme circumstances, a product recall of an unsafe product already supplied to consumers will reduce or eliminate further lawsuits.

The business can also issue disclaimers relieving them of responsibility from any damage caused by the use or improper use of their products (i.e., buyers use the product at their own risk). This will, however, likely reduce their sales.

The risk of product liability can also be lowered by effectively investing in information. Conducting research to identify any potential hazards a product may cause to consumers, and subsequently reducing those hazards by redesign. Firms may also sub-contract the manufacturing of their products to others to diversify risk and reduce losses that might occur. To avoid potential exposure to risk, firms should also ensure that their products are legally acceptable. For example, the production of cannabis ('wee' or marijuana) and cocaine is not legal in some countries.

It is also important for the business to check the way that their products are stored. If a product is stored at a temperature higher or lower than it should be, the quality can be affected.

One advantage of external risk management over internal risk management is that it relieves management of the burden of implementing appropriate risk management techniques and monitoring their effectiveness thereafter. This allows the management of a business to focus on its core operations while outsourcing risk management to specialists who have the skills and expertise to manage it.

Internal Risk Management Techniques for the Family

Instead of involving external sources in its risk reduction techniques, a family can reduce its exposure to risk internally.

Installation of Alarm or Sprinkler Systems

A family can install a smoke or burglar alarm system in the household to help detect early signs of fire or intruders. Sprinkler systems are another useful tool to help avoid or reduce the damage caused by fire. These devices not only reduce the chances of properties being damaged but also those of neighbours (third-party risk) in the event of a fire spreading outside the home.

Safe Practices

There should be fire extinguishers in critical areas of the house. The family should train its members on the use of automated fire sprinklers, fire extinguishers and the use of cooking gas in the home. Keeping gas cylinders in an enclosed space should be avoided as it increases the likelihood of fire. All of this will help the family combat the risk of fire to an extent and minimise the damage that could be caused. There should also be regular maintenance of electrical equipment and gas cylinders because when they are not maintained they can cause serious damage to life and property.

Families can also reduce the frequency of losses through theft by constructing transparent walls around their houses. This will enable neighbours and passers-by to have a clear view of what happens on the premises. While this measure reduces the family's privacy, solid walls will make it difficult for anyone to notice the presence of suspicious characters at the home. Walls also prevent children from straying onto busy streets. If the house has a swimming pool, it should be enclosed to prevent children from falling into it and drowning. Keeping house keys in obvious places such as under flowerpots and doormats should be avoided.

Security Systems

Burglary is a threat to all households. Families can protect themselves by buying a guard dog to alert them to the presence of intruders, especially at night. CCTV cameras can also be installed on the exterior of the house to monitor the comings and goings of people. This is an effective deterrent. Families can also install security doors at the entrance of their house so that only approved faces will be allowed in thus reducing the families' exposure to risks such as assault, theft, burglary and damage to property. Electrical wire mesh can be placed on the wall around the house to prevent thieves and robbers from assessing the home easily.

Personal Hygiene

Good personal hygiene of members of the family will minimise the cost of ill health and exposure to the risks of medical costs. Parents should inculcate in their children the practice of good personal hygiene. Children should be made to take their bath or shower regularly, brush their teeth twice a day and wash their hands with soap before and after eating. Having a good sanitary system in the home and keeping the surroundings clean and dry will reduce the likelihood of mosquitoes. Disposal bins with covers should be used and families should reduce waste by cooking only what they can eat. Items like plastic bags should be limited in use and should be properly discarded to avoid collecting water and serving as breeding ground for mosquitoes. First aid kits should be present in the house, but with all medication secured and kept away from children. These measures will minimise frequent visits to the doctor for minor illnesses or injuries.

Electrical Installations

Electrical wiring systems and lighting systems in the home should be properly installed and maintained. Families should check the background, legality and experience of personnel who do their wiring for them, to make sure that electrical accidents are avoided. This is crucial because faulty wiring can cause accidents at home especially when using electrical appliances. There is also the need for adequate lighting systems to prevent members of the family from running into objects and getting injured because of bad eyesight or darkness.

Regular Maintenance of Vehicles

Regular maintenance of vehicles can assist in reducing the risk exposure of a family to accidents.

Diet

Parents should provide a balanced diet to their families to ensure that they are healthy and avoid sickness. Fruit and vegetables provide vitamins and foods full of protein such as meat, fish and beans help to build the body. Families should reduce the intake of salty, sugary and oily foods that can cause diabetes and coronary diseases. In addition, families should endeavour to cook their own food instead of resorting to fast food. This reduces the exposure to diseases and sicknesses such as cholera and food poisoning.

Regular Exercise

A family can reduce its risk exposure to ill heath by regularly exercising their bodies. This may be done by weekly jogging or visits to the gym for workouts. People who exercise their bodies regularly are generally healthy and strong.

Set Expenditure Priorities

Another way the family can reduce its risk exposure internally is to set priorities and limits on the amount of money they spend on certain goods and services. Families should deliberate on their choice of expenditure so that they do not get into financial troubles. These troubles may arise when the family incurs debts from borrowing too much on credit when the products that they buy do not serve any essential or vital purpose for the day-to-day running of the home. Thus, proper setting of expenditure priorities will minimise the financial risk exposure internally.

Adequate Provision

Adequate provision of the needs of members of the family, especially children, is very important. A parent's inability to provide adequately for the needs of children can sometimes lead them into dangerous situations as they attempt to fend for themselves.

Parents should spend enough time with their children so that they can identify their needs and solve them, otherwise they may follow bad examples set by peers. Parents should encourage their children to be open about their problems. By doing so, the risk of children rebelling because of having to suppress their feelings is reduced.

Location of Residence

A family can reduce its risk exposure by carefully choosing the location of their house. Some areas are typically known to be targets for burglars or are exposed to natural hazards such as floods and earthquakes.

Investment

To combat the possibility of financial problems, a family can use a savings account and invest the funds realised. Profits from such investments can serve as a steady source of income to alleviate difficulties in cash flow. Families can also invest in treasury bills, fixed deposits and bonds that yield interest so that in the event of any loss these investments can be relied upon.

Slippery Floors

Families should avoid slippery floors. In homes where floors are tiled, woollen carpets can be used to avoid someone slipping. Alternatively, floor mops should be placed in easily accessible places in the house so that water that pours on the floor can easily be wiped off. Slippery floors can lead to accidents leading to broken bones and in some cases death.

External Risk Reduction Techniques for Families

Community Watch

There should be a neighbourhood watch scheme within the community where one resides. When members of the community are well known to each other it becomes more difficult for a burglar to pass unnoticed. In addition, families should have the contact numbers of neighbours and the emergency services so that they can be assisted when the need arises.

Security Guards

The family can employ the services of a security guard to protect their property at night or in their absence. While this measure may be costly, it may be costlier in the event of a burglary.

Insurance

The family can also buy insurance policies such as fire, property, education and life policies, among others, so that the financial burden is shifted to the insurance company in exchange for premiums. The premature death of the breadwinner of the family can have a dire financial consequence on a family. Insurance payments can serve as a source of income for the family in the event of the death of the breadwinner.

Direct and Indirect Losses

It is important to consider both direct and indirect losses when a loss occurs.

A direct loss is the loss suffered because of the occurrence of a peril. It is directly related to the loss occurrence, and it is the first loss discovered when a loss occurs.

An indirect loss (or consequential loss) is the loss suffered on account of a direct loss.

Some Examples of Direct and Indirect Losses

i. When a motor accident occurs and the windscreen of Kweku's car gets broken, the direct loss is the broken windscreen. Kweku might miss an important business meeting (an indirect loss) because of the damage to his car (the direct loss).
ii. Property loss because of fire. The cost of the property is the direct loss caused by the peril fire. An indirect loss could be the time lost in looking for a replacement.
iii. Goods stolen from a warehouse. Here the cost of the goods stolen is the direct loss caused by the peril theft. An indirect loss is the inability to supply retail outlets resulting in loss of customers.
iv. Embezzling of funds by an employee of a bank resulting in loss of money. The loss of money is a direct loss. News of embezzlement may cause customers to leave the bank which is an indirect loss by virtue of direct loss of money.
v. When a student does not study for an examination, the direct loss is the bad grade the student will get. An indirect loss may be that the study group may not

be available to support the student in preparation for a re-sit of the paper or may not gain admission to a Graduate School because of the bad grade obtained.

vi. If there is a legal case against an insurer, the direct loss is damages that will be slammed by the court. An indirect loss can be the time lost by the insurer's lawyers in defending the case.

vii. The loss of Ama's house by flood is a direct loss. An indirect loss may be that Ama has to live in a hotel for two months with its accompanying costs.

viii. Eating consistently late at night. The direct loss is sickness. The indirect loss is a person's inability to work when sick.

ix. When there is burglary in a home, the direct loss is the items that have been stolen. The indirect loss is time spent at the police station and loss of valuable work time.

The following provides further details about why it is important to consider indirect losses for an individual and firms or businesses. Risk mitigating strategies are then proposed.

Individual

The extent of the indirect loss could affect the individual more than the direct loss itself. Therefore, considering indirect losses creates room for these losses to be managed and hence a reduction of the cumulative losses that would be experienced. People will be aware of the consequences of certain loses and will improve on their loss control methods to reduce the frequency and severity. There are other reasons why it is important for anyone to look out for indirect loss anytime a loss occurs; these are examined below.

Financial Burden

Financial burden is one indirect loss that can happen to a victim and the family. In case of an accident and the victim involved is the breadwinner of the family, the accident will accumulate cost on the family in obtaining health care for the victim.

Decline in Standard of Living

The loss of one's job has consequential losses of increasing the dependency ratio and thereby reducing the standard of living the person and the person supporting the jobless. The purchasing power or the demand for certain goods and services of the person will be affected.

Increase in Social Vices

When a direct loss occurs such as loss of job, it can trigger social vices. One may resort to illegal or unacceptable ways of earning income. Fraud, armed robbery and prostitution may be taken up as means of survival. Also, when a loss occurs for which human life is lost, it could lead to a broken home especially if the dead person is the breadwinner of the home.

Accidents

Suppose a person's car breaks down on the way to work. The time spent in getting the car back on the road will eat into the time spent at work. As another example, if a house is lost as a result of fire, the house can be replaced in the form of cash, but the indirect loss incurred such as lodging in a hotel, can affect the owner financially.

Frustration

Indirect loss can make a person get frustrated. When a direct loss occurs, a person is already occupied in trying to solve it. The indirect losses may not sit well with a person leading to more frustration which could affect a person's productivity.

Firm

For a firm, indirect losses are very important to consider as they have the potential to affect many people and possibly lead to insolvency. They increase the cost of operation and make up the bulk of expenditure. It is therefore necessary that a firm consider indirect losses if it wishes to remain profitable. A firm's inability to meet its contractual obligation because of a direct loss could lead to legal costs obstructing the firm from achieving its strategic target. Also, considering indirect losses can help the firm put alternatives to ensure operations continue when a loss occurs. There are other reasons why indirect losses are to be studied in greater detail by the risk management function of any business or firm.

Loss Profit

When the plant of a firm breaks down, the loss of customers due to missing deadlines can lead to insolvency. Losses arising out of shut down of machine or power cuts can lead to loss of normal profit as operations seize reducing the output per day. There could be loss of customers to competitors who produce similar goods.

Extra Operating Expenses

When firm productive assets get destroyed through fire, there will be extra operating expenses on the firm. To honour its contractual agreements, there may be the need to rent a machine to continue production. Other expenses the firm may incur may include procurement costs, reconstruction costs or cost of purchasing a generator. A liability cost may arise when the peril that caused the loss affected third parties. These third parties may file lawsuits against the firm.

Brand

An indirect loss can affect the image of a firm. A low pay-out ratio of a bank as a result of shortage of its reserve will make the public lose trust and confidence, thus affecting its corporate image and status. People and other businesses that deal with the firm will be reluctant to do business with it.

Cost of Investment and Obtaining Loan

Another area a firm will suffer indirectly is investment. All investments made in the company's assets will be lost and it will be expensive for the firm to obtain external funds to start operations. This is because financial institutions and other lending institutions will incorporate the information about the loss in their pricing. Also, when a loss occurs, the money spent on replacing the lost items would have been invested to earn interest.

Job Security

No one would like to work in an environment with the potential of incurring losses because when a loss occurs they would lose their jobs. Therefore, seriously considering indirect losses and putting measures in place to mitigate its impact would give the assurance to workers that in the event of a loss, their jobs will be secured. This consideration should be paramount for every manager.

Risk Mitigating Strategies

Individuals

Loss finance can be used to manage consequential losses for an individual. In the event of a loss, a loss financing measure such as retention, or insurance can help reduce the financial impact of indirect losses that could occur. For example, insurance claims can help replace a stolen car and in turn reduce transportation costs using other means.

Loss control measures can be used to manage indirect losses. For example, the use of seat belts in a car reduces the impact of an accident and hence reduces the indirect losses that could have been incurred.

Loss Prevention

Regular maintenance and servicing of one's vehicle is necessary. Individuals should intermittently use public transport to reduce the frequency of usage of one's own vehicle and consequently a reduction of the pressure on the vehicle. Not drinking and driving, parking vehicles to rest when tired, securing homes with fire alarms and good locks and keeping dangerous materials out of the reach of children will assist to prevent loss occurring in the first place.

Loss Reduction

A motorbike can be purchased as a backup to a vehicle so that when the vehicle gets damaged the motorbike can be used to reduce transport costs and ensure that one does not miss out on an appointment.

Firm

For a firm, a loss finance measure such as insurance quickens the regeneration process, reducing the loss of customers and employees when a loss occurs. Liability insurance can be purchased to cater for any legal problems that may confront the firm. The company could also retain money with which it can quickly meet the financing needs when direct losses occur.

Loss control measures can also be employed. Installation of fire extinguishers at vantage points in a firm can help reduce the magnitude of losses should the firm catch fire. Fencing sensitive equipment to prevent authorised entry can also help. For example, securing the server room of an e-commerce company can help prevent consequential losses such as inaccessibility to websites by the company's employees if the server gets physically damaged.

The firm can invest in purchasing assets such as plants or generators. Thus, when there are power cuts or outages, the firm's plants automatically turn on and prevent interruptions in the production process. The firm should consistently check machines on a regular basis and service or replace worn out parts to avoid unnecessary breakdowns or shut down of the production.

Non-insurance transfers discussed earlier can be employed by a firm to reduce indirect losses that can occur.

Employees on the job need training and knowledge about machines being used. Protective clothing especially construction and metal related businesses can save some workers from injuries and consequently save the firm from losses.

Internal risk reduction can also be used to manage consequential losses. A firm can decide to diversify its funds into other different businesses so that if a loss occurs at one area, it does not affect the entire assets of the company. Alternatively, a firm can open different branches at different locations so that if the operations of one branch go bad, it can continue to do business in other branches. A firm can also keep its funds with multiple financial institutions, so that losses that may arise from the failure of one institution will reduce the impact of losses on a firm's finances. Investment in information regarding indirect losses that may arise out of a direct loss can position a firm better in the management of such losses.

Exercises

1. Explain with examples three important meanings of the concept of risk.
2. Why is it important to understand the concept of risk?
3. Risk is embedded in every area of life. Explain three activities in life where risk arises.
4. Explain the difference between loss control and loss finance measures.
5. What is internal risk reduction? Explain five major ways a business can reduce its risk exposure internally.

6. Explain how a business could reduce the risk of product liability caused by consumers injured by the business' products.
7. Explain five ways a family can reduce their risk exposure internally.
8. What is a direct loss? Give three examples of a direct loss, identifying the peril that caused the loss in each case.
9. Present three convincing arguments (in each case) why indirect losses are essential to consider when a direct loss occurs for

   a. A firm
   b. An individual

10. Indirect losses arise in many forms. Discuss three risk mitigating strategies that can be effective in managing losses arising out of covered events.
11. You are the minister of homeland security in your country. Discuss three reasons why you should be bothered about indirect losses that affect businesses.
12. Plasma Company manufactures and sells ladders for companies and individuals that may need their products. Some of its products are also sold to independent retailers across the country. The company's risk manager knows that the company can be sued if a ladder is defective, and someone is injured using it. The cost of product liability insurance has increased significantly in recent years and the risk manager is considering other strategies to minimise the company's loss exposure.

    a. What specific internal risk management techniques in each of the following categories will assist Plasma manage its liability exposure?
       i. Loss prevention
       ii. Loss reduction
       iii. Avoidance
    b. Discuss four specific external risk management techniques that can assist Plasma reduce its product liability exposure.
    c. What advantages do external risk management techniques have over internal risk management techniques? What disadvantages, in your view, do they have compared to internal risk management techniques?

13. PQ Company specialises in the exploration of oil around the Cape Three Points in the Western region of Ghana. Discuss in each of the following cases how PQ can be impeded from achieving its objectives:

    a. Employee practices and workplace safety
    b. Damage to physical assets
    c. Loss of key personnel

    Discuss two mitigating strategies in each case that can be effective in managing their exposure to risk.

Reference

Sweeting, P. (2011). *Financial Enterprise Risk Management*. Cambridge University Press.

Further Reading

Gupta, P. K. (2008). *Fundamental of Insurance* (1st ed., Unit 1: Chapter 1). Himalaya Publishing House.

Gupta, P. K. (2016). *Essentials of Insurance and Risk Management* (1st ed., Part I: Chapters 1 & 2). Himalaya Publishing House Pvt Ltd.

Harrington, S. E., & Niehaus, G. R. (2004). *Risk Management and Insurance* (Chapters 1–3). McGraw-Hill.

Pritchard, C. L. (2015). *Risk Management: Concepts and Guidance* (5th ed., Chapters 1–3). CRC Press, Taylor & Francis Group.

Promislow, S. D. (2011). *Fundamentals of Actuarial Mathematics* (Chapter 1). Wiley.

Redja, G. E., & McNamara. (2016). *Principles of Risk Management and Insurance* (Chapters 1 & 3). Pearson Addison Wesley.

Tchankova, L. (2002). Risk Identification—Basic Stage in Risk Management. *Environmental Management and Health, 13*(3), 290–297.

Vaughan, E. J., & Vaughan, T. M. (2008). *Fundamentals of Risk Management and Insurance* (10th ed., Chapters 1, 2 &10). Wiley.

Chapter 2
Basic Insurance Concepts

Abstract This chapter presents examples of risk exposures that require insurance coverage and discusses the benefits of purchasing insurance products, as well as the characteristics of insurable risks. It further examines systemic and systematic risks and outlines appropriate risk-mitigation strategies for each. Essential insurance terminologies are introduced, accompanied by the information asymmetries that complicate insurance transactions for market participants. The chapter also identifies the implied conditions that must be satisfied before any insurance contract commences. These conditions are considered alongside additional benefits of insurance and a comparison between valued and indemnity contracts. The chapter concludes by discussing techniques for reducing fraudulent activity in the insurance market and the internal risk-management practices that insurance companies can adopt to mitigate fraud.

Keywords And phrases: Implied conditions · Indemnity contracts · Information problems · Insurable risk · Systematic risk · Systemic risk · Valued policies

Introduction

In this chapter, some examples of risk exposures for which insurance are needed are presented, the benefits associated with having an insurance product and some features of insurable risks are discussed. Systemic and systematic risks, a type of risks that affect a large group of people for which insurance companies typically shy away from are discussed together with its risk mitigating strategies. Some insurance terminologies are introduced along with a discussion of the information problems that complicate the insurance transaction on the insurance space for market participants. There are certain conditions, called implied conditions, that must be fulfilled prior to the inception of any insurance transactions. These conditions together with other benefits of having insurance, the differences between valued and indemnity

C. Andoh, *Fundamentals of Managing Risk and Insurance*,
https://doi.org/10.1007/978-981-95-4581-0_2

contracts are discussed. Finally, the chapter end with techniques for reducing fraudulent activities on the market and the internal risk management techniques that can be adopted by insurance companies to minimise fraud.

Examples of Risks

Property Loss Through Fire

Fire can destroy a whole building resulting in financial loss. When a house, office or business premises get burnt down by fire because of bad wiring or some other reason, many assets are lost. In addition, the replacement of these assets is usually necessary, which in turn causes additional financial loss.

Natural Disasters

The flooding of a community results in financial loss. When flooding occurs, assets, buildings and human life may be lost. When there is windstorm, excessive damage may be caused to both life and property. Earthquakes can equally cause the absolute destruction of lives and property. These events cause financial loss to individuals, people and businesses.

Death of a Guardian

When a parent or guardian who supports a family dies, the financial support of those relying on this person ceases. When a partner in a business dies, this deprives the partnership the expertise the person possessed resulting in financial loss. Funeral arrangements and burial expenses can also be expensive.

Theft and Burglary

Thieves or armed robbers may break into someone's home, shop or business taking valuable belongings resulting in a financial loss.

Terrorism

Terrorists can attack innocent lives and property on land, sea or air inflicting damages that may be worth millions of dollars.

Liability

A consumer may sue a manufacturer for the use of a defective product. A business may be sued for the advertisement they put out which may have resulted in bodily injures for persons who might have relied of the information advertised.

Shipwrecks

A severe financial loss occurs when a ship fully laden with goods capsizes, sinks or is shipwrecked in the deep ocean. Pirates can attack innocent lives and property at sea resulting in financial loss.

Accidents

Road accidents, fires and injuries in the workplace more often than not lead to costs and unplanned expenses that reduce the value of a business, a group or person's wealth. Some of these accidents can cause life-threatening injuries which may affect the ability of the person to continue to work resulting in financial loss. When there is a motor accident, damage is caused to the car involved and people in the car. The car has to be replaced or repaired and the people require hospital attention causing financial loss. In a game of football, injuries, such as a broken leg, are expensive for both the player and the team.

Illness

Illness may mean that an individual or a business owner cannot work, thereby creating financial loss. An individual with a terminal illness could be a drain on resources all year round. The breadwinner of a family who suffers from a chronic disease puts pressure on the family finances. When a person falls ill, money assigned for other activities may be used to pay the person's medical expenses leading to financial losses.

Longevity

The longer life one lives the greater one is exposed to risks that may cause financial loss. An older person is more likely to require medical care and more frequent treatment that comes with a cost. Health problems such as obesity and metabolic syndrome are very common with very old people. These illnesses tend to create high medical bills for patients who, in their old age, are living on their savings. These high medical bills drain the savings of the individual.

Benefits of Insurance

Individuals and businesses can never fully eliminate their loss exposure. However, they can adopt measures that reduce the frequency or severity of potential losses or prepare for their financial consequences. Insurance is a key mechanism for managing these financial losses. It protects individuals, businesses, and groups against unforeseen monetary losses by allowing them to transfer the potential financial burden of a loss exposure to an insurer through a contractual arrangement. A major benefit of insurance is the reduction of fear and uncertainty. In addition to financial protection, insurers often provide a range of support services bundled with their products. Insurance also works by pooling risks among a large group of people. This pooling is not limited to a specific geographic area but extends to all who choose to join the risk pool. Ultimately, the very existence of risk is what makes insurance both necessary and possible.

Features of Insurable Risks

Insurable Risk

An insurance company does not insure all types of risk because sometimes, the nature of the risk or the cover being sought for risk exposure is against the interest of the public. Certain risks are generally uninsurable. An insurable risk relates practically to a risk that an insurance company has deemed fit to provide coverage for (i.e., it is the type of risk that an insurer can provide cover for to the requesting applicant). For a risk to be insurable, it must satisfy certain conditions.

Requirements of an Insurable Risk

Before any risk can qualify to be insured, the following conditions must be met.

Fortuitous/Accidental

An insurable risk should be one that is accidental in nature. In other words, it should be a risk that was not intentionally caused to profit from an insurance policy or an occurrence that will definitely happen. It must be unexpected and not engineered by anyone else. Losses resulting from faked accidents, fires or staged or arranged robberies do not qualify to be insured and the insurer will not pay out if a fraudulent claim is made.

Financial Value

Before a risk can be insured, it must have a financial value. In other words, it should be possible to quantify the risk in monetary terms. This explains why subjective criteria, such as one's love for someone cannot be insured. You cannot quantify it since it has no financial value and therefore it is not insurable.

Insurable Interest

Before you can insure any risk, you should have a vital stake in it so that when it is lost or destroyed, you will be adversely affected. In other words, the insured must have a stake in or ownership of the good in question. Thus, it is important that the risk will cause a direct loss to the insured in the event of a peril. This characteristic of an insurable risk explains why you can insure the lives of your children but not those of your friend's children. Also, health risks are insurable as they create health costs, whereas the probability of failing in an interview is uninsurable.

Measurable and Calculable

When a loss occurs, it should be capable of being measured so that the insured will be restored to their previous financial position. A risk of unemployment, by this definition, cannot be insured. This is because there are people unemployed by choice. Disability risk is somewhat hard to measure since some people like to malinger to continue to enjoy the proceeds of an insurance policy. In contrast, life insurance is quite different as the death of the insured is easy to determine. Also, the risk of a motor accident is an insurable risk because the amount of loss can be estimated whenever it occurs.

Pure Risk

An insurable risk should be pure risk. Pure risk is a risk with two outcomes: a loss (adverse), or no loss (neutral). The essence of insuring on the basis of pure risk is that such risks occur randomly and the law of large numbers can be easily applied. The prediction of expected losses becomes difficult when the law of large numbers is not applicable or difficult to apply.

Particular Risk

One important characteristic of an insurable risk is that it must be specific, that is, it is one that affects only a portion of the entire population. This is referred to as a particular risk. The independence of the events triggering the loss is central! It must not be fundamental such as an increase in inflation that may affect an entire population at the same time. If insured losses were to be fundamental, and so all policyholders were being indemnified at the same time (i.e., if losses were correlated) with each claim exceeding the expected loss, the insurer will not be able to serve their purpose of indemnification.

Homogeneous

The risks to be insured should be similar to other risks. Hence, a pool can be formed to encapsulate them allowing for the law of large numbers to help predict the occurrence of the risk. Thus, it should be classifiable with other risks.

Public Policy

No matter the risk you want to insure, it must not be against what society thinks is the right thing to do. This means that anything that is frowned upon by societal rules, public policy and law cannot be insured. For this reason, prostitutes cannot buy an insurance policy to cover the possible health risks of their profession. This also applies to drug trafficking, armed robbery or rape. In civilised countries, an insurance contract will be void when it is found that the risk exposure for which insurance was provided was illegal.

Systematic and Systemic Risks

Systematic risk is the risk that remains after extensive diversification. Systemic risk is a type of risk associated with the losses of a financial institution due to runs on a bank (i.e., creditors demanding their money at once, resulting in the collapse of a financial institution) or cascading failures. Cascading failures exist when the failure of one financial institution is the cause of failure of others.

Systemic risk may happen to one entity but has a ripple effect on other entities with similar operations. This may arise from unnecessary speculation by the financial institution leading to a loss of public confidence in it that may result in customers withdrawing all their savings from a bank at once.

Systematic and systemic risks all affect a large group of people at the same time and so the independence of the events triggering the loss fails. Systematic and systemic risks are both uninsurable risks. One difference between these risks is that the losses arising out of systematic risks can be measured whereas the losses from systemic risk cannot be measured.

These risks can be mitigated through education, loss control measures, government interventions and, in extreme cases, avoidance. People can be educated on loss control and loss prevention measures that will assist in minimising losses resulting from these risks. Governmental intervention on losses arising from these risks will assist greatly in minimising the impact of losses.

To manage cascading failures, managers of insurance companies should carefully select their reinsurers. If a financial institution is suspected of becoming insolvent, a bank run can easily follow and management cannot control it.

Some Insurance Terminology

An ***insurance contract*** is a legal document that represents the agreement between the insured and the insurer. The agreement is usually that the insured pays premiums and the insurer pays claims contingent upon the occurrence of an event that results in financial loss. ***A policyholder (or policyowner)*** is a person/organisation/business that has an insurance contract with an insurance company. The policyowner need not be the insured.

A ***proposer*** is a person/organisation/business that possesses a risk exposure and is seeking protection from an insurance company (i.e., the prospective insured who is yet to be granted insurance cover). The proposer fills the ***proposal form*** that provides the insurer with information about the risk to be insured.

The ***cover*** is the financial value of an insurance policy. If someone says: 'I have cover for theft insurance for my home'. This means that person has an insurance policy in place that compels the insurer to pay for losses that arise from theft, fire or other contingencies in the home.

Benefit is the proceeds that accrue from an insurance policy. Under life insurance, the person to whom payments are made on the death of the insured death is the ***beneficiary***. There is a subtle difference between *benefit* and *cover*. *Cover* relates to the losses that will be compensated for by the insurer when they occur. In both cases a ***premium*** must be paid. *Cover* can also be the amount of insurance purchased by the insured.

An ***agent*** is a person employed by an insurance company to assist with the sale of insurance products. Agents solicit for prospective policyholders and in some cases write the insurance policy on behalf of the insurance company. Two types of agents can be identified: exclusive/tied or captive agents sell insurance products for one insurance company. Independent agents sell for several insurance companies.

A ***broker*** is a legal representative of an insurance purchaser. Brokers advise the prospective insured on which company to sign up to, given the peculiar needs of the customer and the potential advantages offered by different insurance companies.

Information Problems in the Insurance Market

Insurance markets are generally imperfect and particularly characterised by information problems that affect both insurance providers and policyowners. Ideally, a perfect market is characterised by speed of reaction and information transparency.

Below, we discuss several of the problems that arise for both those seeking insurance cover and insurance providers.

Moral Hazard

Moral hazard is a situation whereby an insured entity or individual does not take the necessary precautions to prevent or mitigate losses, because that entity or person has insurance. When this happens, insurance rates or premiums increase which deter others from purchasing insurance. Insurers attempt to combat this behaviour by insurance purchasers by providing less than full insurance so that the risk of moral hazard will reduce. This is based on the premise that if full insurance causes moral hazard, then less than full insurance reduces it. Consequently, insurance purchasers are often made aware that they will bear part of the loss when a covered loss occurs. This makes the insured careful not to cause loss or create conditions that might increase the frequency of loss.

Moral hazard can also occur when high-risk individuals are charged the same insurance rate as those with low risk thereby altering the behaviour of those in the high-risk group.

Adverse Selection

Adverse selection is a situation whereby one party to a transaction has information that is relevant to the other party but deliberately does not disclose it. When adverse selection occurs, insurers wrongly classify applicants and charge a rate that is not commensurate with the risk the applicant possesses. The high-risk individual will purchase more insurance than the low-risk individual. Adverse selection can also occur when the proposer uses their superior information about a particular risk to outwit the insurer. Not all the facts relevant to the pricing for the proposer are disclosed, resulting in the underpricing of the insurance product by the insurer. To solve this problem, insurers use a number of techniques that require high-risk individuals to disclose all relevant material information so that they pay appropriate rates for the risk they wish to insure. By correctly pricing insurance products for high-risk individuals, less risky individuals benefit by paying lower premiums.

The Lemon Problem

Of course, an insurer can also adversely select a policyholder by not revealing the true state of the financial standing of the company. The lemon problem arises when insurers fail to reveal their true financial state and yet commit to a contract with a person or business seeking insurance. A policyholder simply receives a promise that they will be indemnified when a covered loss occurs. Will the insurance company be in a good enough financial standing to honour its side of the contract? An insurer can also use its superior knowledge to overprice the products it sells to consumers. An insurer may decide to exclude or obfuscate vital information on the proposal form thereby misleading the insured. Thus, there is the need for an independent party that understands the technicalities of insurance transactions to oversee the activities of insurance companies. We will discuss insurance regulation as it relates to insurance transactions in a later chapter.

Implied Conditions in the Insurance Market

Implied conditions in the insurance markets are conditions that must be fulfilled prior to the formation of an insurance contract. These are conditions, rules or principles at the insurance market that govern every insurance transaction or contract. The principle of utmost good faith stresses the fact that the proposer will be truthful in revealing all relevant information needed for the proper assignment of the price for the policy being sought. If the proposer violates this principle and a covered loss materialises, the insurer has the right not to honour its side of the contract. It is therefore important that proposers for insurance reveal all relevant information needed for the proper pricing of the risk for which cover is sought. Insurance companies have received negative publicity because policyholders have hidden certain information that would have been material to the contract formation resulting in the company's inability to honour its side of an insurance contract. In almost all cases, the information provided by the proposer is not available to the public for them to make an informed judgement. We discuss four of these conditions necessary for the formation of a valid insurance contract below.

Indemnity Principle

Indemnity means restoring one to the position held immediately before a loss. The indemnity principle states that the insured should not make a profit from a loss. Thus, an insured entity suffering a covered loss is entitled to recover from the insurer an amount not exceeding that which would be necessary to return the insured to the same pre-loss financial position. Therefore, claims are paid to restore the insured to a pre-loss financial position. Without this principle, the insured may be motivated to incur losses knowing that there might be an opportunity to make profits. Also, in the case where the insured has taken double insurance for the same asset, the insurance companies involved will share the loss between themselves to prevent a double recovery and a profit for the insured.

The function of this principle is to prevent the insured from profiting from a loss in the insurance market. If Kofi's home is insured for GH¢150,000 and a partial loss of GH¢25,000 loss occurs, the principle of indemnity would be violated if GH¢150,000 were paid to Kofi. The second function of this principle is to prevent moral hazard. If entities or individuals could profit from a loss, dishonest people could intentionally cause a loss to collect the insurance proceeds.

Principle of Subrogation

Subrogation places the cost of the loss with the wrongdoer. The principle of subrogation states that an insurer is entitled to recover from a negligent third party any loss payments made to the insured. However, to settle the cost of the loss, the wrongdoer may choose to settle amicably with the policyholder. There is always the possibility that after such a settlement, the policyholder may also attempt to recover the same loss from the insurer. Subrogation prevents this from happening because the insurer will exercise its right under this principle to recover or retrieve the cost of the loss directly from the wrongdoer. This also reduces the potential for moral hazard, as it discourages any attempt to collect compensation from multiple sources following an event that causes a loss. The principle prevents this double recovery and thereby helps to hold down insurance rates. Thus, the excess duplicative proceeds are returned to the insurer and the insurer recycles them in the form of lower insurance premiums to all policyholders. This principle exists to prevent fraudulent activities such as collusion between the insured and negligent third parties. The principle permits insurers to recover valuable assets such as salvage vehicles from fire after full damages or claim payments have been paid.

The principle helps in stabilising the finances of an insurer by recovering the costs incurred in indemnifying the insured. Once the insured is indemnified, the right of the insured to pursue the third party for compensation is transferred to the insurer.

One benefit of this principle to policyholders is that it allows the insurer to bear the legal costs on the policyholder's behalf. When a negligent third party causes damage to an insured item, the insurance company will use its legal machinery to retrieve the cost of item from the negligent party. Without the existence of this principle, this cost would have to be borne by the policyholder.

Also, because this principle helps to hold down insurance rates, it makes insurance more affordable, consequently allowing many more people to purchase it. This is also good for insurance companies as the predictability of expected losses are improved.

In addition, because the principle empowers an insurer to recover from a negligent third party any loss payments made to the insured, it assists in protecting the property and possessions of policyholders. Wrongdoers know that wrongs they commit against policyholders will be held to account and this consequently acts as a deterrent against causing harm in a negligent way. For example, any road user understands that damage caused to another person's car negligently will be borne by them or their insurers and therefore will be careful not to inflict such damage.

The principle also combats waste in the sense that a person will exercise due care in their dealings with an insured assets because should anything go wrong and a loss be caused, they would be investigated and if found culpable will be instructed to reimburse the insurer. People with insurance will also not deliberately cause damage to their assets because they will not profit from it and thus reducing or combating wastages.

Principle of Insurable Interest

Insurable interest is the legally recognised relationship a person has with a property that gives them the right to assume insurance for it. It requires a proposer for an insurance contract to have a financial interest in the subject matter of the proposed insurance policy such that the loss or destruction of the subject matter would lead to a financial loss for the insured.

The principle of insurable interest states that the insured entity or person must lose financially if a covered loss occurs. The principle allows individuals who have a direct financial obligation for the insurable item to be provided cover by an insurance company. The insured will hope for such a loss not to occur and so will not deliberately cause the loss to happen. This is a very important principle in insurance because it prevents people from seeking insurance policies on properties or assets they do not care about.

The function of this principle is to prevent people from gambling with insurance. If this principle did not exist, one would be able to insure the properties of others (where one has no financial ownership) and hope for a loss. The second function of this principle is to prevent moral hazard in the insurance market. If the principle did not exist, (dishonest) people could purchase property insurance cover on someone else's property and set fire to it to collect proceeds. A third function is that this principle allows insurers to measure the quantum of insured's potential loss in property insurance. Most property and liability insurance policies are contracts of indemnity and one measure of recovery is the insurable interest.

An insurer must ensure that the principle of insurable interest is preserved before any contract is issued. This prevents fraud at the insurance market.

Insurable Interest and Gambling

Gambling could simply be an agreement between two people or businesses about something whose value depends on the outcome of something else that may result in a gain or a loss for one party. The principle of insurable interest combats gambling at the insurance market. This is because the insurer will determine if the prospective insured stands to lose financially before he/she is insured or given cover. If the individual does not have any insurable interest, he/she will not be insured. If this is not the case, a person can take a fire insurance policy for example on another person's house and hope for the house to burn down so that he/she can collect proceeds on it. When this happens, insurance will be no different from gambling because the insurer loses and the insured wins.

Principle of Utmost Good Faith

This principle emphasises the issue of honesty. The principle states that neither party to an insurance contract should use superior information to take unfair advantage of the other. The principle is supported by three important legal doctrines, namely representation, concealment and warranty.

Representation is simply a statement made to an insurer for the purpose of providing information or inducing it to accept a risk. However, if the information furnished by the proposer is incorrect, a misrepresentation has occurred. The legal significance of representation is that the insurance contract is voidable by the insurer if the representation is material, false and relied on by the insurer.

Concealment is an intentional failure by an applicant for insurance to reveal a material fact to the insurer. For the insurer to deny a claim based on concealment, the insurer must prove that the concealed fact was known by the insured and the insured intended to defraud the insurer.

Warranty is a statement that becomes part of an insurance contract and is guaranteed to be true by the warrantor in all respects.

Utmost Good Faith and Gambling

Because the principle is an implied condition, it alerts fraudsters who want to take undue advantage of insurers by reiterating the issue of honesty. Therefore, people come with clean hands in buying insurance thereby reducing gambling. Representation of statements gives information to the insurer about a potential policyholder. Misrepresentation renders an insurance contract voidable at the insured's option if found. Therefore, it helps to reduce gambling because potential policyholders would be compelled to employ true representations to keep insurance contract.

Other Benefits of Insurance

Peace of Mind

Insurance ensures peace of mind for an insured person or a business that has insurance cover for its risk exposure. When a business enters risky new fields, insurance may serve as a cushion for a firm in the occurrence of a loss.

Guarantee for Loans and Financial Aid

An insured person or business may be granted a loan request mainly on the grounds of insurance availability. Buying insurance is enough assurance to lending firms that a business is sufficiently financially stable to ensure payback.

Lowest Cost of Financing Business Losses

Insurance offers the lowest cost of financing a business loss as compared to generating new funds or through internal funds. Insurance pays for losses that a business may experience with only the premium a business/policyholder pays. This may be lower than the average rate of return in the market if capital is borrowed. The cost of using internally generated funds is the forfeiture of valuable investment projects that are higher than the cost of insurance.

Solvency of a Business

Insurance protects the solvency of a business and in the long run may prevent it from financial distress and its accompanying problems. The direct and indirect costs of bankruptcy are avoided when a business has insurance (Harrington & Niehaus, 2004, Chapter 9, p. 172).

Insurers' Services

By purchasing insurance, the legal machinery of the insurer is automatically available to the insured to cover risks for which their cover has been purchased. Therefore, a negligent third party who causes a loss to occur will be dealt with by the insurer's legal service via the principle of subrogation. An insured business will have legal representation in a law court in the event of a lawsuit against them if they have purchased liability insurance. Consequently, the cost of hiring a lawyer by the insured entity is taken care of.

Insurance provides a policyholder with services such as loss control, loss prevention and claim management services at a relatively cheaper cost than can be obtained elsewhere. An insurance company will advise on measures that can be employed to minimise losses that can occur. For example, an insurer will advise on where to place a fire extinguisher in your premises to minimise loss if a fire breaks out. An insurer may also prescribe a loss prevention measure such as the mounting of security cameras on premises upon the purchase of theft insurance. A business therefore has the advantage of saving extra costs that might have been spent to secure those services elsewhere.

Provision of investment counselling is another service an insurer provides. An insurer will guide a business to make sound investment decisions. This not only benefits the insured but also keeps expected claim costs relatively low since the insured is less likely to make financially unsound decisions.

Valued Policies Versus Indemnity Contracts

A valued policy is a type of policy for which the insurer pays a stated sum irrespective of the actual economic loss. With these policies, insurable interest is needed at the inception of the policy because the policy can be assigned to a third party. Examples of valued policies are life insurance, most disability and long-term policies, insurance for fine arts, rare paintings, antiques, expensive jewellery, etc. With these policies, the insurer agrees with the insured the value of life (or asset) at the inception of the contract. When the policy matures, the agreed amount is paid as benefits.

On the other hand, an indemnity contract is a type of contract in which the policyholder cannot recover more than their economic loss. With these contracts, insurable interest should run throughout the life of the contract and it cannot be re-assigned. Most property and liability insurance as well as medical insurance are indemnity contracts. With these contracts, the insurer assesses the loss at the time the loss takes place and pays that amount to the insured.

Reducing Fraudulent Activities in the Insurance Market

The insurance market can be risky for insurers due to losses they can suffer because of fraudulent activities and inflated claims on the part of the insured. Fraud is costly to the insurer and eventually affects other policyholders, as losses caused to insurers tend to result in higher premium costs for those that wish to be insured. As a result, insurers adopt some mitigating factors to reduce the occurrence of adverse selection and moral hazard. These include the options of coinsurance, indemnity clauses, exclusions, suicide and other clauses.

Coinsurance

Coinsurance indicates the proportion of the whole loss that will be borne by the insured. This means that when a loss occurs, the insured pays a certain percentage and the insurer pays the remaining percentage. The use of coinsurance helps to reduce moral hazard and adverse selection by dissuading fraudulent claims. It ensures that the payment of a claim is not entirely borne by the insurer. The higher the amount of a loss, the higher the amount that is borne by the insured. Since the insured wish to suffer as little loss as possible, such techniques cause them to exercise more care and employ loss control measures.

Exclusions and Clauses

Insurance companies use exclusions to minimise fraudulent activities in the insurance market. Insurers offer coverage that includes exemptions from some type of losses. Exclusions reduce administrative costs, moral hazard and adverse selection and consequently minimise fraudulent activities. Exclusions in health insurance include pre-existing conditions and intentionally inflicted injuries. Life insurance would not be paid out in the event of a suicide typically in the first few years of purchasing insurance. Such clauses seek to prevent or deter people who have fraudulent intentions from purchasing insurance products. The insurer also uses a delay clause to minimise the effect of fraud. The delay clause gives an insurer some time to conduct investigations needed to decide whether a claim is valid or not.

Deductibles

Deductibles eliminate coverage for small losses. Deductibles are also used to reduce or minimise fraudulent activities in the insurance market. For example, a high-risk person might not reveal all the relevant information to the insurer to obtain coverage at a lower rate. An insurer can offer multiple policies with different deductibles and different prices per cedi of coverage. Higher risk people might choose the lower deductible (high priced) policies. On the other hand, lower risk people might choose the higher deductible (i.e., lower priced) policies. Thus, policyholders fall into different groups (see Harrington & Niehaus, 2004, Chapter 10, pp. 188–189).

Policy Limits

A policy limit places a cap on the maximum amount payable to the insured. By limiting the amount payable, the insurer protects itself from exposure to very high claims. Policy limits reduce classification costs when consumers of insurance products have information that is costly for insurers to obtain. Consider a consumer who has jewellery worth GH¢2500 but is reluctant to reveal the value of the jewellery to the insurer. An insurer might limit coverage for jewellery losses to GH¢2000. Those with particularly expensive jewellery would then need to buy special coverage. Policy limits deter the intention of using superior information to defraud the insurer.

Tight Underwriting Standards

Insurers can tighten their underwriting standards to minimise fraud. Since underwriters are the 'gatekeepers' of insurance, they are key players in rooting out fraud in the insurance market. By tightening underwriting standards, the insurer can ensure that only non-fraudulent applicants are admitted into the insurance market.

Vigilance in the Claim Settlement Process

An insurer can strengthen its claim settlement process to prevent fraud. Insurers should conduct adequate investigations into all claims. The insurer can employ the services of a loss adjuster (a person who investigates a claim after a loss has occurred) to ensure that inflated claims are detected and not settled.

Corroboration with Security Personnel and Regulatory Authorities

Authorities such as the Economic and Organised Crime Office (EOCO) in Ghana are very much involved in prosecuting fraudsters. By engaging such bodies and taking advice from them, an insurer can help mitigate the effect of fraud.

Classification

Classification of risk helps to avoid insurers charging both low-risk and high-risk customers the same premium. When risks are not classified, the market favours high-risk policyholders as part of their cost of insurance is borne by low-risk counterparts. This triggers adverse selection as the high-risk policyholders will purchase more insurance, while the low-risk policyholders will switch to other risk management techniques. A good classification of the different risks confronting the insurer will help prevent adverse selection, reduce moral hazard and, by extension, minimise fraud. However, an insurer should use classification only when it is cost-effective because it can be costly to undertake.

Reinsurance

Reinsurance is a mechanism whereby a primary insurer cedes all or part of an insurance policy to another insurer. This improves the underwriting capacity of the insurer and allows it to share the risk of fraudulent activity that can cause stress to the finances of an insurer. A reinsurance company can also provide an insurer with technical advice and strategies as to how best to minimise the effect of fraud. Thus, should any such activity occur, the insurer is itself insured against the loss.

Securitisation of Risk

In this scenario the risk exposure of the insurer is transferred to the capital market. Thus, the possible loss exposure to fraudulent activities is transferred to the capital market (see Redja, 2008, p. 120).

Conditions

Conditions are elements within an insurance contract that render it null and void at the insurer's option if they are not met or adhered to by the insured party. They may be either expressly stated or implied. Express conditions are clearly stated and agreed to by both the insurer and the insured. Implied conditions are implicit, not clearly stated but apply strictly to the contract (see, for example, Holyoake & Weiper, 2002, 184). Conditions help an insurer minimise the effects of fraud because they outline actions, when breached by the insured render the contract void. Conditions included in the policy contract that any fraudulent act noticed or observed will render the contract null and void and will also cause severe consequences for the insured will deter some people from committing fraudulent acts.

A warranty is a condition in an insurance contract (see, for example, Williams et al., 1999, p. 493). Two types can be identified: express and implied. An express warranty is an explicit statement (promise) that a product or service will perform according to some standard. An implied warranty is an implicit performance guarantee that usually accompanies the sale of any product or service (i.e., the product will reasonably perform its intended use). Consumers who are injured because of a product not performing according to implied or express warranties can sue the seller for damages (see Harrington & Niehaus, 2004, p. 608). One difference between a condition and a warranty is that all warranties describe the obligation of the insured. A condition need not describe these rights and obligations, though most conditions do. Also, a breach of a 'condition' usually entitles the innocent party to terminate the contract and claim damages whereas a breach of 'warranty' entitles the innocent party only to claim damages.

Monitoring

Insurers can actively monitor the insured either by doing this themselves or by outsourcing it. For example, an insurance company offering fire insurance as one of its bouquet of products may occasionally ask their representatives or fire officers to do safety inspections on their policyholders to see whether the warranty agreements are being followed.

Experience Rating

Experience rating is another technique to combat fraudulent acts. It is the modification of an insurance class rate based on the previous loss history of the insured. Thus, if someone, having previously been negligent, seeks insurance, the insurer will likely increase the premium to be paid. If the insured knows that their future premiums will be tied to previous loss experiences, they are likely to take actions to reduce loss.

Good Salary and Compensation Packages

An insurance company can reduce the effect of internal fraudulent activities on the part of its workforce by paying them well and acknowledging good work. In a situation where the underwriters, agents, claim adjustors and others are well taken care of by provision of good conditions of service or compensation for their work, they are unlikely to be induced by fraudulent actors to engage in acts that could create a loss to the company. Compensation of employees can be linked to performance or based on the revenue generated by the company.

Association of Insurers

An insurance company can seek information about a policyholder to find whether the policyholder has other insurance in place covering the same loss. This would prevent the double payment of claims to the insured. As part of the underwriting process, an insurer should study a proposer to find out whether the proposer has a history of moving from one insurance company to another after successfully making a claim. Such behaviour is a strong indicator of fraud.

Co-benefit

Co-benefit is a technique used by an insurer in two main ways: pro rata and excess loss. With a pro rata loss, the insurer shares the loss incurred with the policyholder and any third-party insurance in proportion to the amount of the coverage. With an excess loss, the insurer only pays the excess loss of the other policy's limit at the time of the loss (see Redja, 2008, p. 119).

Prosecution of Fraudsters

Legally prosecuting insurance fraudsters and publicising their names will ensure law and order in the insurance market.

Expressing the Effect of Fraud in the Policy

The effect of fraud and its consequences on the insured can be stated in the policy contract. This could be stated as one of the conditions of the policy. The effect of litigation, voidable contracts and null contracts that could result should be made known to the insured. An insurer may refuse to pay claim settlements when an insured person or entity uses fraudulent activities to obtain an insurance policy. Fraudulent activities will cause the insured to forfeit all claim payments. The concept of forfeiture will go a long way to deter fraudulent activities in the insurance market.

Limited Coverage

In most cases, when there is full insurance, the tendency of the insured to take precautionary measures to mitigate a loss reduces. Insurers are aware of this and consequently do not offer full insurance coverage for a requesting applicant. The insured is required to assume responsibility for part of the loss upon its occurrence. This is meant to combat moral hazard (i.e., the effect of insurance on the insured's incentive to reduce losses). The argument is that if full insurance causes moral hazard, then less than full insurance limits moral hazard.

Independent Loss Adjustors

By employing an independent loss adjustor, employees of an insurance company do not know who will be working on a claim. Consequently, an employee of the insurance company cannot connive with an insured entity to dupe the company into accepting a claim. The independent loss adjustor will do a thorough job investigating a claim before deciding. The independent loss adjustor has a reputation to protect and so they are less likely to indulge in fraudulent acts.

Employees as Shareholders of an Insurance Company

An insurance company can make its employees shareholders. Since shareholders act in their own interest, an employee is unlikely to engage in acts that will stifle the growth of the company.

Internal Management Issues to Minimise the Effects of Fraud

Insurers should be very vigilant when recruiting employees especially for very sensitive departments such as claims and underwriting. Historical records and references for the employees should be sought before employment. Recruits with negative work ethics should be shunned.

Senior management of an insurance company should have good communications skills and address the grievances of its employees. Dissatisfied employees are more likely to engage in immoral acts that can harm the growth of a company. Good working conditions should be provided for employees.

Employees should be educated on the negative effects of fraud on the company and the consequences that they could face if they partake in such activities.

Transparency, when adopted by managers of a company can help minimise the effect of fraud. In an organisation where there is no transparency, a number of activities performed within the organisation can give rise to theft, embezzlement and other vices. Senior management of an insurance company should set a high standard for their subordinates to follow.

Exercises

1. How does insurance differ from risk?
2. Discuss implied conditions that minimise fraud in the insurance market.
3. Discuss the requirements for an insurable risk.
4. An insurable risk must meet certain requirements. Which of this/these requirement(s) prevent the pain resulting from a slap from someone uninsurable? Explain your answer(s).
5. Explain how the principle of subrogation assists in protecting the insured properties of policyholders.
6. Explain the functions of the following principles in the insurance market.

    (i) Principle of insurable interest
    (ii) Principle of indemnity
    (iii) Principle of subrogation
    (iv) Principle of utmost good faith

7. Explain how the principle of utmost good faith assists in combating gambling in the insurance market.
8. Explain four techniques that can be employed by an insurer to minimise the effect of fraudulent activities in the insurance market.
9. Discuss three services that a business or an insured person or entity enjoys by employing insurance as a risk mitigating strategy.
10. Explain why the following are uninsurable:

    (i) Unemployment
    (ii) Pain resulting from a slap
    (iii) Loss resulting from spiritual incantation
    (iv) Wear and tear of your vehicle tyres

11. Explain why insurers are often reluctant to insure disability risk.

12. Moral hazard is a pervasive problem in insurance. Discuss two examples in each of the following insurance products where expected losses depend on the insured's behaviour.

    (i) Health insurance
    (ii) Property insurance

    Explain two risk mitigating strategies that can be employed by an insurer to combat them.
13. Some insurance companies' employees connive with those they have insured to inflate claims so that the proceeds can be shared later. Explain five techniques that can be employed by an insurance company to curtail or minimise this problem.
14. Suppose life insurance is an indemnity contract. Explain how donations made to a bereaved person can violate the principle of indemnity and consequently increase the likelihood of death of an insured life.
15. Explain the following terms as applied to insurance:

    (i) Proposer
    (ii) Cover
    (iii) Benefit
    (iv) Policyowner
    (v) Insurance contract
    (vi) Agent
    (vii) Broker

16. Some people purchase life insurance without notifying beneficiaries or contingent beneficiaries. Do you think there should be a law by parliament that compels insurers to notify beneficiaries upon the death of the insured? Discuss each point you provide.
17. How does benefit differ from cover? What differences exist between them?
18. What are the main differences between an indemnity contract and a valued policy?
19. How do conditions differ from warranties?

References

Harrington, S. E., & Niehaus, G. R. (2004). *Risk Management and Insurance*. McGraw-Hill.
Holyoake, J., & Weiper, W. (2002). *Insurance* (4th ed.). AITBS Publishers.
Redja, G. E. (2008). *Principles of Risk Management and Insurance*. Pearson Addison Wesley.
Williams, C. A. Jr., Young, P. C., & Smith, M. L. (1999). *Risk Management and Insurance* (8th ed.). McGraw-Hill.

Further Reading

Black, K. J., & Skipper, H. D. J. (2000). *Life and Health Insurance* (13th ed.). Prentice Hall.

Gupta, P. K. (2008). *Fundamental of Insurance* (1st ed.). Himalaya Publishing House. *Unit 1: Chapter 2.*

Gupta, P. K. (2016). *Essentials of Insurance and Risk' Management* (1st ed.). Himalaya Publishing House Pvt Ltd. *Part II, Chapter 5; Part III, Chapter 5.*

Promislow, S. D. (2011). *Fundamentals of Actuarial Mathematics* (p. 1). John Wiley & Sons.

Redja, G. E., McNamara, J., & Rabel, W. H. (2022). *Principles of Risk Management and Insurance.* Pearson Addison Wesley. *Chapters 2 & 9.*

Vaughan, E. J., & Vaughan, T. M. (2008). *Fundamentals of Risk Management and Insurance* (10th ed.). Wiley. *Chapters 3 & 9.*

Chapter 3
Some Forms of Insurance Products and Bonds

Abstract This chapter provides an overview of the principal types of insurance products available in the insurance market. It explains the nature, structure, and key design features of these products, with attention given to both general insurance and life insurance offerings. In addition, the chapter discusses bonds, three-party contractual arrangements that, while not classified as insurance products, perform related risk-transfer and guarantee functions. Their inclusion serves to highlight important conceptual and practical differences between insurance contracts and other financial instruments used for risk management.

Keywords Bonds · General insurance products · Life insurance

Introduction

This chapter provides a description of the types of insurance products that are generally sold on the insurance market. It is important to point out that the list of insurance products explained here is not exhaustive as depending on the jurisdiction, these insurance products may be designed to cover risks that are peculiar to that market. Also, the benefits accruing to the insurance purchaser may differ from one insurer to the other. However, the description of insurance products presented provides the nature of the products that are sold and covers what is generally included in the design of these products. The types of insurance products described here include general insurance products and life insurance. Discussions on bonds which are not insurance products but are contract between three parties are located here.

C. Andoh, *Fundamentals of Managing Risk and Insurance*,
https://doi.org/10.1007/978-981-95-4581-0_3

General Insurance Products

These are the type of insurance products that cover any loss other than the loss of life. General insurance products are commonly referred to as non-life insurance products and hence do not cover the life of the insured. In most cases, premium paid for general insurance products are usually on a one-time basis. The following are some examples of general insurance policies.

Property Insurance

This is a type of general insurance policy that is designed to provide cover to the owners or renters of a structure and/or its content in the event of loss caused by perils such as explosion or flood. In some other cases, loss of property arising from damage or theft is also generally covered. Property insurance may include earthquake insurance, flood insurance, renters insurance and homeowners insurance. The following are typical property insurance products that exist on the insurance market.

i. Earthquake insurance: This policy covers losses and damage caused by earthquake shocks.
ii. Flood insurance: A typical flood insurance policy is designed to cover losses directly caused by flood.
iii. Renters insurance: This policy is sometimes referred to as tenant insurance. It is taken by renters of facilities to protect their interest, the tenant's property against any liabilities that they may incur. This policy does not cover the rented facility or structure but rather its content. There are, however, some exceptional cases where the policy may cover for the rented structure especially when the renter has made some modifications to the structure.
iv. Homeowners insurance: Generally, homeowners insurance policies are comprehensive and cover a wide range of personal insurance protections. Losses covered may include loss of one's building and/or its content, loss of rent accruing to homeowner because of accident at the home caused by fire, burglary, explosion, etc., within a defined territory as stated in the policy.
v. Burglary insurance or theft insurance: This policy covers loss or damage to property because of theft or attempted theft leading to forceful entry or exit from a premise. That is, the insurance policy offers compensation to the insured because of damage or loss of goods/stocks/property or other items in connection with theft or burglary as stipulated in the insurance contract.
vi. Fire and allied peril insurance: This policy provides cover for losses emanating from damage to the insured property by virtue of fire outbreak, lightning, explosions, windstorm, earthquake, busting or overflow of water tanks, among other perils. Some properties that are often insured under this policy include but not limited to furniture, buildings, fixtures and fittings and other electronic appliances.

vii. Business interruption insurance: This insurance often seeks to indemnify businesses for the loss of income arising from interruptions caused by fire, lightning and other allied perils such as flood, windstorm, strikes, earthquakes and explosions.

Motor or Automobile Insurance

With this policy, the insurer undertakes to cover for any loss that may occur through damage to the property or damage to persons because of an accident involving the motor in question. Apart from the damage or complete destruction of the owner's vehicle or motorcycle, properties of other people may also be damaged or destroyed as a result of the accident. In some instances, lives may be lost, or persons may get injured. Most insurers have three main policies under motor insurance. These include comprehensive motor insurance, third-party motor insurance and motor third-party fire and theft insurance.

i. Third-party motor insurance: this policy seeks to indemnify the insured and any permitted driver in the event of legal liability to third parties resulting in death, body injury or even damage to properties of a third party. Third party as used here may refer to pedestrians, passengers and other road users. The sum insured may also be limited or unlimited depending on the content of the policy.
ii. Motor third-party fire and theft insurance: with this policy, the insured is indemnified in the event of liabilities incurred on third parties because of injury, death or property damage. In most cases, the cover is also extended to damage or theft of the insured's own vehicle. This policy is generally an extension of third-party motor insurance to cover loss of the insured's vehicle as a result of risk of fire and theft.
iii. Comprehensive motor insurance: this policy is designed to provide cover against perils of the road among other perils. The comprehensive motor insurance basically covers all the risks described in third-party motor and third-party fire and theft insurance in addition to damage to the insured's vehicle as a result of accident.

Marine Insurance

Marine insurance products cover for any loss or damage that may occur to ships and cargo. The policy also covers loss or damage of a client's good at sea or air because of collision, bad weather, explosion or stranding. Most marine insurance come in two types, the single cover and the open cover. The single cover is designed to cater for those who engage in imports on less frequent basis and a single cover may be undertaken for each import made. In the case of open cover, importers take up one open cover policy to cover for all imports that will be made.

Goods-In-Transit Insurance

Goods in transit policy is undertaken to indemnify an insured person for any loss or damage to the insured's merchandise in transit due to loss arising from fire outbreak, theft or accident to the vehicle carrying the goods causing damage to the insured's property that is in transit. This policy usually covers damage to insured goods that are being transported from one place to another, usually within the same country.

Aviation Insurance

Aviation insurance policies are usually distinct from other policies covering transportation. Aviation insurance policies come with their own set of terminologies. It is designed purposefully for aircraft and any associated risk that involves aviation. Most insurers provide a wide range of insurance products to cater for the varying needs of various aircrafts. Some general aviation insurance policies include:

i. Hull All Risk: this policy covers all risks associated with loss or damage of the aircraft while in flight, on the ground or even taxing. Generally, spare parts or equipment meant for servicing the aircraft are also covered.
ii. Hull War and Allied Risks: this policy usually covers risks associated with acts of war including invasion, hijacking and insurrection, among other perils.

Mobile Insurance

This policy provides insurance cover for all forms of mobile devices including but not limited to phones, laptops, IPad mobile personal computers and cameras. In the event of damage, loss or theft the insurance company settles claims for the damage, loss or theft.

Cash In-transit Insurance

With this policy, the insurer indemnifies the insured against loss of cash (currency, notes, coins, postal orders, cheques, securities for money, etc.) in transit from a stipulated destination to another. Generally, the cash in transit cover is available for institutions that are faced with the risk of physically transferring cash received from a bank to the business premise towards the payment of wages and salaries.

Money Insurance

Like the cash in transit policy, this policy covers business risks associated with cash in transit, cash held in a safe or even cash held on the premises of the workplace (hold ups). The policy thus covers loss, damage or destruction of money due to unforeseen events.

Plate Glass Insurance

This policy is uniquely designed for all business establishments that have installed plate glass in their business premise. The policy thus covers loss or damage to the plate glass.

Travel Insurance

This is designed to protect the insured from any risk associated with travelling outside one's country. In some cases, travel insurance policy is considered a prerequisite and hence necessary to be undertaken before obtaining a visa. Some of the benefits of this policy include cover for medical expenses and hospitalisation abroad, repatriation of mortal remains, emergency return home due to unforeseen events, location or forwarding of baggage, among others.

Assets All Risk Insurance

This policy is designed to provide a much wider cover for owners of premises. With this policy, the insured, usually business organisations, obtain cover for its premises and/or its content against allied perils, burglary, fire or other accidental or unforeseen losses.

Engineering Insurance

Engineering insurance provides a range of engineering insurance solutions to suit the needs of policyholders. Some of the general engineering insurance policies are described below.

i. Contractors All Risk Insurance: This is a unique policy that is designed to cater for the various risks faced by contractors in respect of damage, complete destruction or loss of their contract works, materials, plants and machinery, removal of debris during construction, temporary buildings used as offices on the site. The policy may also extend to other third parties to cover loss or damage to third-party property because of the execution of the contract work by the contractor.
ii. Erection Insurance: this policy compensates the business organisation for losses arising from the erection, installation of plants and machinery, testing and commissioning of the plant and machinery including steel structure of any kind. The policy may also cover third-party liability in connection with bodily injury and property damage in the event of executing the contract.
iii. Machinery Breakdown Insurance: this insurance policy is basically designed to address issues surrounding the breakdown of machinery in firms whose operations largely depend on these plants and machinery. This policy is thus taken by companies to cover major losses that are likely to threaten the existence of the company.
iv. Electronic Equipment Insurance: electronic equipment comprises all electronic systems and electrical appliances that are used for processing data and transmitting information. The policy thus provides indemnity in the event of loss or damage to the electronic equipment under cover.
v. Contractors Plant and Machinery All Risk: this is usually a comprehensive policy against accidental physical loss or damage to the machine while the machine is at work and in some cases while the machine is at rest or under maintenance.
vi. Machinery Loss of Profit Insurance: there may arise situations where interruptions in business operations may result in loss of gross profit. The Machinery Loss of Profit insurance seeks to indemnify the insured against accidents specified under the policy. The indemnity provided generally covers reasonable expenses incurred in the process of avoiding a reduction in turnover due to the

occurrence of an accident leading to the interruption. The policy may also cover continuing business expenses (business charges), wages and salaries, rent and other expenses that will have been paid for by the insured company if there had not been any interruptions.

vii. Deterioration of Stock in Cold Storage: this policy is basically designed to offer protection to the insured against loss, damage or breakdown of the insured machine, refrigerator or equipment used as storage devices. The insurance company will indemnify the insured if the breakdown in the machine results in deterioration of the stocks (perishable goods).

Professional Liability Insurance

This policy usually provides cover for professional workers such as Chartered Accountants, Actuaries, Doctors, Auditors, Tax administrators, Lawyers, etc., and caters for any legal liability that may arise because of professional negligence, errors or omissions on the part of the insured or that of their employee. The insurance company agrees to indemnify the insured up to but not exceeding the stated limit in the schedule for which the insured is legally liable to pay.

Director and Officers Liability Insurance

The Directors and Officers Liability insurance is taken by directors or officers of a company to protect them against losses arising from claims that may be either jointly or severally made against them by reason of committing any wrongful act(s) in their capacity as directors and officers. Wrongful acts as used here is generally defined as omissions, misleading statements, errors, negligence or even breach of duty of the insured director or officer individually or otherwise.

Bankers Indemnity Policy

The banking sector usually faces high level of risk when dealing with monies and securities belonging to their customers and companies. In the event of loss of money and securities of customers arising from theft, misappropriation, destruction by fire, etc., the insurance company will indemnify the insured bank.

Guarantee Policy

The guarantee policy is generally undertaken by an employer (the insured) to cover for possible fraudulent and dishonest acts of their employees resulting in pecuniary losses. The dishonest act resulting in financial loss must be in connection with the work they perform for the company.

Public Liability Insurance

This policy provides insurance for policyholders against any liabilities arising from accidental body injury, death or damage to property caused by the policyholder or their representative to other third parties in connection with the business of the insured. The cover may also include other legal costs or expenses incurred with the written consent of the company. The policy is generally designed for businesses such as hotels, night clubs and cinemas where large number of customers use the business premise. Also, public liability policies usually cover the insured against his/her liabilities arising from an accident leading to death, property damage or bodily injury to the public.

Workmen's Compensation Policy

Workmen's compensation policies are generally mandatory to be taken by employers to cover occupational injuries and death of their employees. Some companies have however extended the workmen's compensation policy to include cover for disabilities when an employee is involved in an accident at the workplace only. The general trend with this policy requires companies to offer workmen's compensation benefits to cover bodily injury, disability or death of an employee occurring out of or in the course of employment or even outside the course of employment. The policy may even cover all expenses incurred by an employee while defending any claim for such compensation with the consent of the company. This is often known as 'any cause' benefit or 'all occurrences' benefits.

Product Liability Policy

Product liability policies seek to indemnify the insured against accidents leading to death or bodily injury because of consuming the insured's product. The product liability insurance protects the insured business against legal damages in the event of death, bodily injury or illness to a third party or the public arising from the sale or supply of defective products by the business to third parties.

Cyber Crime Insurance

This insurance is basically designed to protect individuals and companies from risks associated with activities involving the use of information technology infrastructure. The insurance thus protects one from internet-based risks. Liability coverage under this policy may indemnify individuals and companies for third-party losses arising from failure to safeguard their data, errors and omissions. First-party coverage on the other hand may include losses arising from loss, destruction, hacking and extortion of data.

Bonds

Bonds are generally contracts among three parties. The parties involved in a bond contract are the principal (employer), the contractor and the guarantor. The guarantor (insurance company/surety) seeks to provide guarantee that the principal (person engaging the service of the contractor) will be indemnified should the contractor default in executing the services as expected by the principal. Should the contractor fail to fulfil the obligations under the contract thereby leading to financial loss, the principal is entitled to call on the bond and the guarantor is obliged to fulfil the promise made in the guarantee. These guarantees are issued by the insurer to the contractor for projects and/or loans granted by the principal.

The following are general examples of bond insurance.

i. Bid Bond: To tender in for a contract, bid bond is mostly required. The bond is thus taken by contractors who wish to tender for projects. The insurance company guarantees the principal who is the owner of the project that the bidder (contractor) will continue to remain in the bidding process until the project in question is awarded. In guaranteeing for the contractor, the insurance company assures to pay the principal an amount up to the bond value should the contractor withdraw from the bidding process or fail to sign the contract.
ii. Performance Bond: This bond is designed to protect persons who have been awarded contract to execute. That is, the performance bond seeks to guarantee to the principal on the contractor's behalf that the contractor will perform the contract awarded to him/her based on the stated specification and within the stated time allocated for the project.
iii. Custom Bond: The custom bond is a guarantee by the insurance company to governing/regulatory bodies such as the Ghana Revenue Authority, that in the event of loss of revenue arising from the failure, default or non-compliance of the insured (usually a company) to pay for custom duties associated with export and imports, the insurance company will become liable to pay. For example, a company that is involved in the import and export of goods from Ghana is legally required to immediately pay for custom duties once the goods leave or enter the country. The body responsible for collecting such duties will, however, allow the importing/exporting company to defer duty payment if there is a custom bond in place to serve a guarantee.
iv. Re-exportation Bond: This bond is usually taken by individuals, businesses and clients who import goods into a country for use during their visit and to send the goods back upon returning to their home country. This serves as a guarantee up to the duty value should the individual or client fail to send the goods back. At other instances, the insurance company issues the re-exportation bonds to clients who intend to re-export imported goods to another country.
v. Exportation Bond: This bond is taken by insured persons who are interested in exporting locally produced goods to other countries. The bond then becomes a guarantee to respective regulatory bodies responsible for issuing export tax. The exportation bond therefore serves as a guarantee such that should the insured fail to export the goods, the insurance company will be liable to pay a sum up to the sales tax that has been lost to the state.
vi. Warehouse Bond: Certain unforeseen events may require companies and individual importers to have their goods to be sent to their warehouse even though duties on those goods have not been paid. When this happens, the warehouse bond serves as a guarantee to pay an amount up to settle the duty charges.
vii. Removal Bond: In the removal of goods from one destination to another, the bond guarantees the individual to pay an amount up to the bond value should

the goods not be delivered at the designated destination thereby resulting in loss of duty to the state.

viii. Advanced Payment Bond: The Advanced payment bond is generally a guarantee that the contractor will perform his/her task with respect to payments given to him/her as advance payment towards the execution of the contract.

It should be noted that bonds are not insurance policies. They are simply referred to as 'guarantees'. The following are differences between bonds and insurance policies:

i. Bonds involve three parties (the guarantor, the contractor and the principal) while insurance policies involve two parties (insurer and insured).
ii. With bonds, the guarantor/insurer has right of recourse after payment of claim. To this end, a counter indemnity is always executed. However, for insurance policies, there is no such right of recourse.
iii. Bonds are irrevocable, whereas insurance policies can be cancelled.
iv. Banks can issue bonds but cannot issue insurance policies.
v. Bonds are specialty contracts and so are signed, witnessed, sealed and delivered whereas insurance policies are simple contracts and so are only signed.

Life Insurance Products

Life insurance products are generally designed to cover the life of a person. It is generally purchased by a sequence of payments, monthly, quarterly or semi-annually. The section discusses some types of products that are generally provided by insurers on the life insurance market.

Education Plan

This policy is usually taken by parents or guardians who are 18 years and above to cover the educational needs of their children. In some cases, the policy is designed as a savings tool that provides a lump sum benefit towards future educational expenses. It may also be taken by individuals to enable them take care of their own education. The policy may also serve as an investment from which the policyholder can make periodic withdrawal towards the settlement of their educational expenses. The most common type of education plan is the Immediate Death Benefit. This is more of an investment account created on behalf of the child to cover the education. In the event of the death of the parent or guardian of the child, the appropriate sum assured is then paid in addition to the investment account and paid to beneficiary to cover for the child's education.

Whole Life

This life insurance policy as the name suggest is designed to protect the whole life of the policyholder. In most cases, this type of policy is allowed to build cash value such that the policyholder may use it as a collateral to secure loan. This policy may have various variations based on the jurisdiction in question. For example, the policy may build cash value over the life of the policy.

Funeral Plan

Funeral plan is a variation of whole life plan designed for individuals and groups to provide funds towards the funeral expenses upon the death of the insured. One key benefit of funeral plan is that upon the death of the insured during the waiting period, the full sum assured is payable to the beneficiaries. One main example of funeral policy is the group policy. This policy provides life insurance cover for groups of people, be it group of employees, an association or society. It is usually a single contract policy that covers the entire group. The policy owner may be an employer or an entity. When for instance an employee covered under the group policy dies, the responsibility now lies on employers and other group members to pay for funeral expenses and other benefits to dependants of the deceased employee. The policy therefore is designed to provide benefits to named beneficiaries. In the event of death of a member of the group, the insurance company pays the sum assured to the employer to enable the employer to settle the financial commitment associated with the death of the employee or group member. In some cases, the benefit may be extended to cover permanent disability where members who suffer injury and become disabled while carrying out their employment duties are given cash benefits as compensation.

Mortgage Protection Plan

This plan is designed for anyone who purchases and/or builds a house by means of mortgage loan to free himself/herself from all financial burdens in the event of critical illness or premature death before the mortgage is fully paid. In the case of premature death, the family members of the mortgagor are freed from all financial obligations associated with the mortgage. The main features of this policy are as follows:

i. insures the life of an individual for a specific period equivalent to the mortgage period
ii. insures against death of the mortgagor but cover can be extended to include critical illness, permanent disability and unemployment.

Retirement Plan

This policy allows individuals to save towards their retirement. Retirement plans are usually defined contribution schemes. Thus, the benefit to be accrued to the insured largely depends on the amount of contribution they have made and the return on their investment made. Some examples include End of Service Benefits. The End of Service Benefits are usually service plans taken up by employees in addition to their statutory pensions. The plan is designed to pay out cash benefits to named beneficiaries. The cash benefit may either be paid to the employee at a maturity date when they retire or it may be paid to another named beneficiary upon the death of an employee before the maturity period. The following are some of the additional benefits a policyholder may choose.

i. Hospitalisation Cash Income: The policyholder may benefit from the end of service policy if within six months of the inception of the policy, the policyholder is hospitalised. In this regard, the insurance company shall pay an amount of money based on the sum assured in the form of *in hospital cash income benefit* for a maximum of three hundred and sixty-five days the policyholder spends in the hospital.
ii. Accident Indemnity: In a situation where the policyholder is involved in an accident and thereby sustains body injuries which causes him to be temporary disabled, the insurance company shall pay the policyholder monthly benefits. On the other hand, if the accident renders the policyholder to be permanently disabled, the insurance company becomes liable to pay a lump sum cash benefit to the policyholder.
iii. Annuity: With this benefit, the policyholder stands to receive regular income be it annually, bi-annually or quarterly for a stipulated number of years upon maturity of the policy.
iv. Gratuity: Upon maturity of the policy, the policyholder is liable to receive a lump sum of money as indemnity.

Micro-Insurance

This type of insurance plan is like a pension plan. The main difference is that micro-insurance plan allows policyholders to pay premiums daily through collectors/agents of the insurance company. Another unique feature is that the premiums collected gives the policyholder access to funds which can be accessed every three months. The micro-insurance policy is generally designed for those in the informal sector.

Keyman Insurance Policy

Keyman insurance policies are designed to offer protection to an employer in the event of loss of a key top executive or employees because of accidents or death that renders them incapable of performing the duties required of them. That is, because most businesses have key personnel whose capital, energy, experience and technology drives the business, the Keyman insurance policy caters for losses that may arise in the event of losing these key personnel. This person could be anyone directly associated with the business whose demise could cause financial strain to the business. The policy allows organisations and businesses to insure their key personnel for business continuity purposes. It is purchased by a company on the life of a key person within the organisation to protect the company against loss of profit or cost of replacing the key person in the event of death. The objective is to indemnify the business for losses and facilitate business continuity. It replaces profit that ordinarily would have been lost and provides funds for meeting the cost of replacing/training a successor.

Loan Protection Policy

Generally, loan protection policies are designed to cover any risk exposed to a bank as a result of death or disability of a borrower (temporary or permanent). Loan protection policies thus cover the liabilities associated with the inability of the borrower to pay back loan if the borrower passes on.

Life Savings Plan

This type of life insurance product is an endowment policy that requires the policyholder to pay regular premiums over a specified period. The insurance company then guarantees to pay a lump sum to the named beneficiary after an agreed number of years (minimum of five years) whether the insured has finished paying his premiums or not.

Family Protection Policy

This policy is designed to provide cash benefits to beneficiaries of the policy upon the death of the breadwinner of the family. This policy ensures that in the absence of the breadwinner by virtue of death or permanent disability, the family continues to enjoy life.

Student Welfare Policy

Generally, insurance companies partner with educational institutions to improve the welfare of the students and their guardians by providing comprehensive life insurance cover for them. The insurance cover may be in the form of a lump sum under a single policy such that in the event of death or permanent disability, the student or guardian may be compensated.

Master Plan Policy

This policy is mostly designed to provide cover to the policyholder upon the death of the assured. The unique feature of the policy is that it provides the policyholder with part of the sum assured on instalment basis even before the maturity date. In the event of death of the insured within the duration of the policy, the policyholder is still entitled to the full sum assured irrespective of the amount already paid out in instalment to the policyholder.

Children Welfare Policy

This is an endowment policy that seeks to provide unique benefits to its beneficiaries. This policy is also designed to provide 2% per annum of the sum assured to cater for the upkeep of the child should the sponsor die before the maturity of the policy. Also, the premium to be paid is waived upon the death of the sponsor before maturity of the policy while at the same time the cover is kept in force until the child is of age and ready for the school for which the policy was bought. Upon maturity, a lump sum is paid to cater for the admission cost of the child's secondary and university level education. The policy also covers the school fees of the child for a maximum of four years.

Life Guaranteed Plan

This policy is a combination of pure investment policy and insurance policy. The policy guarantees to pay a lump sum which is usually a portion of the sum assured to the beneficiary every five years if the assured is to die before the maturity of the policy. However, the lump sum will be paid provided that all premiums from the inception of the policy have been paid in full. Upon the maturity of the policy, the life assured has two options of benefit. The life assured may either opt for the cash option where the amount due the life assured will be paid immediately or the life assured may opt for the retention option where the amount due the life assured will be transferred to a separate fund to generate interest on yearly basis (pure investment policy). The amount retained under this option is credited with interest towards the payment of claim on maturity or death. The retention option is also a default option such that if the life assured fails to choose any of the two options of benefit, then the retention option will be automatically applied.

Wealth Master Plan

This life insurance policy is designed to offer flexible and convenient approach to individuals to ensure that in the case of death, their family income, long and medium-term goals and aspirations do not die alongside. This policy is a conventional endowment policy that offers policyholders the opportunity to create wealth and to financially plan towards accomplishing their lifetime goals. In the event of death, a stated sum assured is payable at the maturity of the policy. The wealth master plus is a term policy and as such the policy expires after maturity.

Personal Insurance Policy

This type of life insurance policy ensures that in the event of death or bodily injury caused by accident, the insurer will pay the insured or his legal representative compensation as stated in the policy. Generally, the insurance company is liable to pay a lump sum to the beneficiary in the event of death or permanent disability/temporary disability. There are, however, variations of this policy based on the terms of the policy as well as the jurisdiction.

Health Insurance

Some life insurance products directly fall under health insurance. Health insurance in some jurisdictions is considered as an aspect of life insurance. Health insurance can be defined as an insurance coverage that seeks to provide payments as benefits to cover for losses arising from accidents, medical expenses, accidental death or disability. The health expenses incurred by the insured may be paid directly to the insured in the form of reimbursement. It may also be paid directly to the care giver by the insurer. General examples of health insurance policies are explained below.

i. Critical Illness Plan

   The critical illness plan is a health policy which pays a lump sum to the policyholder to cover against any diagnosed dreadful disease(s). Critical illness as used here refers to life-threatening diseases including but not limited to stroke, cancer, heart attack and paralysis, among several others. Depending on the age and the class of disease, a premium is quoted. When applying for critical illness plan, the applicant is required to disclose all known medical conditions (if any) to the insurer. Based on the information provided by the applicant, the insurer may request for a medical examination from the applicant carried out by a recommended health centre.

ii. Health Plan

This policy is designed to cover for all the medical expenses (usually up to a sum insured limit) of the insured in the event of sudden illness, hospitalisation or accident. Other related expenses such as rent and utility bills arising from the inability of the insured to settle those expenses because of the illness may also be covered by the insurance company.

iii. Hospital Cash Plan

This plan seeks to provide financial support to individuals and/or their dependents in the event of loss of income arising from hospitalisation. There are basically two types of hospital cash plan. One may either opt for a family plan or an individual plan. For either the individual plan or the family plan, one has the option of including the parents such that they will also be covered. The main benefit of this plan is that the insurance pays daily hospital income to the beneficiary up to a stated number of days every year in the event of hospitalisation of any of the covered lives.

Exercises

1. How does non-life insurance differ from life insurance products?
2. Explain the following general insurance products.

    (i) Property insurance.
    (ii) Third-party motor insurance.
    (iii) Comprehensive motor insurance.
    (iv) Travel insurance

3. You are the manager of a large Insurance Company and have been approached by a service company which has a large clientele that transact business at its premises for advice. The management of the company is worried about its legal liabilities to clients that visit its premises. Advise the management of the service company of any insurance products available that can address their concern, explaining what is covered by the policy.
4. What is a bond? How is it different from an insurance policy?
5. Discuss an insurance policy that will be suitable for the key personnel of a large IT firm. Your discussion should include the benefit such a policy will offer the IT firm.

Further Reading

Black, K. J., & Skipper, H. D. J. (2000). *Life and Health Insurance* (13th ed., Chapters 4–8). Prentice Hall.

Gupta, P. K. (2016). *Essentials of Insurance and Risk'Management* (1st ed., Part III: Chapter 11, 12 & 13–15). Himalaya Publishing House Pvt Ltd.

Gupta, P. K. (2008). *Fundamental of Insurance* (1st ed., Unit 1: Chapter 9, 11, 12, 14, 15). Himalaya Publishing House.

Redja, G. E., McNamara, J., & Rabel, W. H. (2022). *Principles of Risk Management and Insurance* (Chapters 24–27). Pearson Addison Wesley.

Vaughan, E. J., & Vaughan, T. M. (2008). *Fundamentals of Risk Management and Insurance* (10th ed., Chapters 31–33). John Wiley & Sons.

Chapter 4
Risk, Insurance And The Home

Abstract This chapter examines the various risk exposures present in the household and explores the risk management strategies, including insurance, that can be employed to mitigate them. It identifies early indicators of potential challenges in long-term decision-making within relationships, discusses the foundational principles of marital life, and addresses a range of issues that may threaten the family, which is regarded as the core unit of society. Appropriate loss control and loss financing measures are proposed for these threats. The chapter further considers the risks associated with religious fanaticism, outlining corresponding loss control and financing strategies. Defiant behaviour is also discussed, with attention given to the factors that trigger such behaviour, and the role of insurance and preventive measures in managing these risks. Finally, the chapter concludes by examining the risk exposures associated with festive activities, along with the loss control and financing techniques that can be applied to reduce potential losses.

Keywords Defiant behaviour · Festivities · Loss finance · Loss control · Principles of marriage life · Religious fanatism

Introduction

Risk is engrained in every area of our lives and the home is no exception. This chapter examines the risk exposures in the home and the risk management techniques including insurance that can be deployed to provide solutions. It provides the signals to potential problems in a long-lasting relationship decision-making and discusses the principles of marriage and life; a host of issues that threaten the family as a core of every society. Loss control and loss finance measures are provided for these threats. Religious fanatism and the risk it poses are also discussed together with the loss control and loss finance measures to deal with these risks. Defiant behaviour, a type of undesirable behaviour, typically exhibited by young people that have no boundaries is also discussed. Many factors trigger this behaviour, a number of which are discussed, the loss control measures and the role of insurance in its management.

C. Andoh, *Fundamentals of Managing Risk and Insurance*,
https://doi.org/10.1007/978-981-95-4581-0_4

Finally, the chapter ends with festivities, a type of celebration that can be found in the developing world, the risk exposures, the loss finance and loss control measures to mitigate these risks.

Some Signals to Potential Problems in a Long-Lasting Relationship

Marriage can be seen as a risk. Things can go smoothly and the couple can have a good life together. However, things can also go wrong which can lead to divorce. In the case of a divorce the individuals concerned would have wasted a good number of years and funds in a failed partnership. The decision to marry or not becomes an issue of risk.

Maintaining long-lasting relationships is usually not a smooth journey: one generally must be tough and resilient to keep a relationship alive for a very long time. It would be disappointing to realise, after committing to a relationship, that certain undesirable behaviour surfaces months or years down the line. Undesirable behaviour can be difficult to determine at first sight, but some traits are likely to become clear as time passes during the friendship period. These traits should be incorporated in the decision-making process.

One cannot change a person's character overnight or, indeed, in the immediate future. Behaviour once built is hard to change when a person grows into adulthood. Consequently, before one enters a lasting relationship, it is extremely important that certain traits are looked out for.

This section discusses some early warning signs that can assist in identifying some of these undesirable traits before one jump into a long-lasting relationship.

Communication

Clear and open communication reveals a person's true character over time. A person cannot pretend to be someone that they are not forever. Engaging in diversified communication with a potential partner will eventually reveal their true nature. If, for example, discussion reveals that the potential partner has experienced tough times in the past, then most likely this person can stand equally tough times in the future. Also, someone who will readily and happily communicate issues that bother them will always want to voice and resolve issues that arise. Such a person wants amicable solutions to problems that crop up. However, a person who is reluctant to discuss issues may have deeper secrets that could potentially harm a marriage. For example, a person may have children elsewhere and may fear that revealing this information will mar the relationship. Of course, if your future partner is reluctant to accept your children or listen to issues concerning your children you may have had in a previous relationship, then this is a good indication of potential problems ahead.

Another way to discover the true nature of a potential partner is to engage with their friends and tease out needed information. Being familiar with friends or colleagues can help in predicting a person's character and lifestyle. A person who is pampered is more likely to expect from the partner the same treatment and this can imply that in times of need that person may react badly.

A person who never returns calls also signals that there are potential problems ahead. On the other hand, a person who is always arguing and trying to prove their point is likely not the right person for you.

Temperament

A good-tempered person can withstand tough times more easily than a bad-tempered person. Consequently, temperament is one thing to look out for. A snobbish and arrogant person is unlikely to be supportive in difficult moments.

Money

One can also check for signs of the misuse of money or other resources. A person who overspends or does not manage money well will struggle when challenging times arise. However, a person who spends wisely on urgent issues and will readily offer to help is a person that can withstand difficult times.

Someone who saves or invests wisely part of any surplus income thinks about the future, not the immediate situation or condition and therefore would be able to manage loss exposures better because of the ability to withdraw part of any invested funds to address difficulties that may arise.

Financial Demand Approach

The behaviour portrayed by the request of financial support will assist in assessing how a person will behave when money is not readily available and children's needs are not met. For example, one's reaction to intermittent demands for money portrays a lot about how one will behave in times of financial difficulty.

One can also deny money on request on some occasions. During such times, loyal people will tend to behave just as when money was available whereas opportunistic individuals will be upset or even walk away from you.

Another approach (if you have the resources) is to provide a potential partner with a lot of monetary aid. This way, you most likely bring out the true character of the person. If they show modesty in what they purchase and an interest in investment, such a person should be able to stand the test of difficult times.

Future Expectations

One should seek to discover the future expectations of a potential partner to see if their needs match yours. If there are differences, agreements can be made to satisfy both parties. For example, you can propose operating a joint bank account so that both partners are aware of the credits and debits to the account. If your potential partner agrees, then it means that person is ready to sacrifice the privacy for the common good.

Observation

By carefully observing and paying attention to a person's actions and behaviour over a period, one can draw conclusions about behavioural patterns in a variety of settings. Another area for observation is budgeting. It is important for budgets to be drawn up so that impulse buying is minimised. Does the potential partner manage money well, plan for both the best- and worst-case scenarios and stick to the budget drawn?

One can also intentionally commit errors and observe how a person is concerned about one's successes or failures. For example, one can dress shabbily and observe how a person corrects the shabby dressing.

Hardworking

A hardworking person indicates someone that can thrive during difficult times and provide support when the going gets tough. A hardworking person will try as much as possible to support the household and cater for unforeseen problems that may arise.

Other Signals

If you are abused, verbally, emotionally, financially or physically in a relationship, you should terminate the partnership. If emotional blackmail becomes a way of life: your partner belittles you in the presence of other people or lets people know that you are a bad person or uses an occasion to disgrace you, one should leave the relationship. Reluctance to go for marriage counselling to resolve problems in a marriage is a likely precursor of a failed relationship.

Principles of a Marriage Life

Marriage can be considered as a sacred institution that binds two individuals together and brings together their respective families. It is also a means of gaining companionship and arguably a means of productivity. Before a person decides to enter a marriage, it is important certain principles are discussed extensively.

The first principle of marriage life is the principle of *utmost good faith*: each party to a marriage contract should avoid concealing information about oneself to take unfair advantage of the other. There should be total disclosure of all relevant information about oneself in a marriage decision process. For example, an individual intending to get married can undergo a sickle cell test to determine the blood type a person has. If a person is 'AS', then it would be unwise to marry a person with the same blood type as children from the marriage would be at risk of being 'SS' which could pose challenges to a couple. This principle essentially removes the element of surprise from a marriage and helps the couple to have a backup plan once the relevant information is known.

The second principle is *expectation*. This principle states that all relevant needs should be disclosed prior to a marriage. No assumptions should be made by either partner about the needs of the other but should be openly discussed and agreed. This principle settles disputes that might arise from the divergent needs of either partner when the marriage is in force. These expectations may be the number of children to have or the methods to employ in the upbringing of children. Any anticipated interference from outsiders should be discussed extensively prior to the marriage as third-party interference can wreck the marriage. This principle essentially helps to minimise disputes that might arise by virtue of outside factors when the marriage is in force. Issues such as maximum length of time in-laws, friends could stay with the couple should be discussed extensively prior to the marriage.

The third principle is *trust*. The trust principle states that individuals intending to get married should keep their word and stay true to the vows that they make to each other. Trust involves the belief and the conviction that one will do what one says. Signs of mistrust from either the man or the woman should not be taken for granted prior to marriage. When trust is lacking, it threatens any marriage because one party begins to lose the belief and conviction in the other.

Family Life

The family is the core of every society. A host of issues threaten the success of every family or married couple and the success of every home hinges upon the extent to which married couples handle its affairs. In this section, we discuss the major issues and offer techniques to mitigate or eliminate threats.

Trust

Married couples undertake to trust each other because unless they spend all their time together, they cannot monitor each other all the time. When trust is lacking, it threatens any marriage because one party begins to lose belief in the other. Trust helps a marriage to stand strong.

A couple with trust issues must seek marriage therapy as a loss control measure to reduce the effect of this on the marriage.

Communication

Lack of good communication could pose a threat to successful married life. Communication is important because it draws people together. It reveals one's thought processes, feelings and any problems that an individual may have. The absence of communication makes it difficult for any marriage to thrive because the other partner does not know what the other person thinks or feels. If the concerns of either partner are kept to themselves, this eventually widens the distance between the couple. If a partner has an extra-marital affair, it leads to a breach of trust and could create communication barriers.

Also, in dealing with each other, partners may send mixed signals. One partner may expect the other to read his or her actions and may not find it necessary to say out loud what he or she means. This may cause the other partner to be frustrated because not all non-verbal communication can be interpreted accurately. Thus, good communication binds couples together as it prevents ambiguity.

As a loss control measure, couples should read and research about the concept of communication to apply it in their marriage. Couples can enrol in communication lessons or read relevant literature. Couples can also undergo counselling to improve the way that they communicate with each other. By its very nature, counselling requires those undertaking it to sit down together and talk out things with each other. Couples should cultivate the habit of greeting each other in the morning and asking each other how their respective days have been. The family can also have a family Thanksgiving Day where each member of the family could express their love to each other.

As a loss finance measure, couples can retain part of their income to purchase books or other publications on good communication and read them.

Finance

Financial problems are at the root of many marriage problems. When there is little or no money in the home, problems arise as the couple cannot provide for each other as they would like. Also, when one partner earns more than the other, the other person may feel insecure. This pertains mainly to men. This is because most men prefer to be the main breadwinners of their families, and when it so happens that their wives are earning more and providing for more of the home expenses, they tend to feel insecure and feel that their wives are dominating them.

Marriage also leads to the merging of individual finances. Behaviour such as impulse buying, overspending and stinginess can affect the marriage. This is because such behaviour deprives the couple of certain basic amenities or savings. Also, if the regular source of income of the breadwinner is lost, the marriage can be affected significantly. The loss of a job or a disability leading to a similar outcome is one of the major causes of stress in a marriage.

Married couples can go for periodic counselling to assist them in understanding that marriage is built on solid values such as trust, but not on money. The couple can also draw up a budget as a loss control measure to eliminate issues such as impulse buying or other wasteful practices and if they have not yet done so, open a joint bank account to monitor credits and debits. The need to show love and concern especially during a stressful period of unemployment is paramount.

A loss finance measure for protection against such circumstances would be to take out insurance cover for child education or the disability of one or both parties. A couple could also mitigate the effects of future financial problems by having a savings account they regularly pay into when working.

Unemployment

Unemployment can cause the break-up of a successful marriage. Unemployment makes the running of the home very difficult since there will be little or no money for that. It might even be difficult to feed the family.

One key loss control measure is education. When couples educate themselves to acquire the necessary skills and qualifications for work, it will be easier to obtain and retain a well-paying job. The setting up of one's own business can assist in hard times. Also, the installation of smoke detectors at business premises can give an early warning of a potentially damaging fire that might render someone unemployed. As a loss finance measure, one can take out a fire insurance policy for the business.

Sex

Sex is important in marriage because apart from procreation, it consummates the marriage, spices the relationship up and keeps it alive. Lack of sexual satisfaction in marriage can cause the partners to seek satisfaction with others that would likely break the marriage. Such problems might occur because of the disparate experience of the partners, the over tiredness of one partner because of a challenging or stressful job, the lack of time the couple must spend together, or age differentials between the partners.

A loss control measure is to seek help from medical doctors, gynaecologists or psychologists. A married couple should avoid flimsy excuses for refusing sexual advances from each other. Couples can spice their marriage up by going on vacations or holidays together and attend sex education classes or read books on the subject.

A loss finance measure is to save money to purchase materials on sex education that teach partners how to satisfy each other. Possession of health insurance can also help fund the treatment of problems that are health related.

Third-party interference (Outside influence)

Third party's interferences can threaten the success of a happy home. Before two people get married, they evidently have different families but also usually different friends, work colleagues and associations. When they get married, it is usually prudent to merge these sets of people to ensure that harmony prevails. However, situations arise when one partner does not identify with the other's friends or colleagues and believe that they negatively influence the partner. There are instances where marriages break up because of the persistent influence of friends. Friends and in-laws tend to impose their own opinions and this often leads to misunderstandings between the couple. Some in-laws make many demands on married couples without regard to their earning capacity and/or the needs of the married couples themselves.

When in-laws move to live in the home of the couple or vice versa—it causes discomfort for some partners and prevents the couple from having privacy and deciding on issues for themselves. Some women/men share secrets about their marriage with their parents or friends that breaks the bond between the couple, leading to disputes. In addition, there may be conflicts if one partner feels that the parents or relations are not treated well by the other partner. When both husband and wife keep excessive friendship contacts after marriage, they are likely to spend less time with each other. Friends are likely to trigger undesired attitudes, such as jealousy, from one spouse towards the other.

A loss control measure is to discuss and decide beforehand how such interferences should be handled when they occur in the future. The couple must agree on specified periods any relative may wish to live with them. The couple should avoid sharing their marital issues with others and they should not give third parties the opportunity to control what goes on in their home. The couple should know each other's friends and associations. If one partner does not agree to a particular set of friends and it will cost the other nothing to disassociate from them, then this should be agreed to. Each partner should treat the relations of the other respectfully. Couples can also communicate to their extended families that the marriage needs privacy and that only when the partners fail to reach an amicable solution to a problem should they be invited to resolve issues. Married couples need to drastically limit the number of friends they individually have as well as the time they spend with them.

Bringing up Children

Another source of possible friction is a disagreement on how to raise the children from the marriage. Since married couples may be from different backgrounds, they may have varying views on how to raise children. Such views may range from a strict disciplinarian method to a more lenient approach. Couples should agree before having children on how they intend to raise their children as a loss control measure.

Infertility

In many cultures, children are necessities in marriage. If a couple are not able to bear children, problems arise. In many cases, in Ghana, a man divorces his wife, if she is infertile and looks for another partner who can bear children. For men, impotency can be a problem. One cause of this is an unhealthy lifestyle: bad eating habits, bad drinking habits and little or no exercise can all contribute to such problems. When this is the case, women may seek divorce or look for sexual satisfaction with or without the consent of the man.

Couples should use safe contraceptives when they are not ready to start a family to prevent unwanted pregnancies and should agree on the method to use with a health professional. Abortions can adversely affect a woman's chances of getting pregnant in the future. Overworking can decrease sexual drive and so married couples should try to limit the working day, overly stressful work or bring work home with them. Good diets and regular exercise can help with sexual drive. Couples can increase the frequency of sexual intercourse to ensure that their chance of successful procreation is increased. In addition, if there are fertility problems, couples can undergo fertility treatment. Advancements in science have made it possible for those who have fertility problems or are past the usual age of childbirth to give birth to their own biological children. Therefore, if a couple has problems conceiving, medical treatment should be considered. Artificial insemination is one technique available to assist couples. Adoption is another option that could be classified as a loss control measure.

The cost of treatment for infertility is usually very high. Couples might therefore take out medical expense insurance to offset such costs. Setting funds aside for the adoption of a child is a loss finance measure.

Arrival of a new baby and the demands of growing children

The arrival of a new baby puts extra stress on the home. When this happens, men may feel neglected by their wives who are taking care of the new baby. Some men feel that the baby is taking all their wife's time, while others cannot put up with the physical changes in their wives during pregnancy and after delivery. This leads to arguments and potential infidelity that can easily break up a marriage.

A loss control measure is for men to educate themselves about how a pregnancy affects their wives. Some prenatal classes are open to both the father and mother. Women should also make a conscious effort not to neglect their husbands after a birth. Richer families might consider hiring a nanny so that the couple can have more time together.

Respect

When there is no mutual respect, couples usually quarrel and use abusive words on each other. Love without respect is not really love. Human beings are egoistic and crave respect. If one feels constantly disrespected by your partner, divorce is the likely outcome. This may happen when one or the other of the couple loses their job and cannot provide for the family.

As a loss control measure, married couples should always treat each other with respect Conflicting ideas should not be the basis for insults and fights in the family. The tone used between married couples should be one that shows respect.

As a loss finance measure, money can be set aside to pay for the services of a marriage counsellor to work with the couple on how they relate to each other.

Health issues

Sometimes married couples face unexpected health problems. It could be stroke, typhoid, cancer or many other things. These ailments can seriously drain the resources of a happy home if the person that becomes ill is the main breadwinner in the family. The death of a partner can be devastating for the surviving spouse.

As a loss control measure, couples should care about the food they eat and the water they drink. Food and water should be clean for consumption. They should also keep their home clean and tidy. It is also good for both partners to be employed so that when there is a problem, the other can take over. Couples should also note that nothing lasts forever and should not over rely on their partners. Going for counselling to support each other in such circumstances as well as getting emotional support from friends and family can also help.

As a loss finance measure, married couples can purchase health insurance for unexpected medical expenses. Taking a disability and dread disease insurance policy can help provide income for the home when one of them becomes incapable of earning income. Life insurance can also be purchased to provide for the needs of the home should the unfortunate event of death occur. Partners should make a will to transfer their assets properties to the surviving spouse.

Loss of assets

Property belonging to a married couple can be lost to fire or flood, leaving them homeless. A burglary might mean that they lose valuable belongings. A couple may decide to end their marriage because all that they laboured for has been lost.

As a loss control measure, couples should avoid the exposure of combustible materials close to fire. This involves the safe positioning of gas cylinders in kitchens and turning off electrical gadgets when not in use. There should also be a good drainage system around the house. Couples should ensure that all doors and windows are properly locked before leaving the house or going to sleep. They may also consider obtaining a dog to warn off possible intruders. Couples can purchase home and liability insurance to cover such possible losses.

Longevity

A married couple may live longer than expected and outlive their resources. A loss control measure is to seek retirement planning from financial advisors. The purchase of an annuity or other investments can also help mitigate the costs of old age.

Divorce

Divorce may be caused by external influences, interference by other family members or by an internal problem between the couple. An extra-marital affair is likely to cause the dissolution of a marriage. As a loss control measure, couples can seek counselling from other married couples, good pastors or Imams.

Some funds can be set aside to offset any expenses or legal liabilities resulting from a divorce. A partner may be held liable when a lawsuit ensues. Legal expense insurance can be purchased to fund any legal costs arising from divorce proceedings.

Abuse

There are instances where married couples physically abuse each other. In certain cases, both partners are culpable, but in most cases, the woman is likely to be on the receiving end of the physical abuse. Such a development will pose a serious threat to a successful marriage.

As a loss control measure, the partners should go to their religious leaders for spiritual guidance and prayers. In Ghana, the Commission for Human Rights and Administrative Justice must become involved in such abuses in marriage and should punish and prosecute such offenders.

The Domestic Violence and Victims Support Unit (DOVVSU) of the Ghana Police Service provides free service to the members of the public that are abused by any member of their families.

As a loss finance measure, one can take up a health insurance policy to cover medical expenses in the event of such abuse happening.

Addiction

The addiction of either partner to certain behaviours can affect the marriage. If either partner is unable to stop an action that is intolerable to the other such as smoking, excessive drinking or drug taking, the marriage is in jeopardy. There are certain adverse effects of both smoking and alcohol. These include the risk of liver cancer, abuse due to drunkenness and the use of family resources to finance such addictions.

If a partner is addicted to alcohol, the other partner should enrol the alcoholic in alcoholic anonymous groups that can help get over the addiction. Also, it may be prudent to relocate as the addictions may be caused or influenced by other alcoholics or smokers in the neighbourhood where the couple reside. An addicted person can also be sent to a drug rehabilitation centre.

Technology

The advent of technology has brought several gadgets such as computers, television sets, mobile phones and tablets that people have become attached to. Excessive use of these gadgets can be annoying for a partner. Refusing to pay attention to your partner and their needs because a phone is ringing or there is a programme on TV could lead to quarrels.

A couple can create a family day and spend time together away from all technological gadgets. A loss finance measure is to try to set some funds aside to meet the costs of family days.

Laziness

The standard of living is rising partly due to advances in technology. Higher disposable income is required to cope with this increasing standard of living. Hence there is an increased pressure on families to work hard. When one or both partners are lazy, there will be problems as there will be little money to meet the basic needs of the home. Squabbles about money are likely and could eventually wreck the marriage.

A loss control measure is simple hard work. Both partners should find work so that the provision of the needs of the home will not fall on the shoulders of just one person. The services of a home help can be sought to help maintain the cleanliness of the home. Couples should find ways of cutting down on their expenses such as switching off all lights when not in use, using public transport or walking instead of driving their car so that they will have enough money to spend on more essential services.

Urbanisation

Urbanisation has made people very busy. Most people spend long hours at their workplaces and their children also spend more time in school attending extra classes. As a result, families rarely spend much time together or have time to talk properly.

A loss control measure is for families to set aside a day in which they can all spend time together, for instance, on Sundays, and make use of public holidays.

A loss finance measure is to self-insure by setting money aside that can be used for family gatherings and holidays.

Bad behaviour of the couple's children

When the child of a married couple brings problems home from school, it can adversely affect the marriage. Issues such as a suspension from school for activities such as fighting, smoking, drinking, etc., are difficult to manage. Stepchildren can be problematic, if they do not have a good relationship with the new partner of their birth father or mother.

As a loss control measure, children must be shown love and care by the couple. A married couple must treat their biological and stepchildren equally to ensure that they feel part of the family. The couple should invest in their children's education to ensure that they have the best opportunities to be fulfilled in the family and succeed in society at large.

As a loss finance measure, an education plan can be purchased to ensure the continuity of the children's education should some mishap befall one of their parents.

Democracy

Democracy is essential in a marital home because everyone should be at liberty to express his or her opinion without infringing on the rights of the other. When there is lack of democracy in married life, it can hamper the success of a marriage. One partner, usually the man may want to make all the decisions and expect everyone in the family to accept them. When some decisions are not accepted, he may become angry. An autocratic partner only stifles and destroys a marriage.

A loss control measure is for the couple to undergo counselling.

Achievement of a new social status

Sometimes when people climb higher on the academic ladder or attain new positions in their career, they develop new attitudes that are unhealthy for their marriage. These attitudes include disrespect, disregard and looking down on the other partner. It could be that the new status comes with more responsibilities that will lead to spending less time at home. In addition, when the educational gap between the couple widens, there is the possibility that it will pose some threat or challenges to the success of the marriage.

As a loss control measure, encouragement or financial support can be given to a partner to seek further educational advancement.

Distant relationships

Distance is another major threat to a successful relationship. If one partner lives and works in a different country or town for financial reasons, communication may only be possible through the phone or other electronic gadgets. There is little personal attachment and the couple do not share quality time with each other. This can cause instability in the relationship that can lead to a break-up.

As a loss control measure, a couple should make some savings and visit each other every quarter for persons living in another country or on a weekly basis for persons living within the same country.

Religious Fanaticism and Married Life

Most people in Ghana today identify themselves with one religion or the other. These religions shape who we are and what we do, and often urge us on to become better people. Religious fanaticism is a situation where one becomes overly involved in religious activities to the neglect of other equally important matters. Religious fanaticism is proving to be a growing problem in our society today. The fanatic is mostly seen as one involved in religious activities more often and neglecting their families. The religious fanatic, out of the blue, starts strictly adhering to the accepted religion's beliefs and expects everyone in the family to behave in a similar fashion. Today, many marriages are feeling the effects some of which are outlined below.

Lack of time spent with the family

One of the most direct effects of religious fanaticism is that in spending so much time at religious meetings and being involved in other religious activities, one minimises the time spent at home. This can create a rift between a husband and wife because of minimal communication and lack of quality time spent to develop the marriage. This could make one partner suspicious of the other and could lead to break-up of the marriage. Children also need considerable time and care. Some parents go to religious services and leave their children at home with no one to care for them. Religious fanaticism can lead to children lacking time both with their families and their peers.

As a loss control measure, it is important that couples set specific time to be spent with the family and limit the number of church activities in which they are involved. Heads of religious groups could also make their followers understand the advantages of spending time with families.

Employment

If one is overly committed to several activities in religious gatherings, one's job may be at risk. Some religions have programmes on working days and this prevents those who partake in these programmes from holding profitable jobs. There is nothing wrong with prayer, but there is time for everything. Also, some religious activities serve only as an avenue for people to gossip instead of using the time productively. This may place the financial burden of the family on only one spouse while the other spends all their time at religious meetings.

As a loss control measure, couples must agree on times to spend at religious meetings and must agree on the importance of employment for each spouse. Praying at lunch breaks or after the working day is over will solve some of these problems.

Financial burden

Taking part in so many religious activities will cost a lot in the form of dues and fees. If the new religious convert begins to divert most of his or her resources into religious activities and shirks other financial responsibilities in the home, it may increase the pressure and stress on the other partner. Though it is good to contribute to a religion financially, it is not justified if one has difficulty making ends meet at home.

As a loss control measure, couples should budget their funds and make sure all obligations are met before donations are made to religious bodies. Couples can also create a common account and plan how money is spent together.

As a loss finance measure, insurance companies could design policies that benefit religious leaders and members of religious bodies. For example, a funeral policy for religions would help to take care of the expenses for a member who dies. In addition, education policies can be taken out for children so that even when a substantial amount of one's income is used on religious activities, the children's education will not be jeopardised. Also, products such as life insurance policies have a savings component which when tapped into can provide some financial cushion in times of need.

Demands by some religions

The unreasonable demands of some religious sects put stress on marriages. Religious fanatics may take a conservative view regarding dress and grooming. A wife/husband who is a fanatic might view jewellery and other things used for beautification as sinful. Other sects may prohibit certain activities such as eating during certain periods that may be contrary to the expectations of the other partner. Couples should make their expectations regarding religious beliefs clear at the beginning of their marriages so as not to have any surprises down the road.

Divine intervention in times of ill health

Some religious fanatics may refuse to seek medical treatment when ill in the belief that divine intervention will cure the sickness. Some of these religious fanatics believe that whatever happens in one's life is God's will and do not care much about their health when indisposed. They may refuse a blood transfusion either for themselves, their spouse or children when a medical doctor prescribes it. Such decisions can lead to death leaving the other spouse a widower/widow.

As loss control measure, couples should become enlightened about the benefits of health and life insurance. Taking a health insurance policy will help in times of sickness. Life insurance will provide for the rest of the family in the event of the death of one partner.

Inadequate parental attention

The children of strongly religious parents can be left alone for long periods under little or no supervision. When this happens, the children may be influenced by their peers to engage in immoral practices such as stealing. Children do not learn from their parents as either one or both are frequently engaged in religious activities. This poor parental care is not in the interest of society and could lead to broken homes and delinquency.

As a loss control measure, married couples should spend quality time with children and assist with their children's homework. Alternatively, parents can involve their children in their religious activities.

Sex

Sex, a bonding agent and stress reliever for couples, is also a major factor that can be affected by religious fanaticism. Since couples hardly see each other, procreation activities become non-existent. The issue of fasting is also problematic as some religious leaders ask their followers to not only fast but also refrain from sexual relations over a period. This may lead to infidelity or other stress-related behaviour by the shunned partner.

A loss control measure is for married couples to agree that one is only allowed to fast during normal lent periods and that any abstinence from sex for religious reasons must be indicated well in advance.

Frequent quarrels and arguments

Another effect of religious fanaticism is the frequent quarrels and arguments it can cause in the home. Most religious fanatics tend to be overly judgemental of their partners and children. They are always on the lookout to point out the 'sins' of their family members and want everyone to act in accordance with their religious beliefs. If members of the family do not agree with this and still act as they please, unpleasant quarrels can result. Misunderstandings also occur when the couples have different beliefs. For instance, when a Christian gets married to a Muslim, there may be disagreements on which faith the children should adhere to, what food the family should eat, or what dress is appropriate. These conflicts do not create a happy home. A fanatical partner may develop a holier than thou attitude and disregard the opinions of the other spouse or try to impose the views on the other. We live in a changing world with new technological discoveries every year. A religious fanatic may hold on to old beliefs and reject modern ways of doing things.

As a loss control measure, a counsellor's advice may be sought, as effective negotiation skills are a necessary factor in managing such complex problems. Religious compatibility can also help minimise misunderstandings about the belief children should follow. If one partner decides to opt for the other partner's religion, these problems can disappear.

Counselling

Many married couples seek counsel from their religious leaders when they encounter problems in their relationship. Before taking this step, couples should try to discuss and resolve the problems themselves. This is not to say that religious counsel is wrong but sometimes pastors, deacons or imams make the wrong recommendations that can further aggravate problems. If every little misunderstanding is reported to the religious leader for spiritual intervention or counsel, then the marriage may be compromised. A religious fanatic would always adhere to what the pastor thinks is right rather than what the spouse proposes on the matter irrespective of the situation.

Effective communication in the home can reduce these problems. Peer group counselling sessions with other married couples or a professional counsellor can also help.

Poor home management

As very religious people seldom stay at home, they neglect responsibilities in the home such as cleaning, washing, ironing and helping their spouse. This does not help in enriching family life because a sound mind lives in a healthy body and cleanliness is next to Godliness.

Enrolment in a home management school can assist in minimising the impact on the home and a cleaner can be employed to assist in the cleaning of the home.

Role models

A religious fanatic can be a bad role model for children. As children naturally learn from their parents and most importantly want to imitate them, they simply pick up these attitudes as they grow older. Some religious beliefs allow individuals to marry more than one wife. Strict adherence to this practice can cause rivalry between wives and jealousy between children.

As a loss control measure, the leaders of religious groups should educate their followers and encourage them to put a stop to these practices.

Perception

Some people have been religiously indoctrinated either for or against a belief system. This entrenched position hampers meaningful marital relationships.

As a loss control measure, people should have an open mind and learn about other religions to understand and appreciate them.

Forms of prayer

Praying at home could bring about problems in the home. The traditionalist wants to pray by pouring a libation, while the Christian or Moslem has other ways of praying. These differences in the form of prayers can bring disputes in a marital home.

As a loss control measure, each partner should accept their way of prayer without demeaning that of the partner.

Childbearing and family planning

There are certain religious doctrines that oppose contraception and family planning (managing the number of children one should have).

A loss control measure is to seek help from a counsellor who is well versed in religious and family issues.

Defiant Behaviour

Defiant behaviour is behaviour by children and young people that is not accepted by society, though it varies from society to society and has no boundary for the rich or the poor. Some of these behaviour patterns include extreme alcoholism, smoking, substance abuse, pilfering, rape, robbery, burglary, murder, prostitution, fighting and fraud. These behaviours may be caused by a lack of parental control, too much freedom given to children, the imposition of stringent limits on children, a lack of love and support from parents, peer pressure and copycat actions, among others. A child who lacks a good education or drops out of school has the tendency to go down the delinquent path compared with his/her peers with good and solid education.

Often delinquent activities by children influence society through the mental and physical health problems experienced by the children and the loss of human capital.

Families also suffer financially if their offspring are on the wrong side of the law. Such behaviour is caused by numerous factors some of which are enumerated below.

Lack of parental control

The children of parents who do not have the time to act as responsible guardians are likely to engage in delinquent activities such as bullying and stealing. At times, the stress of work weighs parents down. Taking the time to talk, observe and teach good behaviour to their children is a prudent loss control measure. Parents should also talk with the teachers of their children, to discover if there are any problems. Parents should ensure that there is devoted family time by turning off phones and computers at weekends so as not to be disturbed by any work duties. If there are problems, these could be discussed with family and friends.

A loss finance measure is for parents to set aside holiday funds, so that when they take break from work, they can spend quality time together as a family.

School dropouts

Most defiant behaviour comes about because a child has a lot of spare time to spend. Children may, for many reasons such as poverty or bullying, decide not to go to school. Sitting idly at home may cause such children to engage in deviant behaviours to occupy themselves.

Parents should support their children in going to school and resolve any issues that may exist as a loss control measure. Besides, school dropouts may be able to enrol in training for work programmes.

Parents should set aside funds for their children's education. Parents can also insure the education of their children, so that should a parent become incapacitated or die, the child's education is secure. Schools should ensure that they foster a safe and positive environment for children.

Orphaned children

Orphans who are left on the street to take care of themselves are at risk of entering deviant behaviours such as stealing to survive.

A loss control measure is for society to invest in social services to care for orphaned children.

Parents should make it a priority to take out a life insurance policy that will cater for their children when they die.

Bad parenting Skills

Parents must make a conscious effort to develop good parenting skills. Punishments should only be handed out to children when they misbehave. In general, more democratic ways of bringing up children make them feel that their views are being heard and minimises the risk of rebellious activities. If a child does not receive praise from their parents, the child tends to be more receptive to bad influences.

A loss control measure is for parents to go for counselling to learn good parenting skills. Parents can also purchase books on parenting and apply the lessons to their lives.

Freedom without limits

Parents sometimes give their children too much freedom allowing children to do what pleases them and encouraging children to exhibit defiant characters.

As a loss control measure, parents should limit the kind of freedom given to their children where necessary. Parents can move their children to a moderately strict school, for example.

Limits without freedom

If there are very strict rules in the home that hinder the freedom of the child, then there is the chance of rebellion. Some parents are too authoritarian in their approach to parenting, and this can make their children uncomfortable and unhappy and consequently defiant at the least opportunity.

As a loss control measure parents should give their children some freedom to make their own choices and have a voice in the family.

Ambitious children of uneducated parents

Ambitious children of uneducated parents can also be problematic. Sometimes young people with high ambitions tend to be defiant because they feel their parents are failures and therefore tend to disrespect them.

As a loss control measure, parents of such children should endeavour to ensure that their children are in high quality schools where good moral behaviour is encouraged. Parents must also learn to discipline their children when they are wrong. In disciplining their children, parents should make their children aware of the reasons they are being punished. Parents should have an open relationship with such children to help them appreciate that in their quest for success they will respect the less accomplished.

Peer Pressure

Children who associate with bad influences often experience negative peer pressure from such peers leading them to pick up negative habits such as smoking, indecent language or other forms of defiant character. The negative influence of friends can alter the otherwise good behaviour of individuals.

Peer counselling is a loss control measure. If an individual becomes deviant through the influence of friends, then it is likely that they may take advice from other friends against such behaviour. Consequently, parents should endeavour to know the friends of their children to help caution them on 'bad apples'.

A loss control measure would be for parents to arrange an outing or a meal to get to know the friends of their children.

The influence of the media and western culture

What a person reads, watches and sees others do are determinants of how that person will act. Watching violent movies and seeing parents and friends portray deviant behaviour often influences a person's way of life. Through uncensored movies and articles published by the media, the young can be exposed to unacceptable behaviour that they may imitate. Also, when the young are exposed to western culture in the form of music, movies or online content, there is the tendency to copy what they see.

A loss control measure would be to avoid watching violent and other negative movies. The National Media Commission should enforce the censorship of things that are shown on media outlets. This will help to regulate the negative influence of the western influences on the youth. The National Communication Authority should also place restrictions on certain Internet sites so that underage children will not have access to them.

As a loss finance measure, the National Media Commission should set up a fund to be used for regulation and its enforcement.

Poverty

People who are from poor backgrounds may have a low sense of self-esteem because people look down on them. When young people are from such a background, they may covert luxurious items but not have the means to pay for them. This may lead to illegal acts such as stealing.

A loss control measure is to provide counselling to these youth to build a positive self-esteem.

Excessive and unrealistic expectations and ambitions

People who have unrealistic expectations and ambitions, but have no capital, nor education, may often resort to activities such as stealing. A desire to be accepted and to meet expectations of parents will sometimes lead children to behave in unacceptable ways. For example, if children are expected to achieve an unrealistic grade in an exam that they are not capable of, the pressure from the family could lead them to cheat.

Counselling people to be content with what they have can help. Involvement in a religious activity can help a person to adopt the right measures to achieve realistic ambitions in due course. Parents should set goals that are attainable for their children instead of pushing them to overachieve.

Drug or substance abuse

When alcohol and drugs are taken in excessive quantities, it induces a person to engage in unacceptable behaviours.

As a loss control measure, the sales points of alcohol and drugs can regulate their sales to people below eighteen years of age.

As loss finance measure, companies or outlets that sell alcohol or drugs to underage people should be fined to generate revenues to counsel the young affected by addiction.

Breakdown of family systems

The breakdown of the family as an institution is a major cause of deviancy among the youth. High divorce rates have led to a corresponding increase in delinquency.

As a loss control measure, proper pre-marital and post-marital counselling should be instituted either by the government or the religious bodies. This would help check the high rate of family disintegration.

As a loss finance measure, religious bodies could institute a fund to provide personnel and educational materials to assist married couples in danger of divorce. Divorced parents can also continue to share the responsibility for the upbringing of their children.

Unemployment

Unemployment plays a contributory role to deviant behaviour in society. Without employment, young people roam the streets and some of them indulge in unproductive activities such as stealing.

Institutions could be set up to provide the youth with the necessary skills for meaningful employment. In addition to this, the government should invest in employment programmes.

As a loss finance measure, the government could set aside a budgetary allocation to establish institutions that provide these skills. With these funds, training centres can be established to equip the youth with work skills. Governments should also ensure that the right policies are in place that will make the private sector thrive and ensure that more jobs are created.

Curiosity and the search for adventure

Some children are just curious and want to experience certain practices. They want some adventure as they consider their lives boring and unexciting.

As a loss control measure, parents could get their children involved in extra curricula activities such as football, swimming, hockey, basketball, boy scouts or girls' guides. Such activities are involving and exciting for children and keep them busy.

Parents must set money aside so that they can afford to send their children to these activities.

Teenage pregnancy

In the case of a teenage pregnancy, the mother may not have enough life experience to care for the child. The child may be at risk of delinquency.

Education on the prevention of teenage pregnancy is a loss control measure. Teenage mothers should seek counselling from their parents or other elderly people to develop good parenting skills.

Societal laws or rules

When laws are established without incorporating the views of the young, their rights may be infringed upon and they may engage in defiant behaviour to make their views and concerns heard.

A loss control measure is to incorporate the views of the youth in setting societal laws or rules.

Boredom with a rich life

A child from a rich home who does not find this life exciting or stimulating may want to find ways to make it so. Also, some parents from rich homes do not allow their children to mingle with others they perceive as less fortunate. Such children may feel isolated since they are caged from the real world most of the time, and at some point, in their lives defy their parents.

A loss control measure is to reduce the amount of money that is available to the child and keep the child busy with activities such as being a member of the girls' guides, boys' brigade, etc. Allowing children freedom with limits so that they can associate with and play with friends who may be from lower classes in society can mitigate the likelihood of defiant behaviour.

Lack of education

When children are not sent to school, they are likely to learn only bad habits. They may associate with delinquent groups and when they get older have no qualifications or skills to obtain a job.

As a loss control measure, parents should endeavour to educate their children. Corporate bodies and philanthropists should set up endowment funds to take care of educating children in the community. Governments can make it a policy to offer free universal basic education up to the secondary level for every child, paid from the taxes citizens pay. Governments can institute a compulsory tertiary education insurance policy that all parents must acquire for their children. This will ensure that a large pool of funds is available for educating children who wish to pursue technical, vocational or tertiary education.

Morality and the clergy

Ghana is largely a religious society and most people either go to church on Sundays or to the Mosque on Fridays. If preachers focus on morality and minimise emphasis they place on money and prosperity, the country will benefit with a reduction in delinquent behaviour.

Unstable economy

When the economy of a country is not stable, the youth can be particularly badly affected. Some may be compelled to engage in defiant activities such as fraud, stealing or engaging in dangerous journeys abroad in search of opportunities that may not exist.

As a loss control measure, leaders of a country should work hard to attain a better economy for all. They should ensure that the taxes people pay are put to the best use of the people they represent so that people have the opportunity for fulfilled and economically sustainable livelihoods.

The Role of Insurance in Managing Deviant Behaviour in Society

Insurance has certain basic functions including indemnifying against loss and providing advisory services. Insurance practitioners are well vested in risk management techniques and methods. Consequently, they have a vital role in providing solutions for deviant behaviour. The following section discusses the role of the insurance industry in providing some solutions to such behaviour.

Insurance companies provide products such as cover for educational needs, health and life insurance to ensure that future generations have security.

Insurance companies also offer loss prevention and reduction advice to policyholders to help minimise the risk of theft and robbery that are a consequence of delinquent behaviour.

Insurance companies, through diversification and the investments they make create job opportunities to reduce the impact of unemployment. Currently, a lot more insurance companies are investing into real estate and other business that create direct employment for unskilled workers who are most often the victims or perpetrators of defiant behaviour.

Defiant behaviour can arise in society when employees think that their safety is of no importance to employers, resulting in strike action and damage to company assets which affect society. Insurance has provided solutions through worker compensation policies and other worker related products.

Another cause of deviant behaviour is inadequate finance to support the family. Through insurance, parents can purchase pension schemes that will provide the needed protection when they become older.

Insurance plays a role in reducing the legal costs and expenses one could incur should a child negligently cause harm to others or their properties. By purchasing liability insurance, parents can mitigate any liability arising out of the damage caused by their children to others.

Other Opportunities for Insurance Companies

Insurance companies can partner with educational authorities to set up schools so as to help youngsters and adults get enrolled to develop their skills and talents and be useful to society. Tailor made packages can be designed by insurance companies in partnership with schools to provide the essential stages of education. Also, microinsurance products could be offered by companies to schoolchildren to form financial security groups and foster a culture of saving. These funds would be managed by insurance companies on behalf of pupils until they get to an age when the funds are made available to them.

Social centres can also be set up by insurance companies to include internet cafes, research libraries, basketball courts and other recreational facilities to harness the talents of young adults. Insurance companies can also liaise with religious institutions and other related bodies in establishing rehabilitation centres to work with young people suffering from addictions.

Defiant behaviour has existed in society for a very long time. The availability of insurance provides society with assurance that in the event of any loss occurring as a result of this, a reliable partner will readily come to their aid.

Festivities

Festivities are celebrated by many different groups and for a variety of reasons. These include the commemoration of a religious event, a reunion or as an opportunity to raise funds to help society. Easter, Id-Adhar, Christmas, Ramadan and Sanla are all such celebrations as well as other ethnic festivals that happen throughout the year. Festivals are fun times. They are occasions during which people can relax and be revitalised. Festivals have the potential to draw large crowds of people and enhance societal growth and togetherness. However, they also have the potential to cause losses to society. Some of the threats posed by festivals are discussed below.

Accidents

Most festivals are organised by natives of a particular ethnic group who live in the large cities. Some people tend to drive recklessly under the influence of alcohol during these festivities. As such accidents can occur that may lead to injury or loss of property or lives. Accidents have several indirect losses including higher labour turnover, increased medical expenses and loss of wages. Some festive occasions are characterised by activities such as hunting and the use of firearms. These activities can pose a threat to human life: they can cause severe bodily injury or even death.

As a loss control measure, people should be educated against drunk driving. Travelling in general should be better timed for other times of the year when they are fewer—possibly intoxicated—drivers on the road. There should be restrictions on events that encourage the firing of guns during festive occasions. There should also be frequent police patrols to stop speeding and drunk driving.

As a loss finance measure, comprehensive motor insurance policies should be taken so that all injured parties can be indemnified after a loss. Life insurance policies and personal accident insurance policies can be purchased to fund losses that may occur.

Loss of Property

In Ghana, year after year, festivals continue to record damage to property running into millions of cedis. This is especially the case in areas that have chieftaincy disputes. Aggrieved factions usually choose festive occasions to register their displeasure by destroying properties. Typical examples are the Homowo festivals of the Gas and the Fire festivals of people in Tamale in Ghana. Loss of property can occur because of over excitement and/or drivers running into people's property. Property damaged may belong to the state or private persons. Another aspect is that roads can be blocked or damaged in the process, increasing commuting time and government expenditures.

As a loss control measure, functions should be organised in open spaces away from valuable properties. There should be education and laws to govern acceptable noise levels. Security forces may be deployed to control the loss of property resulting from festivities. CCTV cameras can be installed to identify robbers/intruders who enter people's homes to steal. Since properties are insurable, taking insurance can serve as a loss financing measure.

Loss of productive man hours

Loss of productive hours is another possible loss from festivities. This is because some festive days are declared as public holidays. When this happens otherwise productive days are lost especially for the formal sector (private and public). Some people also leave their jobs to participate in these festive activities that could last for days or weeks.

As a loss control measure, the number of holidays should be reduced. When holidays fall on weekends, they should not be extended to the next working days. Festivals should be held over the weekend so that participants can still work and take part in the festivities. There should be increased supervision at the workplace and employers should have an electronic system that can check the presence of employees daily. Companies can formulate policies that allow them to deduct any day of work missed from an employees' salary. Companies can also negotiate with, reward and motivate workers who choose to work during these times.

Financial strain

Festivals are characterised by heavy spending with people showing off their wealth. As such, most people tend to spend all their savings during festivals, and this has detrimental effects on their finances. During such times, individuals spend heavily on goods and services. People want their homes to look as welcoming as possible and so will spend on decorating for the upcoming festivities. Also, new clothes, jewellery and shoes are purchased during these times for the celebration. All these costs may leave a person bankrupt or financially distressed when the festivities are over.

As a loss control measure, people should draw up a budget before participating in festivals.

As a loss finance measure, people should retain part of their earnings for hard times. Through self-insurance and retention, individuals can save money for contingencies so that in situations where they run out of cash, they can rely on the monies they have saved to avoid financial hardships for themselves and their family.

Teenage pregnancy and the spread of diseases

A typical feature of festivals is the drinking of alcoholic beverages. People tend to misbehave sexually under the influence of alcohol. This generates unwanted pregnancies and the spread of sexually transmitted diseases such as AIDS, gonorrhoea and syphilis. Some of these pregnancies result in unwanted children posing a burden on the society. In addition, many people converging at one point to celebrate could also be a platform for the transmission of airborne diseases including covid-19.

As a loss control measure, people should be educated on the consequences of teenage pregnancy as well as the advantages of abstinence or contraceptives. Condoms can be provided freely to people at bars and restaurants.

As a loss finance measure, health insurance policies can be purchased.

Theft and robbery

Festivities tend to be characterised by thefts and robbery. People carry along with them much money and other precious possessions to either show off to friends or present to relatives and loved ones. Therefore, thieves are attracted to such gatherings.

As a loss control measure, punitive measures should be meted out to culprits to deter other robbers. Security patrols should be increased. People should avoid walking alone in dark and secluded places. People should be very vigilant in handling their belongings and avoid leading a flamboyant lifestyle during these periods. The installation of alarm systems in vehicles will alert owners to any unlawful entry into their vehicles. The formation of neighbourhood watchdog schemes is also a good idea to deter robbers. Losses can be financed by insurance (for example, motor, fire and theft insurance).

High prices of goods and services

When there is an increase in demand—as happens at festivals—without a corresponding increase in supply, the sellers of goods and services will generally increase prices. Everything one purchases at a festival tends to be more expensive.

A loss control measure is early purchase. Products or commodities should be purchased far in advance.

A loss finance measure is retention (i.e., saving some money to be able to purchase at higher prices during this period). Hedging can also be used to finance losses.

Health hazards

During festive times, some people drink too much, overeat and gamble. Some people fall sick as a result. Food poisoning is another possibility and could result in one being incapacitated, hospitalised or even dying in severe cases. When people drink excessively, they tend to behave badly. Smokers also pose a danger to non-smokers through passive smoking. This could result in lung related illnesses. Diseases such as Ebola and covid-19 can be spread through contacts such as hand shaking. There is also an increase in social vices such as prostitution. For example, at the 2010 World Cup in South Africa, there were stories of an increase in prostitution. Festive occasions bring about higher traffic on the roads, with traffic jams slowing down the movement of people, goods and services thereby increasing the stress people go through in performing their daily activities. Excessive stress is unhealthy for people.

As a loss control measure, education is paramount. People should be educated on the negative consequences of excessive drinking and smoking, inordinate expenditure, and bad hygiene practices. Taxes on alcoholic drinks should be increased to deter large alcoholic drink purchases during these periods. A ban on the sale of alcoholic drinks during festivities can also help. Bonuses for employees should be paid in non-festive seasons. People should be mindful of the food they eat, water they drink and the surroundings in which these are purchased. Smokers and non-smokers should be advised on the consequences of smoking on their health. There should also be efficient traffic controls like the use of traffic lights and additional police to direct traffic to reduce the stress people go through during these periods.

A loss finance measure is health insurance. Self-insurance can be adopted to fund hospital bills from ill health.

Pollution

Pollution is a real problem during festivities. The land is polluted through the indiscriminate dumping of refuse and other waste materials. Festivals also bring about air and noise pollution. The air is polluted through fumes from vehicles and smokers. People play loud music at parties, beaches and other functions held because of the festival. Noise pollution has the effect of triggering disputes and hampering students from studying.

As a loss control measure, there can be a ban on playing loud music during festivals in order not to infringe on the rights of others. Regulations prohibiting excessive noise making could be enacted by law enforcement agencies. Dustbins should also be provided at festive grounds for people to use to avoid excessive waste.

A loss finance measure would be to have an account made up of contributions from members of a community or society to clean up the environment after major festivities. Compensation should be awarded to people who might suffer because of the noise pollution through insurance paid by people who indulge in the act.

Nuisance

Some of the festivities are a nuisance to both individuals and the public. A private individual may be denied the usage of his or her property because the property is near the festival site. The public is at times denied some rights as roads are blocked.

Exercises

1. Explain five ways in which interferences in the affairs of a married couple can be curtailed without offending the person interfering.
2. You have graduated from UGBS and have obtained a demanding but well-paying job that is keeping you away from your family. Make arguments both for quitting the job and continuing with it and sacrificing the time you can spend with your family. For each point raised, suggest a loss control measure and a loss finance measure where appropriate.
3. Discuss the functions of the principle of married life.
4. Discuss five things that are important for a marriage to stand the test of time.
5. Explain the role of insurance in providing solutions to defiant behaviour in our society.

6. Discuss five things that are important in committing oneself to a lasting relationship.
7. Explain five effects of broken homes in society.
8. Discuss five major threats to a successful married life in our society today.
9. Festivities have the potential to increase losses to our society. Identify five major possible losses from festivities and for each threat identified, suggest a loss control measure and a loss financing measure.
10. Explain five underlying causes of deviant behaviour in our society by young people. For each cause identified, suggest a loss control measure and a loss finance measure where appropriate. In your view does insurance have any role to play?
11. Identify ways in which religious fanaticism can affect married life in our society today. For each point raised suggest a loss control measure. In your view do you think insurance has a role here?

Further Reading

Andoh, C. (2013). The Role of Insurance in Managing Defiant Behaviour in Society. *Africagrowth Agenda, 10*(2), 6–7, April-June.

Desteno, D. (2014). *The Truth About Trust: How It Determines Success in Life, Love, Learning and More.* Hudson Street Press

Driscoll, G., & Driscoll, M. (2012). *Real, Marriage: The Truth About Sex, Friendship & Life Together.* Thomas Nelson Inc.

Hansen, H. (2009). *STTS: Powerful People Skills: How to Form, Build and Maintain Stronger, Long-Lasting Relationships.* Marshall Cavendish International Asia Pte Ltd.

Kolachi, P. A. (2024). Scrutinizing Religious Fundamentalism of Post 9/11 Scenario in The Blind Man's Garden By Aslam. *Iars'international Research Journal, 14*(01), 14–22.

Shahrestani, F., Doroudi, H., & Hajialiakbari, F. (2024). Determining Priority Actions to Manage Deviant and Unethical Behaviors of Employees with the Aim of Improving Brand Value. *Ethical Reflections, 5*(2), 96–126.

Meunier, V., & Baker, W. (2012). Positive Couple Relationships: The Evidence for Long-Lasting Relationship Satisfaction and Happiness. In *Positive Relationships,* S. Roffey (eds.). Springer, Dordrecht.

Oliver, W., & Oliver, E. (2018). Hope for Today's Families. Review and Herald Publishing Association.

Tóth, S. (2024). The Vexing Paradoxes of Christian Life Denial: A Response to Marilynne Robinson's Worldly Gospel. *Zeal: A Journal for the Liberal Arts, 3*(1).

Chapter 5
Risk, Insurance and the Extractive Industry

Abstract The extractive industry offers numerous benefits to a country, including employment opportunities for local populations, revenue generation for governments, and the provision of foreign exchange, among others. This chapter explores key sectors within the extractive industry, highlighting their benefits as well as the risks and threats they present. It further proposes appropriate loss control and loss financing measures to mitigate these risks. In particular, the chapter focuses on petroleum, mining, timber, rubber, and quarrying industries, examining the specific threats associated with each sector and outlining corresponding strategies for effective risk management.

Keywords Mining industry · Petroleum industry · Quarrying industry · Rubber industry

Introduction

The extractive industry has many benefits for a country. The industry provides jobs for the local people, provides revenue for governments and serves as a source of foreign exchange, among others. This chapter examines some of the most important sectors of the extractive industry, their benefits, the threats they pose and proposes some loss control and loss financing measures to mitigate these risks. Specifically, it examines threats the petroleum, the mining, the timber, the rubber and the quarrying industries pose and provides risk mitigating strategies to manage these risks.

The Petroleum Industry

The petroleum industry is one of the most beneficial and lucrative industries for the major oil producing nations of the world. All nations make use of petroleum products such as petrol, gasoline, kerosene or crude oil. Notwithstanding its major economic

C. Andoh, *Fundamentals of Managing Risk and Insurance*,
https://doi.org/10.1007/978-981-95-4581-0_5

contribution to development, there are a number of risks the industry faces. Some of the major threats, along with loss control and the loss financing methods that can be used to mitigate them are discussed below.

Threat to Physical Assets (Property Risk)

The threat to physical assets such as buildings, machinery and equipment could come from the outbreak of a fire, an explosion resulting in a fire, theft, piracy and the activity of rebel or terrorist groups that all pose direct and indirect risks to the industry. As many petroleum products are obtained from the drilling platforms at sea, they are exposed to pirates, who may attack and steal some of their equipment asking huge sums of money in exchange for its return. This could lead a firm to bankruptcy since it relies on its machinery and equipment to operate. If, because of an attack on the assets of the industry, key employees are injured or physically disabled, this will equally threaten the survival of the firm.

The Niger delta region, located in the South-South zone of Nigeria is a classic case. The region comprises the nine states; Abia, Akwa-Ibom, Bayelsa, Cross River, Delta, Edo, Ondo, Imo and Rivers (Obi, 2023). The region is rich in diverse ecological zones, some of which are the mangrove forest, the coastal vegetation zone, the freshwater swamp forest zone, the lowland rain forest zone, derived savannah zone and the montane zone. It also has massive oil deposits that were first discovered in commercial quantities in 1956. Oil provides 95% of Nigeria's foreign exchange earnings and 80% of the government's budgetary revenue. Nigeria's oil production accounts for 8% of the Organisation of Petroleum Exporting Cooperation's (OPEC) total daily production and 3% of the world's volume according to the Nigerian National Petroleum Company.

Although this region of Nigeria is basically holding the country's economy together and should, as such, expect oil revenues to improve the community, it is one of the poorest and least developed regions in Nigeria. It has not seen investments that recognise its contribution to national wealth but instead has been affected negatively by the hazardous consequences of oil exploration activities such as water and air pollution. The rapid development and production of crude oil with attendant increases in population and industrialisation has brought about serious environmental degradation in this region of the country (Nwilo & Badejo, 2004; Fletcher, 2022). This has led to local people demanding compensation and control of the oil wealth. Beginning from the pre-colonial era, the region has witnessed a series of conflicts that originally had roots in the protest against injustice, and in recent years in the quest for resource control (Ajoko-Adebanjoko, 2017). All efforts to resolve conflict in this region failed until the Yar'adua/Jonathan administration, when an amnesty programme which required that militants hand in their arms in return for an unconditional pardon, brought about an uneasy peace. Some of the military groups that contributed to the violence and sabotage of oil production facilities and pipelines include the Movement for the Emancipation of the Niger Delta (MEND) and the Niger Delta Liberation Front (NDLF). These groups kidnapped western oil workers and were involved in series of attacks on oil facilities causing the Delta's oil production to reduce by a quarter in Summer 2008 (Asuni, 2009). MEND is a constantly changing amalgam of groups, some criminally motivated, while others are politically and ideologically driven. It is difficult to distinguish between them. Some started life on the university campuses before spilling on to the streets and engaging in criminal activity. Other groups set out to genuinely address the grievances of the Niger Delta people, enraged by decades of environmental pollution, economic underdevelopment and political marginalisation. However, the involvement of corrupt outsiders soon took their militancy far beyond any ideological goals (Asuni, 2009). Although the amnesty programme brought about peace, it was short lived because of the emergence of new militant groups such as Niger Delta Avengers (NDA), the Red Egbesu Water Lions, Joint Niger Liberation Force (JNDLF), Niger Delta Red Squad (NDRS) and the Adaka Boro Avengers in 2016. These new groups have continued from where the former militant groups left off with renewed bombing of oil installations and the abduction of oil workers (Ajoko-Adebanjoko, 2017).

As a loss control measure on fire outbreak, there should be safety standard training for all personnel in the management of fire, regular education of personnel in fire prevention and routine maintenance checks on machines and pipelines. Industrial plants should be built with fire resistant materials to minimise the effects of an explosion or a fire outbreak resulting from explosion. Oil platforms should be robustly built. The environment should be kept free from combustible materials and there should be an enforcement of a ban on smoking in and around the industrial areas. In a case where a blanket ban on smoking is difficult to enforce, a display of notices where people absolutely cannot smoke should be provided. In addition, fire extinguishers and automatic fire sprinklers should be installed at key vantage points. Evacuation instructions in case of fire should be provided. Automatic smoke detectors fitted with alarms and the installation of water cannon sprinklers will also help. To combat theft from the industrial facilities, security should be beefed up at installation sites and perimeters and security cameras should be installed.

Oil industry management should commit to fulfilling their social responsibilities such as the building of schools, hospitals, recreation centres, the construction of good roads and the provision of safe drinking water in the locality of the operations. These activities will assist in tempering local resistance to oil extraction and limit if not eliminate resistance to the industry. In addition, local people should be given opportunities to work for the industry. Wise and Shtylla (2007) highlights the fact that it is in the best interest of extractive companies to expand economic opportunity in the regions where they operate. In post-conflict and/or fragile states, Perks (2012) posits that corporate social responsibility has implications for conflict and risk mitigation strategies to ensure the protection of human rights. Perks (2012) argue that a public private partnership approach, which entails public and private organisations working together to address commonly defined conflicts and risks in the social environment, can not only mitigate risks for companies but ultimately lead to the development of more coherent social and economic strategies for populations, governments and community development.

Moreover, the transportation of products using unsafe routes and locating industries in unsafe regions should be avoided.

Management should have backups for key operating machines and equipment that could be brought on board should any mishap happen to the assets of the company.

A loss financing measure is the purchase of comprehensive fire insurance, business interruption insurance, keyman policies (for indispensable staff) or any other suitable insurance policy to cover the risks identified.

Spillages

Spillages of petroleum products during their transportation through pipelines or at sea can occur. This results in the reduction of the volume of the product and thereby reduces the returns or the gains from their sale. This could lead to substantial reductions in the net cash flow of the industry. In addition, the spilled products pollute the environment and if the spillage occurs at sea, will have a very adverse effect on aquatic life. Aside from the direct losses, indirect losses could arise from the costs incurred in cleaning up polluted areas and possible legal actions from local communities.

As a loss control measure, the industry should invest in technologies such as radioactive dyes that can detect any potential leakage before an accident occurs. The lids of tanks should also be properly tightened, automatic spill detection systems installed on tanks, containers or pipelines and there should be constant protection of the pipelines using security cameras or humans. Safe vessels should be used to transport petroleum products. In addition, settlements should not be sited close to oil fields and local inhabitants should be rehoused or resettled safely away from any potential dangers.

A loss financing measure is purchase of liability insurance.

Human Capital

The human resources of the petroleum industry also face serious dangers. This is premised on the fact that the continuous inhaling of petroleum products can cause health hazards such as leukaemia. In addition, workers are exposed to the risk of injury either through fire, in the process of working with heavy machinery and from possible spillages of the petroleum products. In all these instances, an employees' life could also be compromised. As some petroleum products are obtained at sea, workers are exposed to the hazards caused by pirates. In some areas, it is difficult to recruit personnel because of such dangers.

As a loss control measure, there should be regular medical check-ups and education on safe operational practices for personnel. In addition, depending on their job functions, personnel should be encouraged or required to wear protective clothing such as facemasks, gloves, boots, helmets and goggles. Good working conditions coupled with attractive salaries and incentives will be a good measure to combat the risk of strike action or the departure of key personnel to other sectors.

A loss financing measure could be the purchase of disability insurance policies such as a worker compensation policy or keyman insurance policies for staff who are indispensable to the business.

Financial Risk

As petroleum products are usually sold internationally, when there is depreciation in the home currency of the petroleum company, profits will be affected since the firm will receive less money for its sales. In addition, interest rates, foreign exchange rates and inflation can have a negative impact on profitability. A rise in inflation will cause prices to increase causing purchasing power to decline. Such fluctuations could threaten the survival of a firm.

A loss control measure to mitigate the impact of price fluctuations is using derivatives. In the case where the price drops significantly an artificial shortage can be created by the industry coming together to limit the amount of oil put up for sale on the world market to raise prices. For the consumer of petroleum products, one might buy more when the price is low. The industry should also engage the services of skilled and honest financial managers and auditors to manage the finances of the industry. By entering into hedging arrangements, the industry should be able to stabilise fluctuations in its cash flows.

Liability

Liability is another threat faced by the petroleum industry. Liability may take the form of lawsuits taken out against the industry by virtue of the adverse effects its activities have on its stakeholders. A legal action may be brought against the industry for improper disposal of waste, an accident or environmental pollution. This threat has the potential of wiping out a substantial amount of a firm's funds.

As a loss control measure, the industry should invest in comprehensive safety and waste management practices and the location of the plant should be far from any settlements. The industry should take a safety-first approach to reduce the severity and frequency of societal losses. Negligence by workers should be punished. A business should also have an experienced legal department to defend it from actions brought against it. Liability insurance can also be purchased to fund losses arising from any lawsuits that may be brought against the company.

Technical Expertise

Without technical know-how, accidents, inefficiency and ineffectiveness can occur in the affairs of the industry. People without the required expertise can harm not only themselves but can also cause both direct and indirect losses to the industry. Negligence on the part of employees could cause a serious fire to break out or even an oil spillage.

As a loss control measure, workers' skills should be frequently upgraded and new employees should be properly trained. The industry should form alliances with institutions that train people in the skills needed and provide them with the necessary expertise. The industry could set up its own schools to train its staff in all the specialised areas that it needs.

Depletion

Once a site has been drilled continuously, petroleum products will become depleted or too expensive to extract.

As a loss control measure, the industry should embark on research to identify new reserves and invest in technology to identify and develop new sources of energy generation in areas such as hydro, solar and gas as a source of fuel for automobiles.

Strikes, Socio-Political Unrest and Instability

Employee action is another area that can threaten the survival of a petroleum company. Employees can resort to strike action to redress their grievances. In areas where there is political unrest, oil companies may be targeted by radical elements and the kidnapping of key employees can occur. Such events lead to a loss of production and losses in income and taxes for governments.

As a loss control measure, workers should be well remunerated with good working conditions. The industry should carry out corporate social responsibility projects to reduce the burden on governments and generate public goodwill.

Unfavourable Government Policies

When a government establishes sound economic policies, the probability of the petroleum industry improving efficiency and productivity is high. When government policies stifle competition or hamper exploration by other players, it allows the few companies that exist to gain market power. This minimises competition and encourages a monopoly. Governments can also issue regulations that stop further exploration by existing players and this can affect the industry negatively.

As a loss control measure, the industry should lobby governments to develop policies that will favour the industry.

The Mining Industry

Mining has greatly contributed economically to countries with mineral deposits such as bauxite, manganese, gold, diamonds and salt. Mining companies offer employment to the local communities in which their mines are situated. Some have taken on social responsibilities such as the provision of clean drinking water, schools, hospitals and creating funds to support the poor and the needy. Despite these major contributions the mining industry is exposed to a number of threats or risk exposures that affect the environment in which it operates. Mining are believed to curtain access to food in many regions worldwide (Wegenast & Beck, 2020). According to ActionAid South Africa report, residents from a mining town in Limpopo, South Africa, lost access to ploughing fields and grazing land as well as other natural resources including fruits, trees and firewood due to the activity of Anglo Platinum (ActionAid, 2016). Among the key findings, in the villages located close to the mine, there are strong complaints about the environmental impacts of the mine. Air pollution, damage to houses, intermittent water supply being a challenge in all four study villages. Many residents associate these problems with the impact of the mine. The negative impacts of extractive industries on food security are also reported for coal mining in Bangladesh (Bedi, 2015), nickel mining within Inuit territories in Canada (Mills et al., 2017) and copper mining in Zambia's Mazabuka and Solwezi districts (Shalala,

2013). Some of the major threats and loss control and loss financing methods that can be utilised to minimise them are discussed below.

Water Pollution

The extraction of gold or diamonds in some instances involves the use of chemicals such as mercury and cyanide. The use of these chemicals in deep mining could contaminate water tables and consequently affect bole-hole water quality and aquatic life.

As a loss control measure, mining companies should undertake research into using harmless but effective chemicals in their operations. Research can be funded by retaining some of the funds the industry generated and specifically earmarked for this purpose.

Physical Assets

The properties of third parties can be damaged or destroyed by the industry's operations. Equipment and other physical assets of a mining company can be stolen. Machinery may be damaged or fire may destroy assets hampering the smooth running of operations. When operational machinery is run down or becomes obsolete, competitiveness and productivity are compromised.

As a loss control measure, staff should be adequately catered for in terms of having a good salary and working conditions and provided with incentives so that they do not act against the company's interest. Installing smoke detectors can help alert workers to the early signs of fire. There should be frequent checks and maintenance of equipment used for operations.

Third-party liability insurance policies can be taken to fund losses arising out of damaged properties of third parties. Fire insurance policies should also be bought. The industry can retain these losses with a reserve fund. Funds can be set aside or invested purposely for the replacement of machines that break down.

Land Degradation

The degradation and loss of land previously used for different activities such as farming is another threat posed by mining to the environment. Mining normally strips the environment of grassland and vegetation and that can affect rainfall patterns and air quality. The use of dynamite in the mining process causes the destruction of roads and buildings.

There are various loss control measures that can be employed to mitigate these problems. An effective and environmentally friendly waste management policy is essential. There must also be legislation that forces mining companies to engage in active afforestation projects and the reduction in the use of dynamite in the mining process. Mining companies should also commit to reclaim land lost due to their activities through tree planting and filling in leftover trenches. The adoption of 'green mining' practices by using technology to determine the deposits of minerals to prevent the destruction of land through trial-and-error mining practices can be adopted. There can be a re-routing of rivers and streams to prevent pollution to the water supply.

A loss finance measure is to set aside financial resources for the purchase of good tree seedlings for planting. In addition, the industry can take out liability insurance policies to safeguard it against lawsuits that may be brought against it.

Human Capital

Another possible threat is the risk to the lives of miners. There are many examples of underground miners becoming trapped resulting in a loss of life. Tunnels can collapse, gas leaks can occur, and fire is a constant danger. Dust inhaled by miners can cause lung diseases such as cancer and other respiratory problems for workers. The industry can experience high turnover because of these risks and personnel in the industry can be attracted by safer jobs elsewhere.

A loss control measure is the provision of alarm and sensor systems to alert workers to danger underground. Regular safety training can be organised by the management of the mining companies for its workers. Safety equipment and clothing should be made available to miners to protect them and help with their rescue in emergencies and disasters. The provision of health centres to cater for the health needs of the workers and collaboration between the industry and educational institutions to help train qualified personnel should be encouraged.

A loss finance measure is the purchase of health insurance for workers. In addition, the industry can insure its workforce under life insurance so that when a loss occurs dependents can be compensated. Miners can themselves take up life insurance policies to safeguard them from the worst. Good conditions of service such as free medical care and free education for miners' children can entice some workers to stay on despite the risks involved in their job. In addition, some funds can be retained to support institutions that agree to train personnel for the industry.

Liabilities

The improper disposal of refinery waste leads to the pollution of water bodies. Surface mining causes the loss of land and leads to the inability of farmers to sustain their livelihoods. When individuals (including employees) and corporate entities file lawsuits against a mining company for an injury, nuisance, trespass or breach of statutory duty it can cause a halt to mining operations and result in some workers being laid off.

Establishing a centralised legal body that deals with the industry's lawsuits will help deter unnecessary lawsuits. In addition, locating mines away from residential areas can help minimise damage that the industry can cause.

Taking out liability insurance policies to help pay for possible losses from lawsuits can serve as a loss finance measure. Work compensation insurance policies can be purchased to indemnify workers who bring suits against the industry for injuries sustained during operations.

Finance

The price of minerals can fluctuate dramatically on the global market causing uncertainty and potential losses to the industry.

Some form of intermittent hedging can be practised by the industry to stabilise income especially in times when they believe prices could fall dramatically. The industry can also refine some mined materials into finished products before exporting. The industry can invest in economic intelligence to obtain superior forecasts of the future market prices for minerals. This can assist in determining the optimum time to sell their products for maximum returns.

Political Unrest

An unstable political atmosphere could endanger the activities of the mining industry and could cause the loss of huge sums of money in riots and conflicts.

As a loss control measure, the industry should constantly pursue political objectives that enhance its security and that of the country it operates in. The industry should commit to community development to obtain goodwill from the community and preserve the assets of the industry even during periods of political unrest.

Illegal Mining

Illegal miners also pose a threat to the industry. Apart from posing danger to their own lives, illegal miners tamper with resources set aside for the industry.

As a loss control measure, the industry can employ the services of these miners. Also, security personnel can be employed to check on their activities. Educating local communities about the dangers of illegal mining can further help curtail some of these activities.

Natural Disasters

Mining can only be carried out when weather conditions permit, to protect both the product being mined and the workers doing the mining. Floods, hurricanes, heavy rains and other extreme conditions such as earthquakes and volcanic activity can halt work and lower productivity and profits.

Keeping abreast of weather forecasts and other climatic conditions can serve as a loss control measure.

A loss finance measure would be to buy weather insurance or catastrophic bonds to cater for losses that may arise through natural disasters.

Operational Risk

The industry faces huge operational risks due to internal inefficiencies resulting in low productivity. Internal and external fraud, technological failures and violations of regulations form a great part of most operational costs. Where precious metals are being mined, some workers are tempted to smuggle some minerals causing financial loss to the company. Fraudulent staff can cause huge losses by embezzling the company's funds as well.

A loss control measure is to institute mechanisms such as monitoring and control systems to regulate the activities of the industry. There should be internal and external auditors to check the books on a regular basis. Those guilty of embezzlement should be imprisoned and made to settle financial losses to deter others.

A loss finance measure is retention with reserve funds.

Government Regulation

The regulation that government imposes on the industry could also stifle the industry's operations. Government regulations can prevent the industry from operating in certain areas of a country even though minerals are known to abound there. Sanctions can be placed on the industry for unlawful practices.

As a loss control measure, the industry should ensure that it operates within the confines of the law to avoid unnecessary lawsuits against it by the government.

A loss finance measure is liability insurance to finance possible lawsuits.

The Timber Industry

The timber industry is an important sector for every economy especially in regions endowed with plentiful forests. The industry is a source of wood for many domestic and industrial uses and contributes significantly to the GDP (Gross Domestic Product) of many countries. Despite its numerous benefits, there are detrimental effects of logging on the environment. Some of the threats posed by the industry are discussed below.

Deforestation

This is a major threat caused by the industry. Illegal timber operators cut down trees any way they deem fit and destroy other vegetation and habitats in the process. This leads to the destruction of essential natural resources and contributes to climate change. Rainfall patterns can be disrupted.

Government regulation should insist that even in legally sanctioned operations at least two trees should be planted for every tree felled. Governments must resource their forestry departments to be able to enforce regulations, inspect the operations of timber companies and run educational campaigns to emphasise the important role forests play for all life.

As a loss finance measure, government should fund the activities of forest departments from taxes. Government regulations compelling timber operators to set aside funds solely for replenishing the trees felled and ensuring that these trees grow will also help. The industry can insure themselves against possible lawsuits from governments or the public for causing harm to the environment by purchasing general liability insurance.

Land Degradation

One of the consequences of deforestation is soil erosion. When trees are cut down, the forest disappears and the land is left with little or no protection. Such land is exposed to erosion, be it by rain, wind or flood. When topsoil is washed away, the land is no longer able to support plant life which consequently makes it difficult to use for cultivation.

Afforestation is a loss control measure. Other measures include applying fertilisers, mulching or leaving the land fallow to regain its nutrients. Lumbering can also be restricted to particular areas and a nursery for planting trees can be established where seedlings could be protected. There should be constant inspections of the market by the security forces to seize any wood supplied by unlicensed operators. There should also be the institution of stiff penalties for those found guilty of the illegal destruction of trees or forests.

Loss of Wildlife and Biodiversity

Many rare and endangered animals dwell in forests. Wildlife serves as a tourist attraction and provides revenue for both the private sector and governments. When forests are destroyed, animal life can be decimated by the loss of natural habitat.

As a loss control measure, governments can create more natural parks and forest reserves where no tree felling is allowed so that wildlife can be protected.

As a loss finance measure, the industry can retain some funds to pay for fines imposed by governments or lawsuits brought against it by the public.

Risks to Professions

The continuous plundering of forests and destruction of trees will in the long run render some professions such as carpenters and other craftsmen who depend directly on wood for raw materials jobless, as over-logging will deplete natural resources to a point of scarcity. The activities of pharmaceutical and herbal medicine companies who require forest-based ingredients for their products may also be affected.

As a loss control measure, vigorous afforestation efforts by the key industry players will help to preserve the forests in the long term.

As a loss finance measure, the industry can set aside funds for the purpose of planting and nurturing trees to maturity.

Rivers and Water Bodies

Trees act as a protection for many rivers and water bodies. Some rivers have their source in forests. For example, rivers such as the Ayensu and Densu have their source in Atiwa forest in Ghana. As the tree cover is removed, rivers dry up quickly, especially in the dry season. Aquatic life can also be affected in the process.

As a loss control measure, forest reserves should be established by governments and policed and protected.

As a loss finance measure, the activities of a monitoring team to ensure that illegal loggers do not encroach into these reserves can be funded from the taxes people pay.

Extinction of Plant Species

Because of the haphazard way in which certain timber fellers operate, many species of plants and other flora will become extinct. Creeping plants rely on large trees such as odum and sapele among others to survive. Consequently, when these large trees are felled the creeping plants will die and their medicinal value will be lost.

As a loss control measure, forest reserves can be established in different parts of a country to preserve these endangered plants.

As a loss finance measure, governments can provide funds to the Forestry Commission to monitor the activities of illegal loggers to ensure that they do not encroach into these forests.

Absorption of Toxic Air

Trees absorb toxic elements such as carbon dioxide and therefore help to clean the air that we breathe. If trees are lost, these harmful elements stay in the atmosphere contributing to global warming and worsening air quality.

As a loss control measure afforestation should be embarked on vigorously by all relevant stakeholders.

As a loss finance measure, tree planting can be funded from the taxes that people pay. Health insurance can also be purchased to deal with the ailments associated with poor air quality.

Damage/Injuries to Third Parties and Properties

Felled trees sometimes fall on people, houses, businesses or farmland destroying or interrupting their operations. There are many instances where trees have fallen on timber workers resulting in injuries, disability and death in some cases.

As loss control measure, timber should not be cut near residences; otherwise, extreme care has to be taken in order not to destroy a property. The industry should purchase land for their operations far from where people live. Workers in the industry should be properly trained to know how to appropriately fell trees. In addition, masks should be provided for workers to limit the amount of dust inhaled.

As a loss finance measure, the industry can purchase third-party property insurance policies. Workers compensation insurance policies should be purchased to cater for injuries caused to workers.

Health Hazards

The continuous inhalation of wood dust at sawmills can cause serious health problems. Chainsaw operators can experience severe impairments to their hearing as a result of the noise generated from the chainsaws used in their operations.

As a loss control measure, masks should be provided for workers in the industry to minimise the inhalation of dust in the lungs. Earplugs can be used by chain saw operators to minimise the noise levels of their machinery.

Purchasing health insurance cover is a loss finance measure. In addition, personal accident insurance can be purchased to protect against any accident resulting from a worker's activities. Employer's liability insurance can be purchased to cover losses that may be brought against the industry.

Pollution

Timber generates a lot of noise because of the felling and the heavy machines involved in the sawing process. Chainsaws also emit some smoke and noise that pollute the environment. Air pollution is created by the trucks used for the transport of lumber. Sawmills also pollute the environment through the dust at sawmills and emissions from machines used for operations.

As a loss control measure, the felling and sawing of trees should be done far away from residential areas. Banning of all trucks that emit excessive fumes from the roads will also help. Machines that generate less noise should be used in sawmills.

As a loss finance measure, the timber companies should insure against public or general liability to take care of the lawsuits for the noise they make.

Tourist Attractions

Some forests serve as tourist attractions. For example, Ankasa in the Western region of Ghana covers 500 square kilometres and Kakum forest reserve in Central region, near Cape Coast covers an area of about 375 square kilometres. Ankasa is the richest in terms of biodiversity in Ghana and Kakum is one of only three locations in Africa with a canopy walk. Thus, when such forests are damaged by the action of timber industries, such activities pose a threat to the tourism industry and biodiversity.

As a loss control measure, more forest reserves should be created and properly policed.

The Rubber Industry

The rubber industry is one of the most important industries in promoting the growth of an economy. The usage of rubber materials has become part of our daily needs. Such products are convenient, durable and cheap. The industry also provides significant avenues for employment. Storage bag manufacturers produce products ranging from jute bags to polythene bags (popularly known as plastic bags). These products have the same disposal issues as the sachets made by the water manufacturers and so tend to create waste and pollute the environment. Despite the many advantages that rubber extraction has it poses a number of threats as well. In this section, these threats are examined and loss control measures and loss finance measures are proposed to cover the industry's activities.

Pollution

Rubber takes a long time to decompose. The dumping of rubber in water bodies facilitates the breeding of mosquitoes and causes malaria. Fumes from the production of rubber may cause air pollution in surrounding communities and ill health to employees. Animals and humans that reside nearby such facilities can develop respiratory tract diseases. The industry's operations require lots of water to cool off heated rubber and so they are mostly in areas where water is accessible. During these operations, wastewater is emitted into water bodies, thus polluting them. This can also lead to a lack of potable drinking water and the spread of water borne diseases. Also, noise pollution from the industry's operations can be a nuisance to communities where the industry is sited. This is because most production sites house and utilise huge machinery in the production process. In addition, in most areas where rubber factories are situated, bad smells are released into the environment. This becomes a nuisance to residents in the neighbourhood of the factory.

Education on the proper disposal of rubber products and their effect on the environment can help reduce the growing problem of waste. For example, pasting instructions on products providing information on the methods of disposing of rubber products can help. Waste disposal bins should be put at key vantage points so that people can discard of such materials correctly. The industry could assist by providing disposal bins that households could use to separate rubber waste from other rubbish generated for easy collection for shredding and recycling.

The industry should invest in technologies to eventually reduce the amount of liquid waste created. In addition, efforts should be made to create additional water resources for the industry, for example, by harvesting rainwater. Where pollution occurs, the industry should assist in clean-up efforts. In addition, educational programmes should be undertaken to enlighten people about the harmful effects of the industry. Processing plants should be sited far away from residential communities. Better drainage systems can be built to reduce the effect of water stagnation and its attendant problems. Workers should be provided with ear plugs to minimise the impact of noise and face masks to protect against impure air. Governments should legislate against the burning of rubber products such as tyres that pollute the atmosphere.

Companies could make storage bags from paper which is more environmentally friendly. There could also be legislation to increase their investments in plastic recycling plants.

The industry requires comprehensive liability insurance to protect itself from any claims from the public. There should be legislative efforts to enforce the rubber industry to put money aside to alleviate the environmental impact that the industry has.

Flood

When rubber products are indiscriminately disposed of, materials can block gutters and sewage systems stopping the free flow of wastewater. Flooding can result especially in the rainy season.

Education on the proper disposal of rubber products can help reduce this problem. The industry can set up recycling plants to recycle the rubber waste resulting from their activities.

Health Problems

The burning of rubber releases harmful emissions that can cause certain lung diseases into the atmosphere. Other by-products and chemicals are sometimes improperly disposed of and have the potential of endangering local communities. Some factories produce rubber products that may not meet quality standards. It has been found that rubber products used in the preparation and storage of food can, when hot, sometimes release chemicals that are harmful to human health into food or water. Certain types of baby bottles were recalled for leaking dangerous chemicals into the baby formula contained in the bottles. In May 2022, Abott Laboratories (one of US major suppliers of baby formula) in Sturgis Michigan recalled certain lots of 2 fluid ounce/59 millilitre bottles of ready-to-feed liquid formula for infants and children because of reports that the formulas have been contaminated with hazardous and potentially life-threatening bacteria including Cronobacter Sakazakii and Salmonella Newport.

As a loss control measure, the rubber industry should not be allowed to site factories close to residential areas. Raising product and consumer safety standards and procedures as well as quality checks on the rubber industry will assist in the banning of dangerous products.

Liability insurance should be used by the industry to protect against lawsuits.

Land Degradation

Rubber waste when indiscriminately disposed of disrupts the growth of plants. There is thus less vegetative cover that enhances erosion in the rainy season. Crop production will obviously be affected.

As a loss control measure, clean-up exercises should be organised by the industry to rid the soil of rubber waste.

Funds can be retained by the industry to meet the cost of financing these clean-up exercises.

Human Resources

Employees of the rubber industry are exposed to harmful gases that can affect their health in the long term. Processing plants emit toxins that can cause serious diseases and other diseases to employees and people living close by.

As a loss control measure, governments should legislate to force factory owners to minimise pollution.

Employee liability insurance is a loss finance measure for the industry. Also, workers in the industry should purchase health insurance cover to meet their health care needs should they fall sick.

Food Security

When polluted liquid waste is discharged into water bodies, the supply of fish for human consumption is scarce. Rubber plantations require vast amount of land and this reduces the amount of land available for cultivating crops. The cutting down of other trees to create plantations can also be a threat to the production of food. In addition, when there is flood because gutters get choked, farming land can be destroyed affecting crop production.

As a loss control measure, there should be a demarcation of areas that can be used for rubber plantations to avoid the indiscriminate planting of rubber trees.

The industry should have liability insurance to cater for losses resulting from possible lawsuits from landowners.

Global Warming

The rubber industry also contributes to global warming including the pollution of water bodies, air pollution and deforestation. In addition, the continuous emission of carbon and nitrogen dioxides further contributes to the depletion of the ozone layer.

Cleaner production methods can lead to the reduction of harmful emissions.

The industry should set up a fund to cater for losses resulting from its activities.

Threats to the Rubber Industry

Lack of rainfall for long periods can adversely affect the yields from rubber plantations. Litigation about where the industry facilities should be sited can affect operations. Also, an inadequate power supply can damage the industry. When prices of the products produced by the industry are low, the sustainability of the industry is threatened. The physical assets owned by the industry can be damaged by fire, stolen or destroyed in transit. Employees of the rubber industry can sue the company for the inadequate provision of safety equipment.

Loss control measures for these threats include the use of irrigation in plantations as a farming strategy; the purchase of generators to ensure continuous operations when there are power failures; the installation of fire extinguishers, smoke and fire detectors and activated sprinkler systems in industry facilities to assist in fighting fire when it erupts; and the provision of safety equipment and protective clothing for workers to ensure the workplace is free of hazard.

A loss finance measure is insurance. Liability insurance, for example, can be purchased to meet the cost of lawsuits brought against the industry. Non-insurance transfers such as hedging in the rubber futures market can ensure that projected revenues are realised. The industry can set up an emergency or compensation fund to make payments or compensations in the event of employees losing their lives in the discharge of their duties.

Aggregates/Quarrying

The quarrying industry is a booming industry in many developing countries. Private firms and governments invest huge amounts of money in the construction of houses, roads, office blocks, skyscrapers and other construction projects. The industry serves as a huge source of employment and contributes enormously to the economic development of nations. Despite these benefits, there are many problems associated with it and these are outlined below.

Pollution

One of the main threats the construction industry poses to the environment is the pollution it creates. Construction waste is left at project sites or dumped indiscriminately. Construction labourers dump water sachets indiscriminately after their use. Construction activities that take place close to water bodies contaminate rivers and lakes due to the disposal of waste. Muddy water generated from construction activities is sometimes channelled directly into streams, rivers or the sea. A lot of dust is emitted when the ground is ploughed and gravelled during road construction before the application of tarmac. Also, air pollution occurs when dust particles from the sand used in construction gets into the air creating health hazards such as asthma for the populace. It is difficult for people living around a construction site to dry their clothing outside. Noise from large construction machinery also creates problems for residents.

As a loss control measure the industry should recycle all its waste. There should be watering of roads during and after construction works to limit the amount of dust emitted into the atmosphere. Alternatively, construction work can be timed for periods, such as holidays and festivals when most people are away from their location to reduce the amount of polluted air they inhale. Filtering systems that limit the amount of pollutants released into the atmosphere should be employed by the industry. The regular maintenance of machines and equipment—and the replacement of older equipment—can help minimise the noise and fumes generated. The industry should inform local communities of their upcoming work to make residents aware of their presence so that measures such as using earplugs and face masks can be utilised to avoid health issues. Workers should also be provided with suitable safety equipment especially those involved in road construction. Wastewater should be properly treated to avoid contaminating streams or rivers that flow through the land. The industry can also take it upon itself as part of its social responsibility to clean water bodies that do become polluted. Alternatively, the industry can sub-contract another company to deal with waste management problems.

A loss finance measure is for the industry to set aside funds from its profits to purchase modern equipment. Liability insurance can also be obtained by the industry against any legal action that may be brought by inhabitants affected by the industry's activities. Health insurance policies can also be purchased by the industry for its workforce.

Sand Mining (Winning)

Sand winning is the activity of mining sand that may harm the environment. Sand winning can cause land erosion making such areas prone to floods especially in coastal areas. The practice also destroys arable soil and leads to a decline in food production. Majority of sand winning in Ghana is illegal.

A loss control measure is the use of equipment and building methods that require less sand. For example, there are some brick building machines that can make bricks without the use of sand or mortar.

Deforestation

The construction industry uses much timber for its activities. There is often an indiscriminate felling of trees and most often the trees are not replaced. When roads are constructed, trees and plants are destroyed. As trees provide shade for water bodies, deforestation can result in the drying of rivers or streams depriving a community of its source of water. Farmland is also destroyed in some cases. Land where the mixing of concrete occurs becomes infertile and inhibits plant growth. Construction activities degrade the land since it is usually cleared before building. These activities lead to changes in climatic conditions and a loss of biodiversity.

A loss control measure is to plant at least one new tree for every tree that is felled for timber. Trees or ornamental plants can also be planted along roads after the roads are completed to restore beauty to the land.

As a loss finance measure, the industry should have a reserve fund for afforestation.

Health Hazards of Quarrying

In mining and quarrying for raw materials to be used in the construction industry, issues such as uncovered trenches, mining, blasting, digging, etc., can pose serious health threats to society. For example, uncovered trenches can become a breeding place for mosquitoes or a danger to children.

This can be controlled by a company by boarding up their quarrying sites or putting warning signs to alert people to stay away. Reflective ropes can also be employed to alert people of possible dangers.

As a loss finance measure, the industry can take up liability insurance against third-party injury or death. Funds could also be set aside by the industry for all forms of eventualities.

Damage to Property

Most construction activities involve the use of large machines to create foundations, move building materials and drill holes and trenches. As a result, the properties of others can be damaged. Windows can be broken and walls may get broken or weakened. The movement of trucks, tractors and caterpillars may also damage the vehicles of other road users. Water pipes and underground electricity cables can be damaged disrupting the supply of water and electricity into people's homes. Some homes are sometimes destroyed or demolished to make room for road construction.

As a loss control measure, major construction activities should be undertaken in industrial areas and generally not in residential areas. Contractors should liaise with the operators of electricity and water supplies so that cables and pipes are not damaged during construction projects.

As a loss finance measure, public liability insurance should be sought. In cases where the properties of others are destroyed by construction activities, public liability insurance will be essential.

Relocation of Residents

There are times when construction work may necessitate the relocation of people. During the construction of the Bui Dam in Ghana, inhabitants living in the vicinity had to be relocated. A total of 1216 people within the project area were resettled and 444 square kilometres of land was flooded. The construction faced protests from residents and environmentalists who say that Ghana rare black hippopotamus populations were threatened by the dam.

As a loss control measure, people must be notified about the relocation years or many months in advance. People should also be educated not to build close to major infrastructure sites. Accommodation and support should be provided for affected people in any relocation exercise. Sites should be carefully chosen to limit the frequency and severity of a displacement.

Funds must be set aside by the industry for this relocation exercise.

Human Capital

The industry poses threat to humans as well. Working in the construction industry can mean working in dangerous conditions: at great heights, in direct contact with live wires, welding and heavy machinery. All these make the work risky and the possibility of injury or death high. Also, labour laws can be violated by the industry in employing underage people, paying workers below the minimum wage and general exploitation.

As a loss control measure, the industry must provide its workers with safety equipment such as helmets, gloves, goggles and face masks so as to reduce the number of accidents at construction sites. The industry must also ensure that its workforce abide by safety rules such as wearing the appropriate protective clothing when undertaking jobs such as welding. Purchasing an employer's liability insurance policy will avail the industry expert advice from insurers about loss control measures that can be adopted to reduce the possible loss the industry is exposed to.

As a loss finance measure, workers' compensation insurance could be bought to compensate both workers and their family in the case of an accident.

Improper Supervision of Construction Works

Negligence on the part of site supervisors and the improper training of construction workers pose societal threats. Poorly constructed buildings can collapse due to the use of sub-standard materials. An example is the collapse of the Melcom Building in Accra in November 2012. A collapsed building can lead to the immediate loss of life and environmental hazards from the debris left behind. This can lead to pest infestations in nearby buildings. Poor drainage systems created by the construction of roads sometimes impedes the free flow of water bodies. This brings about flooding during the rainy season and affects lives and properties.

As a loss control measure, the industry should employ qualified and trained contractors and employees. Strict safety standards should be complied with in the construction of all buildings. The soil where buildings are to be constructed should be tested to ensure that the right materials are used. In addition, the supervisors of road projects should ensure that the construction of roads does not impede the free flow of water to cause flooding.

As a loss finance measure, the industry should set aside funds to train and develop its workforce to enable them work efficiently and effectively. Also, liability insurance can be purchased to cater for such losses.

Delays

The operations of the construction industry may cause travel delays and traffic jams for road users.

As a loss control measure, alternative routes should be planned and people or signage should be used to direct road users on diversions.

Land Litigation

Land litigation is another problem posed by the construction industry. In most communities where construction projects take place, there are issues about how land is being used. In some cases, land used by construction companies is not properly acquired. This results in litigation that can take long periods of time.

As a loss control measure, the industry must make every effort to acquire land lawfully and from the rightful owners.

Production of Sub-Standard Buildings and Road

Some construction companies can be cited for producing poor roads, poorly constructed buildings and other related construction works. Poorly constructed roads are costly to governments and the public at large.

As a loss control measure, the industry should employ the best modern technologies in the projects that they execute. The industry can purchase liability insurance for lawsuits that may be filed against it.

Exercises

1. Identify six major ways the operations of the timber industry can harm the environment. For each point identified, suggest a loss control measure and a loss finance measure.
2. Explain five threats that the construction industry poses to the environment. For each threat identified, suggest a loss control measure and a loss finance measure.
3. Identify and explain five major threats posed by the construction industry to a country's development. For each threat identified, suggest loss control and loss finance measures.
4. Identify and explain five negative consequences of the petroleum industry.
5. Pollution is a major problem for the extractive industry. Explain how pollution affects society and suggest loss control and finance measures.
6. Explain how financial risk occurs in the petroleum industry.
7. What are some of the measures that can be put in place to control the outbreak of fire?

References

ActionAid. (2016). *Precious Metals II: A Systemic Inequality*. https://www.miningweekly.com/article/actionaid-south-africa-launches-report-highlighting-human-rights-violations-at-anglo-platinum-mine-2016-06-23.

Ajoko-Adebanjoko, A. (2017). *Towards Ending Conflict and Insecurity in the Niger Delta Region: A Collective Non-violent Approach*. African Centre for Constructive Resolution of Disputes. http://www.accord.org.za/

Asuni, J. B. (2009). *Understanding the Armed Groups of the Niger Delta. Council on Foreign Relation*. https://www.cfr.org/sites/default/files/pdf/2009/09/CFR_WorkingPaper_2_NigerDelta.pdf

Bedi, H. P. (2015). Right to Food, Right to Mine? Competing Human Rights Claims in Bangladesh. *Geoforum, 59*, 248–257.

Fletcher, E. R. (2022). *The Niger Delta's Harsh Lessons: Fossils' Harm to People and the Plant*. https://healthpolicy-watch.news/fossil-fuels-harms-health-as-well-as-the-planet/

Mills, S., Tuglavina, J., Simmons, D., & Claus, R. (2017). Food (In)security in Northern Canada. *Northern Public Affairs, 5*(1), 39–41.

Nwilo, P. C., & Badejo, O. T. (2004). *Impacts and Management of Oil Spill Pollution along the Nigerian Coastal Areas.* https://www.researchgate.net/publication/242327944_Impacts_and_Management_of_Oil_Spill_Pollution_along_the_Nigerian_Coastal_Areas

Obi, O. (2023). *Oil Among the Mangrove Trees: A Portrait of the Destruction in the Niger Delta, Then and Now.* Harvard International Review (pp. 1–12). https://hir.harvard.edu/oil-among-the-mangrove-trees-a-portrait-of-destru.

Shalala, P. (2013). *My Nomination for The Africa Story Challenge Award and the Journey Ahead.* The Zambian Analyst.

Wegenast, T., & Beck, J. (2020). Mining, Rural Livelihoods and Food Security: A Disaggregated Analysis of Sub-Saharan Africa. *World Development, 130,* Article 104921.

Wise, H., & Shtylla, S. (2007). *The Role of the Extractive Sector in Expanding Economic Opportunity.* Harvard University and John F. Kennedy School of Government.

Further Reading

Boulanger, Y., Arseneault, D., Bélisle, A. C., Bergeron, Y., Boucher, J., Boucher, Y. Danneyrolles, V. et al. (2024). *The 2023 Wildfire Season in Québec: An Overview of Extreme Conditions, Impacts, Lessons 2 Learned and Considerations for the Future.* Canadian Journal of Forest Research (Forthcoming).

Buchholz, P., & Stürmer, M. (2011). An overview of geological resources in Sub-Saharan Africa: Potential and opportunities for tax revenue from the extractive sector. *Geological Resources and Good Governance in Sub-Saharan Africa: Holistic Approaches to Transparency and Sustainable Development in the Extractive Sector*, 17.

Gupta, P. K. (2008). *Fundamental of Insurance* (1st ed.). Himalaya Publishing House. *Unit 1*: *Chapter 1.*

Gupta, P. K. (2016). *Essentials of Insurance and Risk Management* (1st ed.). Himalaya Publishing House Pvt Ltd. *Part I*: *Chapter 2.*

Harrington, S. E., & Niehaus, G. R. (2004). *Risk Management and Insurance.* McGraw-Hill. *Chapters 1.*

Ogri, O. R. (2001). A Review of the Nigerian Petroleum Industry and the Associated Environmental Problems. *The Environmentalist, 21,* 11–21.

Onyshchenko, S., Hlushko, A., Maslii, O., & Skryl, V. (2022). Risks and Threats to Economic Security of Enterprises in the Construction Industry Under Pandemic Conditions. In V. Onyshchenko, G. Mammadova, S. Sivitska, & A. Gasimov (Eds.), *Proceedings of the 3rd International Conference on Building Innovations.* ICBI 2020. Lecture Notes in Civil Engineering (Vol. 181). Springer.

Perks, R. (2012). How can Public–Private Partnerships Contribute to Security and Human Rights Policy and Practice in the Extractive Industries? A Case Study of the Democratic Republic of Congo (DRC). *Resources Policy, 37*(2), 251–260.

Redja, G. E. & McNamara. (2016). *Principles of Risk Management and Insurance.* Pearson Addison Wesley. *Chapters 1.*

Whitehead Jr., R. & Block, W. (2000). *Environmental Justice Risks in the Petroleum Industry*, 24 Wm. & Mary Envtl L. & Pol'y Rev. 67.

Chapter 6
Risk, Insurance and the Transportation Industry

Abstract The transport sector encompasses road, water, air, rail, and other modes of conveying people, goods, and services from one location to another. This sector plays a pivotal role in the economic growth and development of nations, serving as a significant source of government revenue through taxation, given the constant movement of people, goods, and services. This chapter examines the economic benefits derived from key segments of the transport sector, identifies the risks and threats inherent to its operations, and proposes appropriate loss control and prevention measures to mitigate these risks.

Keywords Air transport · Rail transport · Road transport · Water transport

Introduction

Transportation has long been the backbone of human civilisation, shaping economies, cultures, and connections across the globe. From the earliest exchange of goods along rivers to the modern marvels of aviation, the story of transport reflects humanity's enduring pursuit of speed, efficiency, and accessibility. Beyond its role in linking people and places, the transport sector also serves as a vital engine of national revenue, providing governments with significant tax income as people, goods, and services move across networks every day. Yet transport is not without challenges: while it fuels growth and opportunity, it also brings risks that demand careful management. This chapter explores the four fundamental modes of transport namely road, water, rail, and air. It examines the economic benefits each sector contributes, the threats they may pose, and the importance of effective strategies for loss control and prevention measures.

C. Andoh, *Fundamentals of Managing Risk and Insurance*,
https://doi.org/10.1007/978-981-95-4581-0_6

Road Transport

Road transport provides employment for many people both directly and indirectly. The road transport system has created jobs for mechanics, drivers, bus conductors, car dealers and traders, etc. This has consequently helped to broaden the tax base of governments because these income earners pay taxes.

One other benefit is that it provides a convenient method of transport for both private car owners and those using public transport such as bus services.

Furthermore, road transport is widely used for the transportation of goods with short lead times such as fruits and vegetables. Farmers in rural areas are therefore able to bring their goods to towns and cities quickly.

For businesses, it is easy to monitor the routes, mileage and fuel consumption of their drivers using tracking devices. This enables them to effectively plan deliveries and make use of efficiencies in getting goods to market in the fastest and cheapest way possible.

The major threats posed by road transportation, along with loss prevention and loss control measures are discussed below.

Pollution

Air pollution is one of the major problems caused by road transport. Excessive fumes from the exhaust pipes of vehicles pollute the environment. Old and badly maintained cars emit thick fumes as ambient particulate matter causing severe health problems in many African cities. In Lagos, for example, a city of 21 million people, smog is a daily fact of life. Carbon dioxide emissions also contribute to global warming and climate change, distorting rainfall patterns.

Motor vehicle emissions of sulphur dioxide (SO_2), carbon monoxide (CO), nitrogen dioxide (NO_2), soot, dust and fine particulate matter (PM) contribute to deteriorating air quality in most Africa's largest cities (Haq & Schwela, 2012, pp. 1). In addition, pedestrians, hawkers, drivers and passengers can discard waste when using the road leading to further pollution. Noise pollution is another issue for people living close to major roads and motorways.

The regular maintenance of vehicles is a loss control measure. Governments should enact laws banning the use of old vehicles that pollute the atmosphere. A task force should be set up by the law enforcement agencies to ensure that only road-worthy vehicles can use the roads. Governments should invest in research for cleaner fuels or alternative types of fuel rather than petrol and gas, such as electric vehicles. Trees should be planted along roads by the transport ministries of governments to absorb some of the pollutants emitted by vehicles.

As a loss finance measure, fines collected from cars with high emissions can be used to fund the activities of the task force. Hawkers found littering should be fined and the funds realised used to pay for the services of waste management companies to collect waste. Health insurance can be used to finance the cost of illnesses resulting from the inhalation of dirty air, such as respiratory diseases, including asthma.

Deforestation

Many road construction projects result in the loss of virgin forests. Many people like to reside alongside roads and as a result, trees are destroyed to provide shelter and firewood. Shortages of timber and wood for industries such as furniture making can arise.

As a loss control measure, governments should enact laws banning new settlements along major new roads especially in forested areas.

As a loss finance measure there should be budgetary allocation for the planting of trees along roads by governments.

Loss of Agricultural Lands

Lands that could have been used for agricultural purposes are also lost in road construction projects as they are converted into fuel stations, lorry parks and rest areas. To enable road construction, aggregates are quarried or mined which can also cause a loss of farmland.

Efficiency in land usage is paramount. Governments (through their town and city planners) should ensure that lands earmarked for agricultural purposes are protected and not encroached upon.

As a loss finance measure, governments can make budgetary allocations for the construction of flyovers to minimise the loss of land.

Erosion

When roads are constructed but not frequently maintained, gullies and potholes begin to develop that result in damage to vehicles.

As a loss control measure, roads should be maintained regularly to prevent erosion. In addition, vegetation should be planted alongside roads to prevent erosion.

As a loss finance measure, tolls should be charged for road use to fund their maintenance.

Accidents

Accidents are a major problem with road transport. Speeding, human error badly maintained vehicles, faulty brakes, broken traffic signals, the overloading of vehicles, unclear road signals, the poor vision of drivers and bad roads and road conditions are the major causes of road accidents. Accidents lead to injuries and the loss of human life. In addition, goods being transported can be lost or spoiled when accidents occur.

As a loss control measure, proper education must be given to road users about road safety practices especially during festivities when there is a greater movement of people and goods. Drivers should be screened regularly to ensure that they have good vision and are competent to continue driving. Sporadic checks of vehicles by the police to check the particulars of drivers and the state of their vehicles to ensure roadworthiness will assist in minimising accidents.

Regular checks on the traffic lights should be undertaken to ensure that they are working properly. Insurance companies also have a part to play. For example, they may reduce the premium for a driver should that individual take a driving education course. By so doing, they will encourage greater driving proficiency. Not only will this reduce the number of road accidents; it will also reduce the number of claims made to the insurance company.

Motor insurance is evidently a key loss finance measure. Motor policies provide compensation for injuries and deaths caused by accidents. Life policies also provide benefits to the dependents of a victim. Governments should invest in the development of rail infrastructure and the air transportation system that are generally safer than road if well managed.

Congestion

This serves as one of the major threats to efficient road transportation. Road congestion and traffic jams prolong journeys unnecessarily and result in the delay of the arrival of goods and people to their destinations. It is a huge issue in African cities such as Accra, Nairobi and Cairo and gridlock on the roads results in high levels of pollution. Productivity is also adversely affected since workers not only get exhausted getting to and from work but arrive late. Slow moving vehicles results in car crimes such as the snatching of phones and handbags. Besides, commercial vehicles carrying perishable goods risk their loads becoming spoilt.

Governments need to invest in better road infrastructure and legislating on the standard of emissions for vehicles. Carpooling should be encouraged by the government which will eventually reduce the number of vehicles of the road. Public transport should be improved where needed in terms of comfort and reliability and the populace encouraged to use it for commuting. Parking tickets should be introduced at workplaces to encourage people to either carpool or patronise public transport.

As a loss finance measure, the government should fund additional road infrastructure from public taxes.

Car Crime

Highway robbers are a threat to both people, the vehicles they drive and goods being transported in some major cities of Africa. For example, the transport Minister of Southern African, Sindisiwe Chikunga and her two protectors were ambushed and robbed while travelling on the N3 highway near Johannesburg in November 2023.

As a loss control measure, drivers should desist from travelling at night. Agencies responsible for transport should ensure that all roads have streetlights that work properly.

As a loss finance measure, insurance products such as personal accident insurance can be purchased.

Water Transport

Water transport like any transportation system has created large numbers of jobs, in this case for boat and ship builders, craftsmen, sailors and seamen whose lives depend on it. Water transport is a critical element in international trade. Most goods traded across borders are conveyed by ship and international sea freight continues to grow. This assists a country to boost its foreign exchange reserves and serves as revenue to the government in the form of duties charged on goods transported by sea.

Second, water transportation is an efficient and economical means for the transportation of large quantities of goods over long distances.

Third, water transportation in the form of cargo and container ships is usually well planned: the sea vessels are generally in good condition and captains are usually well-trained professionals. Consequently, there is a reduced risk of accidents.

Fourth, the cost of construction and maintenance is relatively less. Unlike road transportation, water transportation generally operates on a natural track (such as the sea, lagoons, lakes, etc.) and hence may not require any extensive construction work—other than port infrastructure.

By means of water transportation, a country's navy or marine police can defend a country from attack from the sea.

Despite all these benefits, water transportation still poses certain problems. Some of these are as follows.

Slow Form of Transport

Water transportation is generally a slow means of transporting goods over long distances. Ships can stay on the water for awfully long periods before getting to their destinations. Perishable items are at risk on such journeys if refrigeration systems malfunction.

A loss finance measure is for owners to purchase insurance policies for the goods that they are transporting to help reduce such losses.

Weather Conditions

Bad weather conditions at sea can trigger accidents and the malfunctioning of a ship. The exposure of a ship to the perils of the sea such as storms or tsunamis can lead to the loss of a vessel, its cargo and possibly its crew.

Cargo ships should have the most modern technologies to predict bad weather.

Pirates

The resurgence of piracy in some areas of the world is another major threat to water transportation. Pirates can hijack ships and take the crew hostage. This will endanger the lives of those on board, the vessel and the safe arrival of goods to their owners.

As a loss control measure, a ship should employ experienced security personnel to help guard against such occurrences.

Life insurance can be purchased by crew members, and other insurance products can be taken to cover the goods on board.

Pollution

The leakage of oil into the ocean is a source of pollution. This is hazardous to both aquatic and bird lives. Container ships also emit huge amounts of pollution. It has been estimated that just one of these container ships, the length of around six football pitches, can produce the same amount of pollution as 50 million cars. The emissions from 15 of these mega-ships match all the cars in the world. And if the shipping industry were a country, it would be ranked between Germany and Japan as the sixth-largest contributor to global CO_2 emissions.

As a loss control measure, old vessels should be maintained and repaired frequently by owners to prevent leakages. In addition, the overloading of vessels should be avoided. Cleaner fuels should be used wherever possible.

As a loss finance measure, funds should be set aside by owners to replace old ships. Marine insurance can be taken to finance the liability and cost of oil spillages.

Rail Transport

The rail sector provides jobs in areas such as train drivers, ticket collectors, mechanical and electrical engineers, among others. As with container ships, trains can be used to carry heavy goods such as timber, bauxite, manganese and other heavy metals both internally and for export to neighbouring countries. It can transport large numbers of people and goods at the same time and for long distances. This means of transport can save considerable time especially in congested cities where road traffic congestion abounds. It reduces pressure on the road sector and can get commuters and goods to their destinations faster than road vehicles. It is also a relatively safe mode of transport compared to road transport. The industry creates revenue for governments from taxation (if privately owned) or from profits (if nationalised). Rail transport also pollutes less.

A good rail network and infrastructure leads to the economic development of towns and cities in a country as it entails the construction of systems that assist the work of other industries.

There are, however, numerous problems that hamper the smooth running of the rail sector.

Maintenance

The rail sector is the most expensive of all land-based transport systems to maintain. It costs lots of money to replace, repair and maintain trains, rails and carriages. Huge maintenance costs can create problems for the viability of a rail network. The alternative, however, is a dangerous rail system.

As a loss control measure, it is important to induce a maintenance culture in the people who manage or work for rail networks. Training workshops should be conducted for staff to keep abreast of modern methods for maintaining rail operations.

As a loss finance measure, internal funds can be used to train employees or personnel.

Accidents

Train accidents diminish the trust of the people who rely on this mode of transport. Train derailments, collisions or fire outbreaks pose a threat to users. People can sustain serious injuries and goods may be damaged or get destroyed. Unsafe signalling systems can be a hazard for pedestrians and vehicles crossing train tracks. Inexperienced or poorly trained drivers can cause accidents through speeding, misreading of signs and technical glitches, among others. In addition, workers are prone to serious accidents because of the heavy nature of the equipment the industry uses.

The proper training of train drivers and personnel directly involved in signalling and communication and rail truck maintenance is crucial. The carriages of goods trains must be covered so that in the event of an accident some goods can be salvaged. In the absence of automatic signalling and crossings, staff can be deployed to man intersections where road and rail lines meet to direct vehicles and trains when they are approaching intersections. Footbridges can be constructed over rail lines (or tunnels built underneath) to allow people to safely cross rail lines. A training institute can be set up for drivers to attend and only those that pass the requisite examination should be permitted to drive trains. Safety staff should follow strict protocols in examining the condition of trains. Train operators must heed weather forecasts and advice given by meteorologists to avoid accidents that may be triggered by the weather conditions.

As a loss finance measure, the rail transport industry can purchase liability insurance to cover losses that might be brought against it by third parties and/or the industry employees. Train users should ensure that they have personal accident insurance to cover losses they may be exposed to. Management of the industry should reserve sufficient funds to repair and maintain the infrastructure.

Restricted Access

In regions where the rail network is restricted or unavailable people and goods will travel by road or air, putting pressure on road maintenance costs.

As a loss control measure, the rail industry should constantly review its network and the viability of new routes.

As a loss finance measure, a government could set up funds to assist in developing new lines and routes funded through taxation or as part of the ticket price people pay.

Disease Outbreak

In times of an outbreak of a contagious disease, people will be reluctant to use rail for fear of being infected.

A loss control measure for the industry is to employ the services of highly trained medical professionals to identify people with diseases and prevent them from getting on trains.

Funds can be set aside by the industry to fund the needs of these professionals to operate efficiently.

Terrorism

Rail transport cannot exclude itself from the threat of terrorism. Armed robbers have been known to attack a train and rob passengers of their belongings.

As a loss control measure, security cameras can be installed at train stations, guards placed on trains and suspicious characters searched and questioned or even prevented from boarding the train.

Commuters can be educated to purchase personal accident insurance so that any injury or financial loss they experience is covered.

Pollution

Pollution is another threat posed by the rail sector when older steam trains are used. Diseases such as bronchitis and other respiratory diseases can be inflicted on people that reside close to busy rail lines. Noise pollution is another issue.

Proper engine maintenance is critical in minimising the amount of polluted air emitted by trains. Rail lines can also be constructed underground in cities to minimise the noise created by the moving train. Modern trains can be powered by electricity that does not pollute the environment in the same way as coal.

Health insurance policies can be purchased by people that reside close to train tracks so that the cost of any illness is borne by an insurance company.

Land Degradation

Building rail lines can degrade forests or other natural areas and its flora and fauna. The metals used to construct the track can rust leading to soil degradation.

As a loss control measure, trees cut down for construction must be replaced. The metals used for the rails can be coated to prevent rusting.

As a loss finance measure, funds can be set aside by the industry or the government for the planting of trees to replace those lost. Funds can be set aside by the rail sector to carry out research on improved methods of minimising land degradation.

Trains Departure and Arrival Times

The perpetual unreliability of a rail network can be a threat to the trust users have in it and its viability.

As a loss control measure, infrastructure should be maintained to minimise delays, investment in new trains should be done and employees trained to stick to schedules. In situations where delays are inevitable, replacement buses should be made available to convey passengers to their destinations.

Funds can be set aside for the purchase of such buses and used to organise workshops on time management for the employees of the rail sector.

Vibrations

The movement of trains creates vibrations in the ground that can cause cracks in nearby buildings and other assets making them unsafe.

As a loss control measure, buildings and assets should not be sited close to rail lines. The government can enact regulations that forbid constructing buildings close to rail lines.

As a loss finance measure, businesses and houses that are sited close to rail lines should be relocated with costs funded from taxes.

Company's Directors

Directors of a company are to ensure indirectly the effectiveness and efficiency of the operations of a company. Appointment of incompetent directors to manage the affairs of the industry can threaten the sustainability of the rail sector. Some incompetent directors appointed to manage the affairs of the sector brought the previously vibrant rail networks in Ghana to its knees. Ghana lost its vibrant rail networks in the sixties and seventies because of dubious activities of some of its workforce.

As a loss control measure, the recruitment process for these sensitive positions should be stringent. Well qualified people should be employed to manage the affairs of the industry.

Overcrowded Trains

Overcrowding on trains reduces the comfort of passengers making them less likely to travel by train. Additionally, in the event of a sudden brake application by a train driver, serious accidents can happen because of the overcrowding.

As a loss control measure, there must be a safety limit on the number of passengers or cargo a train can carry.

As a loss finance measure, liability insurance can be taken by the industry to pay losses that might arise from lawsuits brought against the industry by the public. Commuters can also purchase personal accident insurance to protect themselves.

Air Transport

Air transport is generally the fastest mode of transportation for people and goods over a long distance. It is free from physical barriers and follows the shortest and most direct route. It is the only means of transport to areas that are not easily accessible. The industry provides employment for people, generates revenue for governments and reduces the pressure on other means of transport such as road, rail and sea. Moreover, the industry promotes or facilitates regional integration and commercial trade. The world has become a global village partly because of advances in air transport. Some airline operators in Africa undertake corporate social responsibility initiatives such as the drilling of boreholes and the building of schools and hospitals in the communities or regions in which they operate.

Despite the many benefits that air transportation has for the economies of the world, there are risks that we will discuss and suggest ways to mitigate.

Weather Forecasts

Sometimes meteorological forecasts may not be accurate posing a threat to the safety of air transport. The loss control measure is equipping meteorologists with modern instruments to make forecasts as accurate as possible. The loss finance measure is to indemnify people who get killed or who are injured through a plane crash because of a poor weather forecast. Thus, passengers should be encouraged to buy insurance policies so that in the case of loss of life, an insurance company will compensate their dependents.

Pollution

Air pollution is an issue for airline companies. The fumes from planes pose health risks to residents that reside close to airports. Planes emit particles and gases such as carbon dioxide water vapour, hydrocarbons, carbon monoxide, nitrogen oxides, sulphur oxides, lead and black carbon which interact among themselves and with the atmosphere contributing to global warming. Noise pollution is another threat for those close to airports or on busy flight paths. The high-pitched noise that airplanes make during landing and take-off can affect the hearing of workers, residents and passengers.

As a loss control measure, the regular maintenance of aircraft is required. Old engines should be replaced to minimise the amount of fumes they emit. The wearing of ear protectors should be encouraged, especially for workers on the runways of airports.

As a loss finance measure, funds should be set aside for aircraft maintenance. Health insurance should be compulsory for workers at airports.

Accidents

A major concern in airline industry is plane crashes. Plane crashes, though rare, are generally fatal to those on board as well as to property and people caught up in accidents on the ground. Fire can break out during flights due to electrical malfunctions; engines can fail and human error by pilots can be a problem. Poorly constructed runways at the airports can cause planes to skid off and fail, damage the aircraft and properties.

As a loss control measure, the proper inspection of an aircraft by qualified engineers must be mandatory before take-offs. Airline operators should employ experienced pilots. Safety gadgets such as fire extinguishers, parachutes and life jackets should be provided aboard an aircraft and passengers instructed on their use.

Everyone that uses air travel should purchase life insurance. In addition, liability insurance should be mandatory for airline operators to fund compensation claims because of an accident. Travel insurance can also help fund some losses when accidents occur for the travelling public.

Improper Management of Air Transport

Airlines are expensive to maintain, and the replacement of aircrafts is costly. Consequently, care must be taken in the management of the operations of the industry because poor practices can cause a company to fail. The lack of infrastructure development at an airport can affect patronage. If the buildings at an airport are poorly maintained, access is poor or there are regular delays, travellers will be discouraged.

Baggage management is an important service aspect of air travel. When a passenger's baggage arrives late or is damaged in transit, it creates additional costs for an airline.

As a loss control measure, the management of an airliner should train its staff to avoid unnecessary cancellations or overbooking of flights so as not to create bad will from passengers. Travelling light is good loss control measure so that in the occurrence of a loss, the impact will not be high.

As a loss finance measure, a fund can be set aside specifically earmarked towards the training of an industry's staff regarding customer service. Periodic renovation and improvement of the facilities at an airport will encourage patronage.

Drug Peddlers

The smuggling of drugs by air is common. When drug mules are arrested at airports, it can tarnish the image of the airline.

As a loss control measure, airport staff should be trained in baggage inspections to identify suspicious bags or passengers before they embark. Security cameras and other security systems should be employed to assist identifying such people. Long jail sentences and heavy fines should be imposed on people peddling drugs to help serve as a deterrent to others.

As a loss finance measure, funds should be set aside for the purchase of security cameras and other security systems that an airport may need. State-of-the-art security systems should be put in place by narcotic control boards. Funds realised from the imposition of fines for drug trafficking should be used to indemnify third parties who innocently suffer from their actions.

Spread of Diseases

Another threat posed by the air transport sector is the introduction of people with contagious diseases into a country. Diseases such as Ebola and Covid-19 can pose a significant threat to the health of the citizens of a country.

As a loss control measure, the industry should stop flights to countries with outbreaks of highly contagious diseases. Also, the presence of well-trained medical staff to inspect passengers in areas of high risk can help stop people with contagious conditions from infecting other passengers.

As part of its corporate social responsibility policy, an airline could retain funds for treating diseases in countries affected with highly contagious diseases.

Hijacking

Hijackers pose a threat to the airline industry. When airplanes are hijacked, the passengers, crew and airplane are at risk. The following are examples of attacks on aircraft by hijackers.

On November 23, 1996, Ethiopian Airlines Flight 961 crashed into the Indian Ocean near a beach in the Comoros Islands after hijackers refused to allow the pilot to land and refuel the plane. Out of a total of 175 passengers on board, 125 of them died and the remaining 50 passengers survived with minor injuries. On February 17, 2014, Ethiopian Airlines Flight 702, a scheduled flight from Addis Ababa to Rome, was forced to proceed to Geneva airport. According to the airline, the Boeing 767-300 (ET-AMF) was flying north over Sudan when it changed its transponder to squawk 7500 indicating a hijacking. Nearing Geneva, the pilots communicated with air traffic control to inquire about the possibility of hijackers receiving asylum in Switzerland. The aircraft circled the airport several times, before landing at around 6:00 in the morning with one working engine and less than 10 min of fuel remaining. The airport remained closed as the aircraft stayed on the tarmac. At 7:12 am local time, the pilots communicated to air traffic control that they would be ready to disembark passengers in five minutes. The hijacker who was the co-pilot was arrested. On October 14, 2000, Saudi Arabian Airlines Flight 115, flying from Jeddah to London was hijacked en route by two men who claimed they were armed with explosives. The hijackers commandeered the Boeing 777-200 to Baghdad, Iraq, where all 90 passengers and 15 crew members were safely released. The two hijackers, identified as Lieutenant Faisal Naji Hamoud Al-Bilawi and First Lieutenant Ayesh Ali Hussein Al-Fareedi, both Saudi citizens, were arrested and later extradited to Saudi Arabia in 2003.

September 11, 2001 was probably the worst attack in the history of air travel. The 9/11 attacks were a series of four coordinated terrorist attacks by the Islamic terrorist group Al-Qaeda on the United States. The attacks killed 2,996 people, injured over 6,000 others and caused at least $10 billion in infrastructure and property damage. Four passenger airliners operated by two major US passenger air carriers (United Airlines and American Airlines)—all of which departed from airports in the Northeastern United States bound for California—were hijacked by 19 Al-Qaeda terrorists. Two of the planes, American Airlines Flight 11 and United Airlines Flight 175, were crashed into the North and South towers, respectively, of the World Trade Center complex in New York City. Within an hour and 42 min, both 110-story towers collapsed, with debris and the resulting fires causing partial or complete collapse of all other buildings in the World Trade Center complex, including the 47-story 7 World Trade Center tower, as well as significant damage to ten other large surrounding structures. A third plane, American Airlines Flight 77 was crashed into the Pentagon (the headquarters of the United States Department of Defence) in Arlington County, Virginia, leading to a partial collapse of the building's western side. The fourth plane, United Airlines Flight 93, was initially steered towards Washington, D.C., but crashed into a field in Stonycreek Township near Shanksville, Pennsylvania, after its passengers tried to overcome the hijackers. The September 11 attack was the single deadliest incident for firefighters and law enforcement officers in the history of the United States, with 343 and 72 deaths respectively.

As a loss control measure air marshals should accompany flights to disarm any hijacker that may slip through security checks. There is the need for greater security checks at airports before passengers are allowed to embark aircrafts.

Limited Number of Airports

The limited airport numbers in some areas of the world can hamper the operations of the air transport sector. In an emergency where an aircraft must necessarily land, an airport may not be readily available in the vicinity resulting in a possible hazard for the plane. Limited airports may also mean that flights must be delayed because of high levels of passenger numbers and flights or bad weather. Aircraft may need to circle until a landing slot is available. The delays can be costly to businesses.

As a loss control measure, new or larger airports, or additional runways must be built in some areas to facilitate the speedy transport of people, goods and services. Governments could fund such large-scale construction projects from taxation.

Difficulty in Acquiring Visa or Travel Documentation

Difficulty in acquiring visas for certain categories of people reduces the likelihood that they will travel thereby hampering regional integration and commercial trade. This in turn reduces the funds that otherwise would have been available to governments through taxes.

As a loss control measure, education about visa requirements and processes should be widely disseminated through foreign embassies.

Exercises

1. Discuss the advantages water transport has over each of the following modes of transport:
    a. Road
    b. Rail
    c. Air
2. Discuss the threats that water transportation poses for a country. What role does insurance have in combating these threats?
3. Discuss the constraints to the development of train transport in developing countries.
4. Explain three techniques that can be effective in combating the hijacking of aircraft.
5. Discuss five threats posed by road transport.
6. In what ways can the government curb migration?
7. Discuss why it is important to properly manage airlines and explain the effects of poor management on the airline industry.
8. What role does insurance have in ensuring that the rail sector thrives?

Reference

Haq, G., & Schwela, D. (2012). *Transport and Environment in Sub-Saharan Africa.* University of York. Chapter 1.

Further Reading

Andoh, C., Mensah, L., & Quaye, D. (2020). Road Pricing: A Solution to Ghana's Traffic Congestion. *African Journal of Management Research, 27*(1), 129–150.

Edwards, F. L., & Goodrich, D. C. (2024). *Introduction to Transportation Security* (2nd ed.). CRS Press.

Gupta, P. K. (2008). *Fundamental of Insurance* (1st ed.). Himalaya Publishing House. Unit 1: Chapter 1.

Gupta, P. K. (2016). *Essentials of Insurance and Risk Management* (1st ed.). Himalaya Publishing House Pvt Ltd. Part I: Chapters 1, 2.

Harrington, S. E., & Niehaus, G. R. (2004). *Risk Management and Insurance.* McGraw-Hill. Chapters 1.

Redja, G. E., & McNamara. (2016). *Principles of Risk Management and Insurance.* Pearson Addison Wesley. Chapter 1.

Shah, I. A., Jhanjhi, N. Z., & Brohi, S. (2024). Cybersecurity Issues and Challenges in Civil Aviation Security. In I. A. Shah & N. R. Jhanjhi (Eds.), *Cybersecurity in the Transportation Industry* (pp. 1–23). Scrivener Publishing LLC.

Chapter 7
Risk, Insurance and Other Industries

Abstract This chapter examines several industries characterised by significant risk exposures, highlighting how the strategic use of insurance can provide effective risk management solutions. It explores the benefits of the fishing industry, the environmental threats associated with its operations, and the role of insurance in addressing these risks. Similarly, the chapter analyses the alcohol industry, discussing its advantages, associated hazards, and loss control measures. The hawking enterprise is also considered, along with the risks inherent in its operations. In addition, the chapter addresses the societal risks posed by drug trafficking and outlines corresponding loss control strategies. The discussion extends to the waste management sector, providing measures to mitigate the risks it presents, and concludes with an examination of the scrap industry.

Keywords Alcohol industry · Fishing industry · Hawking · Scrap metal sector · Waste management sector

Introduction

This chapter discusses other industries where there is considerable risk exposure and where the acquisition of insurance can provide some solutions. The benefits of the fishing industry, the threats posed by the industry to the environment and how insurance can provide some solutions are discussed. The benefits and the threats of the alcohol industry are also discussed along with loss control measures that can be adopted. In Section “3”, the hawking sector, a form of trade common in developing countries, is examined. Section “4” confronts some of the threats posed by drug trafficking and the loss control measures that can be deployed to mitigate its impact on the society. Section “5” deals with waste management and provides ways to mitigate risk. Finally, section “6” covers the scrap industry.

C. Andoh, *Fundamentals of Managing Risk and Insurance*,
https://doi.org/10.1007/978-981-95-4581-0_7

The Fishing Industry

The fishing industry is a vibrant element of the economy for countries with long coastlines. It provides employment and fish for both local consumption and export. It is one of the fastest developing sectors in a number of developing countries. However, despite the benefits that the industry provides, its operations sometimes endanger and threaten the environment.

Pollution

Water pollution is one of such threats. As fishermen carry out their activities on water bodies, they release pollutants (for example, boat fuel) that are harmful to humans and to sea, bird and plant life. The use of Dichloro Diphenyl Trichloroethane (DDT) as a means of obtaining increased yields in Ghana (though banned) pollutes the water and kills all flora and fauna within a particular catchment area. Sometimes, fishermen leave unwanted fish ashore. These rot after a while and are washed back into the sea leading to contamination.

Air pollution also occurs. As the catch is processed, various substances are released into the atmosphere that makes the air unsafe. Processes such as the smoking or canning of fish, to preserve it, can cause respiratory problems. The spoilage of fish also releases some pungent smells into the atmosphere that causes inconvenience to communities and residents nearby.

Noise pollution is also an issue at canneries. The use of dynamite in Ghana (also banned) is a further hazard as it indiscriminately kills both wanted and unwanted species of fish.

As a loss control measure, laws and regulations must be passed and enforced by governments to ensure that safe fishing practices are employed. Fishermen should be compelled to use Liquefied Petroleum Gas (LPG) instead of firewood that emits smoke into the atmosphere. The price of LPG should be subsidised by government so it will be affordable. Factories can be built in such a way that most of the noise emitted is retained within it. Alternatively, fish processing factories can be sited far from residential areas.

A loss finance measure is retention. Health insurance can be taken against health issues that might ensue. The industry can take out product and liability insurance to cover any lawsuits resulting from its operations. This will ensure that those who become ill because of consuming fish and drinking from water bodies contaminated by the industry's actions are duly compensated. The government can also add support by providing funds for the clean-up of polluted water bodies and preventing the fishing industry from locating processing plants in residential areas.

Food Poisoning

Food poisoning can result from the operations of the fishing industry. When chemicals that are harmful to humans are used in fishing, illness or death can result. Also, the supply of expired fish products by the industry can put lives at risk.

As a loss control measure, fishermen must be educated on safe methods of fishing and fish processing.

Overfishing

Fishermen in pursuit of big harvests sometimes use nets that are too tightly woven together and catch even very young fish that results in the depletion of fish stocks. Pair trawling is another fishing technique that depletes the stock of fish in the ocean. This is a practice whereby fishing vessels embark on fishing expeditions in pairs. The two vessels essentially trap and drive shoals of fish into their nets. Some fishermen use very bright lights to lure fish into their nets. Usually, many fingerlings are caught in these traps. This again reduces the reproductive potential of fish in that area.

Education is a loss control measure. Fishermen must use the correct and approved nets for fishing. The regulatory authorities must enforce legislation to ensure that this happens. Larger nets provided by the Ministry of Fisheries could ensure that young fish caught by accident can slip through back into the ocean. Routine checks should be made on fishermen at sea to verify the nets being used are legal. Industry bodies must instruct fishermen to avoid trawling at times of the year when fish species are reproducing. Sanctions and fines should be placed on those that violate the law.

As a loss finance measure, a monitoring team to police the industry should be established by the government.

Ghost fishing

Ghost fishing is another threat the fishing industry creates for the environment. It occurs when fishermen abandon or lose the gear they use to fish at sea or in water bodies (such as nets, long lines, fish traps, etc.) and this continues to trap or kill sea creatures.

As a loss control measure, the Ministry of Fisheries should inspect water bodies for abandoned fishing equipment and enact clean-ups. Fishermen should also be properly trained to ensure that they do not carelessly lose their fishing equipment.

As a loss finance measure, fishermen should get liability insurance so that claims against them from environmentalists may be adequately catered for.

Land degradation

The demand for wood in African countries for the construction of fishing canoes and especially for firewood and charcoal for smoking fish can lead to deforestation. Improper disposal of harmful chemicals used for fishing can also have adverse effects on the fertility of the soil.

As a loss control measure, stringent measures should be put in place to ensure that trees felled are replaced before further felling takes place. Instead of using charcoal, LPG can be used for smoking fish.

As a loss finance measure, governments can release funds yearly for the purchase of trees to be planted.

Endangered species

The fishing industry has caused the killing of many endangered species such as turtles and whales. Climate change has resulted in warming ocean temperatures in some seas such as around Alaska, disrupting the habitat of some species. In some countries, whales or turtles are fished for food. This practice has drastically threatened the lives of many endangered species making them face possible extinction soon.

As a loss control measure, international governments and NGOs should constantly pursue programmes that reduce the fishing of endangered species. Governments need to be particularly strict on the fishing of endangered species. Offenders should be severely dealt with and prosecuted.

Occupational hazards

Another threat is the occupational hazard to workers in the industry. Fishermen on the seas are exposed to harsh weather conditions and the risk of equipment failure. The machines operated by people working in fish processing factories can cause harm to operators. Fishermen are also at risk from attacks by pirates who may seize fishing vessels or hold them hostage for ransom.

A loss control measure is that safety measures such as life jackets should be provided on all fishing vessels. Fishermen should also listen to weather forecasts before going to sea. The use of goggles to protect the eyes, the use of gloves and frequent maintenance of machinery can help reduce injuries to people working at the fishing industry. Fishermen should avoid fishing in conflict areas especially where pirate attacks are reported.

A loss finance measure is to take out health insurance cover. Liability and worker compensation insurance can also be taken out by the industry. The industry can consider the payment of ransom in case of pirate attacks of its workers at sea and insurance may be purchased for this purpose.

Health

When fish is allowed to go bad or is not preserved early enough, it can rot attracting pests that transmit diseases such as cholera. The waste from the dressing of fish, when improperly disposed of also attracts insects. The canning of spoilt fish or canned fish consumed after its expiry date can result in health problems. Also, the use of radioactive rays in large-scale fishing can cause harm to people who consume the fish over time.

A loss control measure is to store fish quickly as they are caught. The proper disposal of waste from fish processing can help reduce the risk of disease. Other means of processing fish such as the use of electric and gas ovens reduce their exposure to smoke. The use of radioactive rays in fishing must be prohibited.

A loss finance measure is for the industry to take out liability insurance to cover legal costs resulting from lawsuits brought against it by consumers. Health and disability insurance is useful for anyone working in a hazardous industry.

Bad disposal practices

It is common practice in some developing countries for the coast to be used as a refuse dump. Fishermen, during their operations, dump waste into water bodies. In addition, many fishermen and residents along the coast use the coastline as a toilet. These practices severely affect the health of the fish in these water bodies. Some consumers of tinned fish do not properly dispose of the empty tins, which can result in the creation of breeding grounds for mosquitos in rainy seasons.

As a loss control measure, fishermen should be encouraged to keep the coastline clean. Waste management companies can help by cleaning up beaches. In addition, communities along the coast can form communal groups that will oversee clean-ups. Waste management companies should make waste containers available to the public so that waste can be properly disposed of. Residents can also build public toilets. This will help reduce the use of the coastline as a place for defaecation.

As a loss finance measure, people along the coast should be encouraged to take up health insurance policies to safeguard their health against cholera and respiratory diseases. Governments should establish proper sanitation and sewage systems along coastlines and avoid releasing sewage into the ocean. Governments can also support waste management companies with funding from taxation.

Development of slums

Every industry needs people to manage its affairs and the fishing industry is no exception. Fishing companies employ a lot of people to undertake various activities. Many people therefore move to coastal areas either temporarily or permanently in search of work. They put up temporary structures all along the coast and these gradually develop into slums.

As a loss control measure, governments should demarcate certain portions of the coastline to be free of development.

Underdevelopment of harbours and tourist centres

Excessive fishing activities along coastlines have prevented the development of harbours and tourist resorts. Some years ago, an initiative by the government of Ghana to build a harbour in the Ada Rural Area was stopped by local fishermen who protested about the likely decrease in their catch and sales, attacks on their autonomy and more government interference in their activities.

As a loss control measure, the government through the agencies responsible for fisheries should properly demarcate fishing areas and increase the supervision and control of fishing activities in rural areas. Governments should embark on the creation of more harbours along the coast to facilitate marine activities as well as increase exports. They could also provide subsidies and tax incentives to fishermen so that they would be unaffected by such developments.

Child labour

Some fishing communities employ the services of young men and women below the age of eighteen. Because these young people earn some money at a tender age, their desire to go to school is diminished. Some of these young people fish on the high seas and at times are thrown aboard to remove trapped nets under the seabed. There have been instances where children have been rescued from the hands of child traffickers who sell them to people in fishing communities.

As a loss control measure, governments should enforce regulations regarding child labour. Governments should institute laws to severely deal with child traffickers and those who engage children in activities that prevent them from schooling. Also fishing associations can assist when more hands are needed to perform certain tasks. Fishermen should be educated on the importance of education.

As a loss finance measure, free education funded by taxpayers can be offered to children in the fishing communities. Parents of children in the industry can be educated to take out life insurance policies in groups so that funds will be available for the education of their children.

Superstitious beliefs

Fishermen have promoted the superstitious belief that fishing should not be done on a certain day or days. In Ghana, people have a preconceived idea that one should not go fishing on Tuesdays.

As a loss control measure, these days should be used for other activities such as farming or other income generating activities to support one's finances.

Cost of living

The fishing industry can create an increase in the cost of living by failing to store excess fish caught during bumper seasons. During lean seasons, fish and fish products become expensive increasing the cost of living for people.

A loss control measure is the building of warehouses where fish can be stored when in abundance to sell during periods of scarcity.

The Alcohol Industry

This industry is primarily involved in the manufacturing, distribution and sale of alcoholic beverages. The activities of alcohol manufacturers have a great impact on the environment due to the poor disposal of bottles. There are no laws compelling these companies to recycle and so consumers and the companies themselves create a waste problem. There should be legislation directing alcohol manufacturers to find more environmentally friendly ways of packaging their products.

Pollution

The manufacturing process of alcohol creates pollution of the environment. Water pollution is the most serious issue. The discharge of liquid waste after the brewing of alcohol into water sources such as rivers and streams make such water unsafe for domestic purposes and affects aquatic life. The operations involve the use of chemicals that can be harmful to humans or animals. In situations where chemicals are accidentally spilt into water bodies, they can cause harm and losses to society. There can also be noise pollution because of the heavy machinery used in the industry. Small-scale brewers use firewood in the process of alcohol extraction and this creates air pollution. The brewing process can also generate a large amount of heat that is released into the atmosphere causing the surrounding environment to be very warm and uncomfortable to live in.

The industry can initiate proper waste management systems by converting its waste products into something beneficial that will reduce its effect on the environment. In addition, breweries should be sited far away from towns to reduce the likelihood of accidental spillage of waste materials into water bodies. Small-scale brewers should utilise alternative sources of energy, such as gas, to minimise the pollution they cause.

A loss finance measure for the industry is liability insurance to cover losses for those who may be affected directly from their operations.

Addiction

Alcohol is addictive and can have grave consequences on consumers especially the young. When the major income earner of a family dies in a motor accident because they were under the influence of alcohol or causes the death of another person there are social consequences for the family. The growth of the sector and how alcohol is marketed also has the potential of increasing the addiction rate of the population.

Education on responsible drinking is a loss control measure. The prosecution of people found guilty of drink driving can serve as a deterrent to others. Stringent rules can be put in place by governments to make drink driving a serious crime.

Motor insurance policies are essential for all drivers. Life insurance policies can be purchased by those who drive to provide income to surviving dependants in the case that they are the victims of a fatal accident caused by a drunk driver.

Productivity

The excessive intake of alcohol for even regular drinkers can affect their productivity. A person who drinks excessively may feel weak and lacking in alertness leading to a loss of productive hours at work. The death of a person through alcohol poisoning or an alcohol related disease has the potential of reducing a country's productivity. This is a large societal problem in many areas of the world.

Education aligned with a regulatory regime can serve as deterrents. Governments should enact laws and implement policies that regulate the sale and the use of alcohol. More taxes should be imposed on alcohol manufacturing industries and on their products. The industry could also be encouraged to reduce the percentage of alcohol in their products and promote responsible drinking.

Depletion of natural resources

The activities of the industry in Ghana especially the small-scale brewers involve the complete uprooting of palm trees, thereby destroying other plants in the process. Animal habitats are destroyed as other trees are cut for firewood for brewing. Large amounts of water are utilised in the industry's operations.

As a loss control measure, mandatory tree planting enforced by the government can help. When a tree is destroyed or cut down to produce alcohol or used as firewood one should be planted in its place.

A loss finance measure is for the industry to retain part of its income to purchase seedlings to nurse and plant new trees in place of the trees cut down.

Accidents

There are many ways accidents can occur with the use of alcohol. Firstly, alcohol is flammable and production sometimes causes the outbreak of fire when spilled in an electrically or mechanically lighted environment. This poses danger to workers and people and properties nearby. Secondly, excessive consumption of alcohol by drivers increases the likelihood of motor accident. Alcohol can cause blurred vision and can reduce concentration considerably.

As a loss control measure, the public should be educated on the safe handling of alcoholic drinks. The provision of fire control devices such as fire extinguishers, automatic fire sprinklers will help reduce the damage caused should a fire occur. The government should pass legislation prohibiting drink driving.

As a loss finance measure, fire insurance and other allied peril insurance can be taken out to cover losses that might occur. Motor insurance policies should be mandatory to cover losses to third parties and injured drivers.

Crime and anti-social behaviour

The use of alcohol is the cause of much anti-social and deviant behaviour including violence, robbery and rape. Excessive drinkers often disturb the peace in their communities, causing arguments with people and misbehaving.

One solution is the enactment of laws preventing minors from consuming alcohol and making the excessive consumption of alcohol a crime. Laws requiring the age identification of a buyer before sales of alcohol are made are common in Western countries. Young people should be educated on the adverse effects of alcohol by parents, schools and government public safety campaigns.

One can purchase a personal accident insurance policy to cover losses that may be caused to another because of the influence of alcohol. The risk can also be retained and funded from savings.

Health risks

The excessive consumption of alcohol is a serious health hazard. Heavy drinkers risk liver and kidney disease and are more prone to heart disease. Infertility in women can result as the womb can be damaged through excessive drinking and it can also render a man impotent. These problems could result in health issues, unemployment or the loss of key personnel for an organisation.

Public education drawing people's attention to the dangers of the excessive intake of alcoholic drinks is one solution. Abstinence from alcohol could rid the human body of these diseases. Regular health checks, labelling bottles with the warning: 'not for sale to people under the age of 18' can also help.

A loss finance measure is to take out life insurance and health insurance policies (though there are increased premiums for alcohol consumers) to cover losses resulting from illness. Also, liability insurance can be taken by the industry to cover claims made against it.

Destruction of relationships and families

The excessive use of alcohol can destroy relationships and families. Where a partner indulges in alcoholism, the needs of the home are not met as in most cases a large proportion of income goes on funding the habit. The children of such parents are not being taught good life lessons. Alcoholics tend to be abusive to their families and in the long run cause the breakdown of families and relationships. Friends and extended family members also try to avoid them and they become isolated.

A loss control measure is for an individual to seek therapy and get sober before the situation gets out of hand.

Threats to other industries

The industry has largely caused a reduction in the patronage of healthy drinks that contain the needed fruits, vitamins and minerals that the body needs to grow and function properly. The government should impose more taxes on alcohol manufacturing industries while subsidies should be given to juice and fruit processing industries to reduce prices and increased consumption.

Destruction of soil structure

The structure of the soil can be made worse by the dumping of non-biodegradable waste such as glass bottles and plastics (including sachets).

As a loss control measure, the recycling and reuse of bottles can be adopted by the industry. The industry could also create depots in large communities where bottles and plastics could be returned for some form of payment.

A loss finance measure is self-insurance.

Quality control

In the process of manufacturing, some quality control measures may not be adhered to especially when the workers' alertness is compromised because of alcohol intake causing harm to consumers.

Stricter testing of the quality of the alcoholic drink production process by government monitoring agencies such as the Food and Drugs Authority is a loss control measure. In addition, the industry must give greater attention to its production processes. Workers should be prohibited from imbibing alcoholic drinks during working hours.

Liability insurance to finance any lawsuit resulting from poor quality control processes should be used by the industry.

Diversion of agricultural produce

The major raw materials used to produce alcohol in Ghana are agricultural produce such as palm, sugar cane and cassava. Such agricultural produce could serve as food for society rather than being used to produce alcohol. One way to deal with this issue is to increase the production of these crops. Mechanised farming techniques if adopted by local farmers through government subsidies would improve yields.

Agricultural research institutions should be contracted by governments to suggest other varieties of crops that could be used for alcoholic drinks.

Competition from the foreign producers

Competition from other alcoholic beverage companies from Europe and elsewhere reduces the market share of locally produced drinks and thus poses a threat to local industry. The local market could be resourced by the government to improve the quality of drinks produced to compete with imported brands.

Taxes and government regulation

The heavy imposition of taxes by the government can make it difficult for a number of players to be profitable. If government policies do not favour an industry, legislation and taxation can stifle its growth.

As a loss control measure, the industry could diversify its operations by entering other lines of business such as the production of non-alcoholic drinks.

The Hawker

Hawkers are street vendors of a wide range of (usually portable) items who, while officially unauthorised, sell goods in most metropolitan areas in developing countries. Their activities range from the sale of iced water, food and non-food items such as clothes and books. Hawkers are normally people who have migrated from rural areas to find a more lucrative life. There are a number of benefits to hawking, to the hawker, the government and the public.

Hawkers do not need to worry about the payment of rent for a shop to do business. They require no registration to start a business. Hawkers enjoy free market entry and exit that enables them to reach their target audience quickly. Hawking provides employment to large numbers of people enabling them to provide for dependants, save and invest.

Street hawkers provide easy, cheap and fast access to items that individuals use in their homes and offices. Consequently, the consumer saves time and transport costs and the effort of having to find a product in a shop. Street hawkers sometimes also have a positive social impact, adding life and colour to a city.

Governments benefit from hawking in the form of the indirect taxes they pay as resellers of goods purchased from other retailers. Hawking serves as a source of income to many people and this helps reduce unemployment and its attendant social issues in a country.

Despite these benefits of street hawking, their presence poses significant threats to both road users and a country. We discuss a number of these threats below and their loss control and loss finance measures.

Accidents

Hawkers normally undertake their activities not only on pavements but also on the streets. Thus, they are sometimes a hazard to drivers, blocking the view as they attempt to sell their products to passengers. Sometimes, drivers hit other vehicles due to these activities and the resulting congested roads. There have been cases where goods fall off the heads of hawkers, damaging vehicles in the process. Pedestrians are also at risk.

As a loss control measure, there should be a law that bans street hawking on all major roads. Instead, a pedestrianised mall could be provided by governments so that hawkers can sell their products safely.

Loss finance measures include the purchase of motor insurance policies by all drivers and health insurance policies for all hawkers. Hawkers who are found operating illegally on the streets should be fined and the funds collected used to construct the pedestrian mall.

Pollution

The products that hawkers sell are usually in paper and plastic wrappers and sachets. Some passengers who purchase these items dump this waste on the street after use. In addition, the hawkers themselves litter the streets with waste. Organic waste causes a stench after a period. Some hawkers also make excessive noise when selling their goods to draw the attention of passers-by.

A loss control measure is to educate people not to purchase items from hawkers on the street and to fine those that do. In addition, the hawkers themselves should be educated not to sell their goods on the street. Refuse containers should be placed at key vantage points on the street so that people properly dispose of the waste that they make.

A loss finance measure is an educational campaign funded by fines that hawkers who flout the rules pay.

Security

Due to the high concentration of hawkers on busy streets, these areas become conducive for criminals and thieves to operate. Some criminals disguise themselves as hawkers and pickpocket pedestrians or rob car or bus passengers when it is least expected. Additionally, hawkers disrupt the peace and cause conflicts. Sometimes conflicts emerge among different hawkers as well as between hawkers and drivers. Areas where hawkers are active in the day may be unsafe at night. Many hawkers are street sleepers and so issues such as alcohol and drug use as well as other social vices may promulgate in such areas.

A loss control measure is the provision of security personnel at bus stops to protect passengers from aggressive hawking. Such security personnel can be empowered to seize goods from offenders. Pedestrians and passengers should be educated through the media to be vigilant and keep their personal assets secure when in areas where hawking is rife. Communities can institute community policing to patrol the streets in their neighbourhood at night to prevent crimes both by and against hawkers.

A loss finance measure is for the government to pay for security personnel who can police the streets and transport terminals from the taxes that people pay.

School dropouts

Many street hawkers are school dropouts and their proliferation on the street encourages more children of school age to join them when they face the least challenge. Thus, hawking on the street has become a viable alternative to school for such children.

A loss control measure is to ban street hawking entirely but in particular to ban children of school going age from hawking.

A loss finance measure is to provide economic benefits to all needy children funded from the taxes people pay.

Revenue losses to governments

The government gains revenue by levying taxes on market sellers to raise funds to renovate markets. However, some street hawkers avoid paying these taxes while continuing to operate by selling on the street. In effect, they do business without paying back to the government to fund investments for societal goods such as waste management.

The loss control measure is to deploy street police to force hawkers to only sell at designated markets to pay the proper taxes.

Congestion (Overcrowding)

The hawkers impede the free flow of individuals who are going to and from work. They occupy both sides of the pavement and sometimes the whole street. As a result, businesses lose productivity and the journey times of workers are lengthened. In such heavily congested areas, the dangers of accidents and injuries are heightened. If pavements are being used for the display of hawkers' goods, pedestrians may need to walk on the road.

A loss control measure is the establishment of designated market sites for hawkers. The hawkers themselves can form cooperatives and have a fund where they contribute money so that they can build markets and shops for themselves.

Illegal and counterfeit products

Many people have purchased illegal and counterfeit products from hawkers. When people are in busy traffic, they have little time to scrutinise the products they are buying. In addition, some of the items sold are either fake or sub-standard.

Disease

Many of the food items sold by hawkers are exposed to an unhygienic environment that may lead to food poisoning and other bacterial infections for the buyers. For example, cholera is caused as result of the intake of unhygienic food substances. A number of hawkers do not have homes and urinate and defaecate on the street. This can cause major health issues for the public.

The Food and Drug Authority should conduct inspections and give permits only to sellers and hawkers that follow hygienic practices. The government should also construct affordable housing to avoid street sleeping. The creation of alternative employment schemes by the government could assist hawkers in leaving the street.

The costs incurred by the authorities can be financed by taxes that market workers' pay. Health insurance policies can be purchased to cater for illnesses resulting from food poisoning.

Fraudulent practices

Some hawkers deliberately delay when giving out change to customers in vehicles in the hope that the traffic lights go green and they no longer need to return it.

A loss control measure is the education of the public about the tricks employed by some hawkers so that they stop buying from them.

A loss finance measure is the setting up of vocational training programmes for these hawkers or offer loans to hawkers from taxation so that they can afford official market stalls or shops.

Combating Street Hawking

One way to combat street hawking is by making educational facilities available to the less privileged in society, especially in communities that record the highest figure in terms of street hawking. The unskilled unemployed can be encouraged to attend vocational and technical schools to develop their skills. A vigorous education campaign should be undertaken by local government to warn the public not to purchase from street hawkers. If people stop purchasing from street hawkers, they will be compelled to relocate to designated sites. When majority of the population are educated about the dangers involved in street hawking it will decline.

The government should enforce already existing by-laws against street hawking. Security personnel or street police can be deployed to arrest hawkers who violate the rules on a sustained basis. Goods should be seized from offenders. In addition, there should be new laws to outlaw street purchases with offenders fined. This will deter people from buying from the street and make hawking a less attractive venture.

Governments should create an environment for people to be effectively trained to identify entrepreneurial opportunities and make the maximum use of those opportunities. Governments, financial institutions, microfinance institutions, businesses, individuals, etc., are all available sources for entrepreneurs to develop their ideas. Loan agencies should put a clause into their policies that prevent the use of funds for illegal activities such as hawking.

Street hawkers should be educated on the dangers of street hawking. When there is a free flow of traffic, street hawkers will have no room to do business. Consequently, the governments should develop other transportation systems such as rail and (where appropriate) water to reduce road congestion.

The government could build markets at locations where business would thrive for hawkers. This should entice them to leave the street. Alternatively, there should be a directive to all hawkers to leave the street and signs erected forbidding the practice. Hawkers who violate the directive should be fined to serve as a deterrent to others.

The government could make private health insurance compulsory for lower income groups but forbid people from hawking on streets. If one chooses to hawk, insurance premiums should be high to dissuade the practice.

The Role of Insurance in Combating Street Hawking

Insurance companies pay taxes to the government on a regular basis. Activities undertaken by a government to combat hawking, such as setting up new markets are indirectly supported by insurance companies. Other activities undertaken by governments such as the opening of new schools for the young also combat street hawking. The free education policy for Senior High School students is laudable but must be strengthened by making it compulsory for all qualified graduates from Junior High School. This will significantly reduce the number of hawkers on the streets.

Some investments made by insurance companies create jobs and effectively reduce the level of unemployment. Also, the provision of alternative livelihoods for street hawkers will decrease its practice.

Insurance products such as life insurance serve to provide for the financial needs of dependants when a policyholder dies. Consequently, insurance combats street hawking in the sense that it provides for the financial needs of a policyholder's dependants who otherwise could have continued to be street hawkers or become street hawkers. The payment of sums to beneficiaries can be invested or used to start a business and generate a good standard of living. Also, the saving components of some life insurance products have made it possible for people to save over a period and to use the interest accumulated to pursue a desired business or trade or to facilitate their educational ambitions. One major excuse for or defence of street hawkers is that they follow this trade because of their inability to stay in school due to school fees. Insurance solves this problem by making available services or product policies that support one in school (e.g., educational policies that parents can purchase) to prevent a person from ending up without any qualifications or vocation.

Insurance companies also provide fire insurance cover for market traders, not available to hawkers. This creates confidence in sellers not to depart from markets and reduces the number of people that may turn to street hawking.

Insurers undertake corporate social responsibility programmes and in so doing make investments into facilities for the nation. Such projects include the provision of schools and vocational institutes which help reduce the number of people (including street hawkers) who do not have access to education. Insurance companies also employ unskilled personnel such as cleaners, security staff and messengers, among others, thereby offering job opportunities to people who otherwise might need to revert to hawking.

Other Ways that Insurance Can Combat the Fight against Street Hawking

Since motor insurance covers third parties, insurers can put in a clause that excludes hawkers from cover. That is, any hawker that sustains an injury or dies because of the actions of a policyholder cannot be compensated because of their illegal operations.

Insurance companies can lobby legislators to pass a law that requires all street hawkers to have compulsory insurance (life/accident). When the hawkers are made to take compulsory insurance cover it will financially deter them from the practice.

As part of their corporate social responsibility programme, insurance companies can build market facilities with the condition that hawkers can sell rent-free but must take out an insurance policy after commencing business. They can also embark on road safety campaigns to inform street hawkers about their risk exposure. Insurers can sponsor high achieving children from poor backgrounds so that they can further their education; create or support training centres to provide hawkers with alternative livelihoods and provide seed capital for budding entrepreneurs. A micro-insurance product can also be designed for hawkers so that after paying a certain amount, funds will be released to facilitate the establishment of legitimate enterprises. Insurance companies can offer business advice and finance in starting up such enterprises. In addition, insurance can be sold to store or shop owners in markets so that in the case of a robbery, the insurer can indemnify the shop owners.

Drug Dealing

A drug dealer or peddler is a person that distributes and sells illegal drugs by either aiding in the transfer of these drugs across borders and/or within a country. Drug peddling poses serious threats to the development of every nation. In this section, we discuss the threats it creates and propose loss control and loss finance measures.

National reputation

Drug peddling or trafficking creates a bad name for a country. When a nation gets flagged as a drug prone country, it sours the relationship it has with other nations. It exposes the citizens of a country to unnecessary checks and scrutiny when crossing borders. This hampers and potentially isolates the nation in many international trade activities.

One loss control measure is to increase security at the entry points to a country. Security personnel should be well resourced and remunerated to enable them to discharge their duties with professionalism. All people of whatever class (including VIPS) should have to go through security procedures. The installation of security scanners at airports and other ports of entry will assist in identifying those illegally importing drugs. Another way to combat drugs is at the source of production. Farmers that engage in the growing of opium and marijuana should be encouraged and financially supported by a government to grow alternative crops.

A loss finance measure is to use taxes imposed on goods and services to finance the purchase of security scanners. Banks and other financial institutions as part of their corporate social responsibilities could provide the needed financial resources to support the work of security agencies.

Crime

Drug peddling encourages robbery and other forms of crime and social vices in an economy. People who tend to use drugs are often involved in violent acts such as vandalism, rape and murder, among other things. Drug addicts from poor backgrounds engage in robberies to fund their habits. Drug cartels often wage wars among themselves that lead to high numbers of casualties. These acts increase fear and panic in drug-addled communities.

A loss control measure is for the police forces to patrol market areas where many peddlers operate to arrest them and seize their drugs.

Finance coup d'états

In many developing countries drug cartels are extremely powerful in terms of their financial and political clout and will act against any government that wages war against them. Consequently, they will finance groups who can mobilise and overthrow such governments.

A loss control measure is to empower security agencies with the latest technology in fighting drug crime to take preventative action where appropriate.

A loss finance measure is to confiscate the properties and assets of drug dealers, sell them off and use the proceeds to fund the needs of the security agencies.

Destruction of societal human capital

People who purchase drugs may become addicted and destroy their lives. An addict may also influence friends and family to take drugs which compounds the problem.

A loss control measure is for the government to enact laws that forbid drug dealing and carry harsh prison sentences. Rehabilitation centres should be available for those who are addicted.

Dissuades investors from an economy

When investors realise that an economy has a major source of its funds from drugs, they tend to turn away. Some international companies shy away from drug prone nations. This is especially true of investors with religious affiliations that view drug prone nations as sinful. Thus, they avoid the risk of having their investments compromised.

As a loss control measure, public education about the consequences of the drug trade on investment from abroad should be vigorously undertaken. Religious groups and Non-governmental Organisations (NGOs) can assist this educational campaign by organising programmes or seminars for its members.

Effects on the young and education

Drug trafficking may be viewed by the young as an easy way to make money. In an economy where jobs are scarce, selling drugs can be seen as an easy way to make money thus diverting the attention of young people from their academic work.

As a loss control measure, those guilty of drug offences should face the full rigour of the law to serve as a deterrent to others. Jail terms for drug dealers should be increased and pardons should rarely be given. Addicts and those that become victims of the drug trade should have their stories widely publicised by the media. Parents should take care of their children and ensure that they do not get caught up in drugs.

As a loss finance measure, parents should have savings to ensure that they can afford medical treatment for their children should they become addicted to drugs and require rehabilitation.

Health risks

A number of psychological and mental disorders such as depression and suicidal tendencies can result from drug usage. Sometimes, dealers swallow drugs to evade detection and this can be fatal. The use of dirty needles spreads serious disease. Overdoses of certain drugs can result in death.

Educating the populace on the dangers of the drug business is key. The Food and Drug Agencies should run public campaigns to warn of the perils and advise people to only obtain legal drugs from pharmacies.

As loss finance measure, health insurance policies can be purchased to fund the costs of illness resulting from drug taking. Governments should assist agencies responsible for drugs with funding to aid educational efforts.

Effects on the labour force

The drug trade is dangerous, and some operatives get injured, become affected by using the drugs that they sell or even die. One of the effects is the reduction of the labour force for a country. Drug peddling discourages people from entering honest ways of making money or doing business. When people see drug dealers making a lot of money they could be lured to join. Drug users are often unable to work, or if they do so, work unproductively.

As a loss control measure increased efforts to stop the entry of drugs into a country is paramount. Security checks at entry points should be increased. High-tech equipment acquired by port and airport authorities will make the detection of drug smuggling easier. The cost of funding the activities of the security agencies can be founded from taxes paid by citizens.

Disgrace to families

Drug peddling goes a long way to tarnish or destroy the image and integrity of families. Someone caught in the drug trade brings shame to the entire family.

As a loss control measure, parents should socialise with their children so that they are involved in the choice of friends to avoid bad influences that may pressure them to engage in drug trafficking. Parents should set up an investment account for their children for which monthly payments are made to help their wards to set up a business in the future so that they will not be tempted by money from selling drugs. In addition, parents should permit their children engage in other vocation training such as carpentry, sewing, hairdressing, during holidays which may be source of income generating for the children in the future.

Sale of expired drugs

Drug peddlers can sell drugs they have obtained after their expiry date at cheap prices. People who take such drugs can develop new diseases or infections while their original illnesses remain untreated.

As a loss control measure, pharmaceutical companies should use marketing and the media to educate people about the need for a prescription from a qualified medical practitioner to obtain medication.

Role of Insurance in Combatting Drug Peddling

Insurance is a legal business and cannot foster ties with an illegal business such as drug peddling. Since drug trading is against the law, insurance companies do not provide cover for it. Drug peddling is therefore a very high-risk venture for those that engage in it. The following are ways by which insurance combats drug peddling.

Information disclosure

The principle of utmost good faith compels each party to an insurance contract to reveal all relevant information prior to the actualisation of an insurance contract. This principle assists in combatting drug peddling because once an insurer knows that the cover being sought is meant to insure against losses caused by drug peddling, the insurer will not provide cover for such risk. Even if the use of drugs is not explicitly expressed by the proposer, the character of the policyholder will most likely depict an increase in risk exposure for certain products such as health, motor or liability insurance with time. This will cause an insurer to review upwards the risk exposure of the insured and consequently an increase in premium and/or the adoption of other risk mitigating strategies such as coinsurance, deductibles, policy limits, etc. These risk mitigating strategies place some risk on the insured. Because an insured person will not want to pay for losses, steps will be taken to minimise the loss occurring. Thus, in this sense, insurance discourages or combats the usage of drugs and drug peddling activities.

Risk assessment by underwriters

Insurance underwriters are the gatekeepers of insurance companies and one of their core responsibilities is to detect and deter adverse selection. To provide cover for any risk, certain basic personal information of a prospective insured person such as occupation is required. The underwriter investigates to check the authenticity of the information provided. If the prospective insured were seeking cover for a house and it is detected that the person is engaged in drug peddling, they would not be provided with cover. Thus, to purchase insurance cover for properties, people will desist from engaging in drug peddling. For health or life insurance, to prevent adverse selection, an underwriter may investigate into the health of the prospective insured. If findings reveal traces of illegal drugs in the body, an underwriter will reject the cover or ask for a higher premium to be paid.

If an individual is a beneficiary of a life insurance policy, this person may not be motivated to engage in drug peddling because she knows she will benefit from the proceeds of the policy in the case of the death of the insured. This person knows that should her bread winner die, there will be a form of income and may not be motivated to get involved in a dangerous and uninsurable risky business.

Insurance as stress relief

Some people engage in drug peddling when they are financially or emotionally stressed. Insurance helps combat drug peddling in the sense that it provides the individual with peace of mind because they know that they, or their family, will receive insurance payments in the case of losses. Such peace of mind can ensure that an individual is not in need of drugs for sedation or escape from reality and neither would they be tempted to take the risk if dealing in drugs to obtain some financial stability.

Insurance as means for accessing loans

Insurance can serve as a source of collateral to access credit from a financial institution. This credit can be used to start a legal business to generate wealth. Therefore, insurance presents another means of accessing capital to start a legal business without which someone may be compelled to enter the drug trade.

Transportation of goods

Insurers do not provide any cover for drug peddlers. Consequently, if a person involved in drugs is transporting illegal goods, they will have to personally bear the risks associated with its transportation. The burden of having to personally bear the risk during illegal transactions may deter people.

Lifestyle

Some people engage in drug dealing because they need money to maintain a certain level of lifestyle. With the provision of life insurance policies, dependants no longer have to worry about maintaining their lifestyle after their main source of livelihood is lost. Hence drug peddling because of the death of an 'economic provider' is combated.

Investigations before claim payment

When a person purchases an insurance product and a loss occurs, investigations are carried out with the help of police officers, medical officers and other third parties that may be needed. If their investigations reveal that the policyholder has indulged in taking or selling drugs the insurance policy would be void.

Insurance encourages a more meaningful life

Educational policies are designed to help individuals to develop and to have a more meaningful life. Insurance as an industry provides opportunities for employment, ranging from research, education to actual practice. Even those who do not possess the necessary skills to take up jobs in the industry are offered employment opportunities since insurance serves as an avenue for raising investment capital that can enable people to start their own businesses. Insurance types such as unemployment benefits paid by the state will reduce the likelihood of a person engaging in drug peddling. Businesses that have good employee compensation plans ensure that their employees are unlikely to turn to drug dealing as an income source. Thus, insurance helps society to raise responsible people to live a meaningful life.

Corporate social responsibility of insurers

Insurance companies as part of their corporate social responsibilities can assist security agencies through the provision of modern security systems that can be deployed at the entry points of a country.

The Waste Management Sector

Improper waste disposal in Ghana is very common. Continual practice of this negative behaviour will affect the nation adversely in many ways. It could result in floods as waste materials choke gutters. It could lead to the breeding of rodents and other pests resulting in the outbreak of diseases such as cholera and malaria. In this section, we discuss the causes of improper waste disposal, propose loss control and loss finance measures to mitigate these risks.

Improper town planning

Most rural and developing areas do not have sites clearly earmarked for waste disposal. As such, some people dispose of waste haphazardly. Poor road networks also make it difficult for people to dispose of waste correctly especially during the rainy season.

As a loss control measure, local government authorities and mayors of cities and towns should ensure the proper planning of their jurisdictions. Well-structured layouts should be enforced on property developers.

As a loss finance measure, funds should be allocated to the budgets of district assemblies by the government enabling them to employ the services of architects and property developers to demarcate townships properly to include areas for waste disposal.

Illiteracy

Widespread illiteracy is also a cause of improper waste disposal by some Ghanaians. Most people are oblivious to the harmful effects on the environment and on the health of individuals. As such, there is a cultural problem relating to waste and the fact that it is not widely perceived as an important issue.

Some people also mix solid waste with liquid thereby causing the gutters and drains to choke. With heavy rainfall, the gutters overflow, causing flood damage to roads and properties.

As a loss control measure, massive educational drives should be undertaken to raise the awareness of the public on the effects of indiscriminate waste disposal and on the importance of a clean environment. Health walks can be organised in communities to educate members of the communities on proper waste disposal methods. Musicians can join the educational campaign by composing songs highlighting the effects of improper waste disposal.

As a loss finance measure, manufacturers of plastics and materials that contribute to Ghana's waste problem could include the funding of such educational programmes in their corporate social responsibility programmes.

Lack of enforcement of existing laws

A lack of enforcement of existing laws is a contributing factor to the improper disposal of waste. Most law enforcement agencies have turned a blind eye to the heaps of waste that keep piling up in the country. On the few occasions an attempt at enforcement is made, it is not sustained and therefore has no substantial effect on society.

As a loss control measure, law enforcement agencies should make waste disposal an important issue and aim to curb it. Teams should be deployed to all parts of the country to enforce the laws on waste disposal. Inspectors can be hired to visit communities and sanction the defaulters of sanitation laws. Local communities can organise their own committees to ensure that their neighbourhood is waste-free. Existing laws should be strengthened to prohibit the dumping of waste.

A contingency fund could be set up from which law enforcement agents could be trained on how to combat the problem. The fund would also finance the tools and resources needed by the law enforcement agencies.

The use of non-recyclable materials

The use of non-recyclable materials by manufacturers also contributes to the waste problem. Items that can be recycled are usually collected and reused or processed to enable other materials to be made. However, materials that cannot be recycled are usually left in unauthorised or improper places.

As a loss control measure, the Standards Board and other regulatory bodies should ensure that manufacturers use recyclable materials in their production processes. After this, consumers could be encouraged to recycle all used products, through public education projects, a reward scheme (for example, for returning used bottles) and the establishment of proper recycling infrastructure and technology.

As a loss finance measure, manufacturers who fail to comply with such a directive can be fined. The proceeds obtained could fund educational and infrastructure efforts.

Inadequate rubbish and refuse containers in public places

The absence of adequate bins and containers for waste in public areas is a major cause of concern. Their scarcity is a key reason why most Ghanaians dispose of waste improperly. Even people with the best intentions will dispose of waste improperly if there are no facilities to allow them to do the right thing.

As a loss control measure, bins and refuse containers should be radically increased in number at vantage points in cities.

As a loss finance measure, town and city authorities should institute fines on those who litter the environment indiscriminately. Funds generated can be used to purchase more containers for those towns and cities.

Lack of proper sanitation and public conveniences

The lack of proper sanitation facilities in people's homes and public places is another reason why people dispose of waste indiscriminately. In some public buildings, the rest rooms are often locked to outsiders making it difficult for people to freely use them. In addition, some landlords do not have toilet facilities in the properties that they rent. As a result, people tend to urinate and defaecate anywhere they please. Some defaecate into polythene bags and dump them. These are sometimes washed into gutters when it rains blocking the free flow of wastewater and providing ideal places for the breeding of mosquitos.

As a loss control measure, governments must ensure that every household in Ghana has a toilet. The restrooms in public buildings should not be locked. Every public building should be legally required to have a restroom including all restaurants. There should also be enforcement of the legislation that makes it compulsory for landlords to provide a toilet for their tenants.

As a loss finance measure, it should be mandatory for everyone to have health insurance so that the cost of health care can be absorbed if they fall sick.

A lack of landfill sites

There are insufficient landfill sites. Therefore, when waste disposal companies collect waste, they find it difficult to properly dispose of it. They therefore resort to illegal activities such as dumping waste in rivers and other water bodies causing water pollution.

As a loss control measure, more landfill sites should be constructed to accommodate the waste that is collected.

Inefficient collection processes

Irregular and non-punctual waste disposal collection can lead people to dispose waste in unauthorised locations. Some waste management companies take payment in advance but do not then collect waste at the agreed times. When refuse bins and containers are full, people dispose of their waste elsewhere.

As a loss control measure, supervisory bodies should impose stricter rules and sanctions on inefficient waste management companies and check and monitor their services. Better or improved routines and schedules should be stipulated. Additional vehicles and refuse workers should be hired.

High cost of waste disposal

The purchase of waste bins and bags is relatively expensive for many people and therefore people resort to bad waste disposal practices. The waste fee collected per month by waste management companies is also quite high. Consequently, some people have no option but to dump their waste where they can.

A loss control measure is to encourage suppliers as part of their Corporate Social Responsibility programme to distribute some of the bins at no cost. The government could also subsidise the prices and invest in the proper distribution of bins to all areas. Waste management companies should also reduce the amount charged for collecting waste. The government could reciprocate by giving tax breaks to waste management companies. Education should focus on sensitising residents to neighbourly behaviour in the disposal of waste.

As a loss finance measure, a resident could set aside funds to pay for the services of waste management.

Lack of sewage channels in some parts of the country

Some communities lack basic drainage systems such as gutters. Consequently, wastewater is thrown into the street.

As a loss control measure, wastewater can be directed to holes dug and filled with large stones to enable the water to sink underground.

As a loss finance measure, residents could contribute to a fund earmarked for community development that can be used for this exercise.

Irresponsibility on the part of successive central and local governments

Government bodies in charge of managing the waste issue in Ghana have failed in discharging their responsibilities. They have not delivered the regulatory or enforcement regimes expected or required of them thereby allowing people to continue to dispose of waste improperly. Over the years, the government has not made proper arrangements with private enterprises that can take on the task.

As a loss control measure, the government can invest in private sector enterprises and assist them with tax incentives to fully engage with the task of ensuring that people dispose of waste properly.

Form of protest

Some people intentionally dispose of waste in public places as a form of protest against the management of or the rules set by an organisation. This occurs, for example, during industrial strikes.

As a loss control measure, the government should spell out the sanctions that will be meted out to such offenders.

Problems in the countryside

Those who live in the outskirts of towns and cities or in the countryside usually do not have access to waste disposal sites.

As a loss control measure, waste disposal sites should be created by waste management companies for people residing in less populated areas. An area development fund can be used to fund this intervention.

Availability of rubber and sachet products

Most products bought in towns and cities are packaged in bags or sachets that cost very little and that people easily throw away after use.

As a loss control measure taxes should be imposed on rubber manufacturers to increase the price of polythene bags and sachets and thereby encourage reuse by consumers. These companies should also offer rewards for people who collect and return waste rubber products.

The role of insurance

Health insurance should be available to all people to ensure that illnesses contracted through the waste problem can be treated.

As part of the loss control activities of insurers, they could engage in educating the public on the effects of indiscriminate waste disposal. Insurance companies can undertake periodic clean-up exercises and donate refuse bins to needy communities as part of their corporate social responsibility.

Insurance companies may also assist in providing bins and other containers for waste collection in their localities. They can also donate tools for clearing waste in rural areas. Funds can also be provided by insurance companies to pay for media campaigns to raise awareness of the problem. Businesses should have liability insurance in case their waste is negligently dumped.

Manufacturers should be sued by the government if they do not adhere to standards on the materials they use for packaging and information on how their waste can be properly disposed of. Public and product liability insurance is therefore needed by manufacturers.

Improper waste disposal affects insurance companies. Those with life insurance policies may die early as result of a cholera outbreak or other illness associated with insanitary conditions created by poor waste disposal practices. Also, those on health insurance may visit doctors or attend hospitals more frequently. Since insurers also act as advisors, they have a major role to play in advocating for a clean environment.

The Scrap Metal Sector

Businesses that collect metallic waste for recycling make up the scrap metal sector. Vehicles, washing machines, motorbikes, bicycles and any other type of machinery or metallic waste is collected by scrappers for recycling or to sell to scrap dealers for export. The sector has benefits for people that engage in this business. It provides a form of employment for scrappers and dealers. People can recycle the scrap and use it for various aluminium products. This has greatly reduced the headache of metallic waste disposal. Scrap can be recycled to produce very useful products such as buckets, cutlery and traps for hunting. The money that would have been used in disposing of the scrap can instead be used for developmental and profitable projects. Scrap generates income for an economy through tax revenue. Individuals and households benefit from scrap because they earn revenue when they sell their scrap to dealers. With the revenue, they can afford more goods and services that offer some stimulus to the economy of a developing country.

The scrap sector can also encourage innovation on the part of producers and entrepreneurs who may use such materials as raw materials to produce other goods like car parts, furniture, ladders and so on. Again, this can boost an economy. A thriving scrap sector can also increase exports and a nation's balance of foreign exchange as buyers recycle waste metal into reusable materials and products. Scrap can be broken down into aggregates that could be used to fill potholes or be used as building materials for construction. Hence, instead of importing raw materials, a country can benefit from the reuse of its own waste materials. By reducing imports, the country rids itself of import tariffs it might have paid increasing economic growth.

Despite these positives, the scrap sector poses threats to the environment. This section discusses these threats and provides some loss control measures.

Waste

One of the major threats posed by the scrap sector to the environment is the amount of waste that it produces. Scrap metal comes in the form of car body parts, electronic devices, white goods and the like. Since these cannot decompose, unsold or unused scrap continues to grow creating a mountain of waste that cannot be taken care of.

A loss control measure is to increase the support for scrap dealers so that they can melt and sell higher amounts to aluminium companies. If their work can be pushed to a larger scale, they can help solve this environmental problem.

Another major threat posed by scrap to the environment is the chemicals that are released when scrap is exposed to air and water. When metals are exposed to water, they corrode and chemicals are washed into the soil and water bodies, polluting them and making water unsafe for humans.

A loss control measure is to locate scrap yards far away from water bodies and farmland.

Unhygienic conditions

Scrapyards are breeding grounds for mosquitos, other insects and rodents. When it rains the metals collect water and thus become conducive for mosquitoes.

A loss control measure would be for scrap dealers to build sheds for their scrap to keep it dry.

Non-insurance transfers can be employed whereby companies that produce the products containing metals transfer the duty of properly disposing of them to the consumer.

Injury

When a scrap worker accidentally steps on a pointed or sharp piece of metal, it can cause cuts and major wounds which may eventually lead to lock jaw, or tetanus.

A loss control measure is for those working with scrap to always wear protective gear in the course of their work. Scrap collectors should also be encouraged to collect scrap that has been improperly disposed of from the environment.

Scrap dealers can insure their staff through an employees' liability policy. Health insurance can also be purchased to cater for such injuries.

Pollution

Scrapyards produce a lot of noise in the course of their work. They can also pollute water bodies as there are many toxic materials in the scrap collected. The runoff of water caused by heavy rainfall can carry polluted materials along its course into rivers, lakes and eventually the sea. Hence, fish and other sea life can become a danger to the health of humans when eaten.

A loss control measure is for scrap yards to be located far away from residential areas and townships.

As a loss finance measure, industries that produce scrap as part of their manufacturing process can collectively take responsibility for the cost of disposing of or storing such waste properly. Scrap dealers should buy state-of-the-art machines that can sort and remove needed metal parts without necessarily causing noise.

Transportation of scrap

The unsafe transportation of scrap from where it is collected to where it is treated could lead to spillages on the road. This could damage the tyres of cars, trucks, motorcycles or bicycles leading to accidents.

As a loss control measure, the government can employ workers to ensure that the roads are free of scrap materials.

As a loss finance measure, drivers should purchase motor insurance policies, preferably comprehensive policies to cover any damage to vehicles. Health insurance can also protect against the consequences of accidents that may occur.

Agriculture

Scrap metal and the chemicals that they can release make the land unfertile for agricultural use. Metals, if dumped on agricultural land do not decompose and reduce crop yield hence leading to low agricultural productivity.

To control this loss, agricultural lands should be guarded to prevent scrappers from using them as dumping sites. Fines should be imposed on transgressors. As a loss finance strategy, farmers can insure their crops against low yield so that such losses could be mitigated.

Exercises

1. Explain five major ways in which the operations of the fishing industry can potentially harm the environment. For each threat identified, suggest a loss control measure and a loss finance measure.
2. Discuss five major threats posed by the dumping of used metallic related gadgets to an economy. For each threat identified, suggest a loss control measure and a loss finance measure. In your view does insurance have a role in combating these threats? Explain your answer fully.
3. Discuss three ways in which insurance combats drug peddling.
4. Discuss how to combat hawking.
5. Outline the role of insurance in combating street hawking.
6. Explain how improper waste management practices affect insurance companies.
7. Discuss the ways that improper waste management practices damage the environment.

Further Reading

Ahmed, A. M. (2023). Architectural Approach to Reducing the Menace of Street Hawking in Kebbi and Its Environment. *Journal of The Nigerian Institute of Architects, BGM 3*, 33–41.

Akunna, G. G, & Lucyann, C. A. (2023). Nigeria's War Against Drug Abuse: Prevalence, Patterns, Ramifications, Policy and Multisectoral Response, Strategies and Solutions. *Studies in Social Science & Humanities, 2*(10), 35–55.

Ezenwoko, A. Z., Oche, M. O., Haruna, A., Bashar, A. G., & Muhammad, S. (2024). Prevalence and Forms of Sexual Abuse among Female Hawkers in Sokoto State. *Journal of Community Medicine and Primary Health Care, 36*(1), 67–79.

Gupta, P. K. (2008). *Fundamental of Insurance* (1st ed.). Himalaya Publishing House, Mumbai. Unit 1: Chapter 1.

Gupta, P. K. (2016).*Essentials of Insurance and Risk Management* (1st ed.). Himalaya Publishing House Pvt. Ltd., Mumbai. Part I: Chapters 1, 2.

Harrington, S. E., & Niehaus, G. R. (2004). *Risk Management and Insurance.* McGraw-Hill. Chapters 1.

Mishra, S., Bharagava, R. N., More, N., Yadav, A., Zainith, S., Mani, S., & Chowdhary, P. (2019). Heavy Metal Contamination: An Alarming Threat to Environment and Human Health. In Sobti, R., Arora, N., Kothari, R. (eds) *Environmental Biotechnology: For Sustainable Future.* Springer.

Omona, D.A. (2023). Alcohol Abuse and Addiction. In Romaniuk, S.N., Marton, P.N. (eds) *The Palgrave Encyclopedia of Global Security Studies* (pp. 26–35). Palgrave Macmillan, Cham.

Patil, K. D., De, J., Patil, V. K., & Kulkarni, M. M. (2024). Environmental Effects and Threats of Waste: Understanding Threats and Challenges to Ecosystem, Health, and Sustainability and Mitigation Strategies. In Arya, R. K., Verros, G. D., Verma, O. P., Hussain, C. M. (eds) *From Waste to Wealth.* Springer.

Redja, G. E. & McNamara (2016). *Principles of Risk Management and Insurance.* Pearson Addison Wesley. Chapters 1.

Toivanen, K. (2024). One Man's Waste Is Another Man's Business: The Early Scrap Business As a Predecessor To The Later Circular Economy. *Tekniikan Waiheita, 42*(1), 6–36.

Chapter 8
Insurance Markets and Competition

Abstract One of the fundamental characteristics of a perfectly competitive market is the unrestricted freedom of entry and exit for both insurers and policyholders. In such a market, participants are presumed to have complete and accurate information regarding the products available, the products are relatively homogeneous, and pricing is governed solely by the forces of supply and demand. In reality, insurance markets diverge from these ideal conditions, as insurers are required to comply with regulatory standards prior to market entry. This chapter provides a detailed analysis of these market imperfections and examines strategies for their effective management. It further investigates the factors that constrain the demand for insurance, emphasises the critical role of insurance in societal risk management, and discusses methodologies for the effective marketing of insurance products. Moreover, the chapter considers the advantages of robust competition within the insurance sector, provides an in-depth assessment of the phenomenon of underpricing, and evaluates its underlying causes, market implications, and potential mechanisms for mitigation.

Keywords Competition · Information problems · Underpricing

Introduction

In economic theory, a perfectly competitive market is characterised by free entry and exit for both sellers and buyers, full access to information, homogeneity of products, and prices determined solely by the forces of supply and demand. The insurance market, however, falls short of these ideals. Entry for insurers is restricted by regulatory requirements, which, while necessary for stability, can also create barriers and opportunities for market manipulation. On the demand side, policyholders may withhold critical information from insurers, exploiting asymmetries that further distort the market. These imperfections highlight the unique challenges of insurance as both a product and an institution. This chapter examines these issues in detail. It begins

C. Andoh, *Fundamentals of Managing Risk and Insurance*,
https://doi.org/10.1007/978-981-95-4581-0_8

with an exploration of imperfections in the insurance market, showing how regulatory constraints and information asymmetry shape the industry. It then considers the factors limiting the patronage of insurance products, addressing cultural perceptions, affordability, and trust as key influences on consumer behaviour. It then discusses distribution of insurance to the market, emphasising strategies for expanding reach and improving accessibility. The chapter also highlights the role of competition in the insurance market, underscoring its benefits for innovation, efficiency, and consumer choice, while cautioning against destructive practices. Finally, it addresses the problem of underpricing, where insurers deliberately charge premiums below market rates. The causes, consequences, and corrective measures for underpricing are analysed, offering insights into how such practices affect market stability and long term sustainability. By weaving together these themes, the chapter provides a comprehensive view of the insurance industry's dynamics, its strengths, vulnerabilities, and the measures needed to foster a healthier, more resilient market.

Imperfections in the Insurance Market

A market where insurance products are traded is an insurance market. Insurance market imperfections are one of the central reasons why regulation exists. These imperfections exist for a number of reasons. When a few insurance companies have control over the market they have the power or influence to set prices or, indeed, price fix the products they sell. When a monopoly exists (i.e., only one company operates in the insurance market) it can set the prices for which policies should be purchased. This is clearly not desirable. In addition, as some companies are larger or more mature than others, they have a competitive advantage over new entrants. A mature firm can act as a barrier to a new entrant because it can sell products at a cheaper cost that may price a new entrant out of the market. Four main imperfections in the insurance market can be identified and are now discussed.

Information Problems

Information problems abound in insurance and arguably constitute the industry's most important market imperfection. In the insurance industry, insurers have superior information about the products that they sell. They also have superior information about their financial standing than consumers. On the other hand, an insurance seeker knows more about their potential exposure to risk than the insurer. In addition, the possession of insurance cover may cause an insured entity to be careless, increasing the frequency of loss for the insurer. In some instances, neither the buyer nor the insurer has sufficient knowledge or information about the risk exposure that confronts them. Information problems emanate broadly from two sources: asymmetric information of the market or the fact that the information does not exist at all.

Asymmetric Information

Asymmetric information arises when one party to a transaction has superior information than the other. This gives one party an advantage and does not foster fairness. We can identify four asymmetric information problems: the 'lemon' problem, adverse selection, moral hazard and the principal-agent problem.

The Lemon Problem

In this situation, the insurer withholds certain information from the insured. An insurer may not always disclose full information on its policies to the insured. For example, an insurer has superior information about its financial status. The policyholder only receives a promise that they will be indemnified when a loss occurs but has little or no knowledge whether the company has the financial muscle to honour its side of the agreement.

Adverse Selection

Adverse selection occurs when policyholders use their superior information to take unfair advantage of insurers. If risk exposures were not completely or fully disclosed by the insured, a loss for the insurance company is more likely. This poses substantial problems to the supply of insurance products because it causes the insurer to underestimate the true risk or the potential loss exposure of an applicant seeking insurance. An applicant could therefore be charged a lower premium than required for their potential expected loss and this could be insufficient to cover losses. When the funds collected by an insurer are insufficient to pay for losses arising out of the pool, an insurer will have to dip into general surplus funds to make up the deficit. In the worst-case scenario or in a market where there are serious adverse selection problems, it can wipe out an insurance company exposed to such risks, and theoretically the whole insurance market. Adverse selection can also occur when insurers cannot classify the loss expectancy of their policyholders and therefore charge the same premiums for customers with different exposures to risk. In this case too, the premiums collected will be insufficient to cover losses. The inability to classify can be due to the costly nature of obtaining the relevant information or because the insurer does not have the technical ability to properly classify the information gathered.

Moral Hazard

Moral hazard is the effect of insurance on an insured entity's incentive to reduce losses. If an insured entity decides that it is in their interest to make a fraudulent claim to realise the benefits of an insurance policy, the insurance company suffers a loss. It complicates the supply of insurance products because it can cause the insurer's claim costs to be much higher than estimated. In the worst-case scenario, an insurer can go bankrupt where serious moral hazard issues persist.

It should be noted that moral hazard does not only emanate from the insured. Insurance companies may, for example, have dishonest employees that work together with an insured entity to falsely claim for a reward.

Principal-Agent Problem

The principal-agent problem is the conflict of interest that arises when an individual or a firm employs an agent to act on its behalf. The agent's incentive in maximising their own wealth may not always be compatible with the objectives of the principal. One example would be the intentional omission of vital information by an agent to benefit from it. Thus, agents use their superior knowledge to their advantage or to the disadvantage of the principal. To combat the principal-agent problem, the following should be done.

i. Drafting of agency contracts: the agent's role should be clearly spelt out in the employment contract. The agent should be required to disclose any potential conflict of interest between them and the principal before employment. If any potential conflict of interest is detected after employment has commenced, the person should be dismissed to serve as deterrent to others. In addition, the insurer should hold the agent responsible for any fraudulent sales so that in the case of litigation the agent will pay for any liabilities that arise. This should also be stated clearly in the employment contract.
ii. Equity in the firm: if an agent has equity in an insurance business, this should minimise the principal-agent problem. If not, agents should be given share options in the company so that if the company does well so will they. This will motivate the agent to work in the interest of the principal.
iii. Good salary with good working conditions: if the agent is paid well and has good working conditions, then it is likely they will work in the interest of the principal.
iv. Tie in incentives with company's performance: incentives constitute one of the key factors that boost the morale of staff. The rewards for agents should be performance related with additional benefits based on the level of profit that the form attains. Incentives such as holiday trips to a preferred destination, annual or sales-related bonuses and other benefits will encourage an agent to work in the interest of the principal.
v. Limits of authority: an agent can be given a limit on the value of business they can procure. High value product sales will thus only be dealt with directly by senior managers of an insurance company.
vi. Performance appraisal: an insurer should periodically appraise their agents. Those who have exhibited due diligence in the performance of their duties should be rewarded. This will serve as a motivation to other agents.
vii. Education: Agents should be required to continually improve their knowledge of insurance and how to best go about their duties through training. Education

on the company's underwriting policies will ensure that they solicit for business based on the firm's underwriting principles.

viii. Monitoring: an insurer can put in place a department that will monitor the activities of agents. Random contacts with policyholders that the agent has contracted for the principal (from time to time) will reveal any misinformation or miss-selling so prompt action can be taken.

ix. Selection of agents: the selection process can always be improved to maximise the quality of agents hired. Agents should not be hired on the basis of a personal relationship or friendship with any senior management of an insurance company. Rather, agents should be hired on competence, qualifications and their ability to do the job.

x. Availability of information to the insuring public: an insurer should make key information about the policies it offers available on its website or through publicity materials for prospective policyholders so that agents are not able to deceive the public.

xi. Provision of logistics: an agent will work for the benefit of the company if the materials and equipment necessary for them to carry out tasks effectively are provided.

xii. Licensed agent: an insurer should recruit agents who are licensed because they are mindful of situations that could result in the revocation of their licence.

Non-Existent Information

Information needed by both the prospective insured and the insurer to operate efficiently may not be available or determined at the inception of the contract. Consequently, there will be an inability for market players to make sound judgements. For example, insurers rely on the rate of interest in pricing of the products they offer, and the investments they do are also affected by the rate of interest in an economy. If the rate of interest is low because price is set before the insured event occurs, insurers lose. On the other hand, if the rate of interest is high, insurers gain at the expense of insurance purchasers. Thus, both the insurance purchaser and the insured face uncertainty.

Externalities

Externalities occur when a transaction or agreement between two parties has effect on a third party. There are two types of externalities: positive and negative. A positive externality arises when the third-party benefits from the transaction between the two transactional parties.

An example of a positive externality is national health insurance which is a result of government and insurers making an agreement to provide society with national health insurance. Another example is when a policyholder purchases theft insurance for a house but is required by the insurance company, as a condition of providing coverage, to install security devices on the property as a loss control measure. This might be additional street lighting or security cameras, for example. Thieves may be deterred from breaking into that property because of the existence of these devices, but neighbours in surrounding houses may also benefit as third parties, despite not having purchased insurance for their own properties. Intellectual property laws, which provide legal protection for the owners of creative ideas or patents, are also positive externalities. However, insurers have rarely sought protection under such laws for their products and innovations and consequently there is a tendency for other companies to copy their products and other innovations.

Negative externalities occur when a third party incurs a cost due to the transaction between the two original parties. An example is an insurance company refusing to pay a genuine or legitimate claim leading to the whole industry suffering from their action as the industry is hit with a lack of trust from consumers. Another example is if someone takes out a life insurance policy and is murdered by the beneficiary. Selling below the fair premium is also a negative externality in that the actions of these insurers can collapse or force other insurers out of the insurance market. These result in a negative outcome for both the purchaser and the insurance company.

Market Power

If one or few providers can control the price of insurance products, then market power exist that needs to be corrected. The problem arises because of entry and exit restrictions, price discrimination, product differentiation, economies of scale and scope. Insurers that have market power stifle competition in the insurance market because they can make decisions over which other insurance companies have little or no control. An insurance company can exercise market power in the following ways:

Entry Barriers

Considerable capital is required to start an insurance business, and this serves as an entry barrier to new companies. Even after meeting initial capital requirements, there are other conditions that must be met for a firm to continue to stay in the market. These conditions also serve as a deterrent to new firms. For example, customer loyalty to existing insurance companies is a barrier to new entrants in the market. Large firms have customers that may be tied to the products and policies of their insurer. New entrants may not be able to provide sufficient incentives to potential customers to cause them switch to a new insurer.

Also, new entrants may find it difficult to gain access to resources that may be needed in the daily running or management of the company. Such resources include cash, assets, expertise and many others. Due to the difficulty in accessing resources, only those companies that have these resources are on the market stifling competition and consequently serving as barriers to new companies.

Exit Barriers

A number of exit barriers can also be identified. They include but not limited to the following:

i. *Difficulty in Obtaining a Reinsurer*

One function of reinsurance is that it enables an insurance company which wants to wind up or exit the market transfer part or all of its risk to it. In the absence of reinsurance who will be willing to take the business of the insurer, an insurance company may find it difficult to exit the market.

ii. *Specialised Nature of the Industry*

Insurance is a specialised field with its unique terminology and assets. Consequently, expertise from this field may not be readily used by other industries, hence making exiting difficult. In addition, its assets may not be needed or bought by other industries compounding the problem to exit especially when it has invested so much in acquiring these assets.

iii. *Unearned Reserves*

Unearned reserve refers to the portion of premium received that have had no claim made on them yet. If an insurer could simply leave the market, customers will be at risk. Thus, these existing contracts make it difficult for the insurer to exit the market.

iv. *Market Power*

An insurer who has a large market share will find it difficult to exit due to the large number of clients or businesses that have insured with it. Market power could emanate from the brand an insurer has attained over the years (i.e., brand name can be a barrier to exiting a market). As a result of rendering quality service to its customers an insurer would want to maintain such good will. Exiting will damage the trust its customers have for it. Also, when an insurance company is a part of a group of companies, the brand name of the group may be adversely affected by the exit. This can result in huge losses for the group and customers may feel the brand name is not as prestigious as before and hence acts as barrier to exit.

v. *Tedious Legal Processes*

An insurer may find the processes involved in exiting cumbersome as it will have to legally disengage itself from agents, brokers, reinsurers, financial institutions, clients and from the regulator. For example, reinsurance provides insurers with the ability to form a pool of risks. Various forms of reinsurance arrangements hinder the insurer from exiting the market.

vi. *Potent Market*

An insurer making a lot of profit in the market will find it difficult to exit the market. Premium received is a source of capital which allows an insurer to expand and enter into other profitable line of business. Also, if an insurer is enjoying certain tax shields, deferred tax payment and favourable conditions in the environment it is operating, it will be difficult for it to exit the market. Thus, profitability of the insurance business can act as an exit barrier.

vii. *Government Imposition*

Government imposition can also serve as an exit barrier. Sometimes the government may insist that a particular industry be provided with insurance through legislation. For such an industry, the government will make it difficult for an insurer who wants to exit.

viii. *Financial Costs*

An insurer who has issued out debt instruments in the form of bonds or has contractual loans from banks and/or other lending institutions must repay its debt obligation before it can completely exit the market. If this is not possible, investors have the right to claim over its assets as compensation for unpaid debt obligations by the insurer. In addition, it would have to hire accountants, lawyers, actuaries and underwriters to make sure that all stakeholders in the company receive their fair compensation or severance package when the company is leaving the market. These financial costs act as exit barrier.

ix. *Shareholder Control*

Shareholders of insurance companies may also restrict market exit. An insurer that is likely to become insolvent may decide that an exit from the market may be the best option, but shareholders can refute this decision because of the control they have over the company. They may want to diversify or continue operations. Disagreement among shareholders about exiting can also stall the idea of exiting.

x. *Court Order*

A court may place an order on an insurer from exiting. For example, if the insurer is found guilty of fraud or a legal battle between a customer and the company exists, the court may place an order preventing it from exiting.

xi. *Labour Organisation*

Labour organisations who are to protect employees also prevent insurance companies from easily exiting. Because employees will lose their jobs when this occurs, labour organisations do everything they can to either seek for compensation or prevent the exit of the company.

xii. *Long-Term Investments and Contracts*

An insurer that has long-term contracts and investments will find it difficult to exit because of possible loss in value of invested funds.

Price Discrimination

Price discrimination happens when an insurance company charges different prices on the same product for different consumers even though the risk exposures are the same. In this scenario, insurers conceal the actual price of certain products and sell to a group of buyers at a higher or lower rate than the actual price because of certain characteristics of the group. For example, an insurer with market power can choose to charge GH¢150 as premium for one customer and GH¢200 for another, even though they bear the same risk, though the actual market price is GH¢160. By virtue of being in the market for long, an insurer knows how to recoup losses from both the lower and higher priced consumers and still make profits. A new firm may not have the ability to do the same and consequently this offers the established player greater market power.

Product Differentiation

An insurance company with market power can distinguish its products by designing different products for different consumers at different prices. Certain features that are advantageous to their customers can be added to the products they produce to set their offerings apart from similar policies being offered for sale. For example, an insurance company can make its products for motor insurance unique from its competitors by providing courtesy cars for its customers in the case of an accident and offer personal assistance that the insured might need. An established insurer could also branch out into an area that is very costly to enter. By so doing, it could create niche products that other companies may not have the needed capital and technical know-how to compete with. An insurer that offers diverse products with lower costs will be preferred to a company that produces just one product. The prompt payment of claims can also be used to attract greater number of customers to an insurer even if the products are priced high because a common concern of customers is slow payment of claims by insurance companies. Other techniques, such as flexible payment options and effective advertising can be employed by an insurer to distinguish its products from those of its competitors. If individuals, companies and other insurance seekers are able to identify a company that offers them better services, they will switch to that company and reward it with higher profits and increasing market share and dominance.

Economies of Scale

Economies of scale refer to the reduction in the average cost of production as output increases. In the insurance sector this can result in only a few firms attaining profitability because of their size. Such firms provide cover at low cost to a high percentage of buyers and remain solvent and make profits. Thus, the average cost of underwriting a new policy reduces because of long-term benefits and the increased expertise market dominance affords. Such a lower cost of production leads to a company being able to influence demand putting its competitors at a disadvantage.

Economies of Scope

When a company can produce many different products or policies by virtue of specialisation or a division of labour, its competitors struggle. Economies of scope could also include the reduction in cost because of producing two products bundled together, reducing the total cost of production. When this happens, expense loadings are reduced and as a result lower premiums can be charged.

Free Rider Problem

A free rider is a person or entity that takes advantage of a service or benefits from an insurance product without paying for it. This arises when insurance products end up selling for very low price or for nothing at all. In this scenario, some participants in the market bear the cost of providing the product or service while others simply get it for free or at a very low cost. For instance, if an insurance company that shoulders the cost of research into a new insurance product, is successful, and subsequently provides cover for the risk, other insurance companies may start providing cover for the same loss exposure even though they did not bear part of the research costs. People who evade taxes and still benefit from social provisions are free riders.

Other Market Imperfections

Inefficiencies on the Part of Regulatory Bodies

There are inefficiencies on the part of regulatory bodies such as governments, regulators and the judiciary in efficiently regulating insurance firms. The courts have not been very effective in solving information related grievances by the insured. Soft regulation and lax enforcement of already existing rules mean insurers who break the rules are generally left off the hook. This is partly due to insufficient budget allocations for enforcement. For example, the regulator should be monitoring insurers to ensure that rules governing the proper classification of policyholders are obeyed. However, it is costly for the regulator to ensure that insurance companies conform to set guidelines on the proper classification of purchasers of insurance products.

Economic Conditions

Changes in economic factors such as inflation, taxes and interest rates can contribute to the imperfect nature of the market. Insurers might alter its pricing to offset its tax liabilities. Harsh economic conditions can also affect the demand and supply of insurance products.

Government Intervention

Intervention by governments contribute to the imperfect nature of the market. The inequitable distribution of income of insurance purchasers means the government will have to intervene in some cases to ensure insurance is made available to its citizenry. When the government intervenes to provide insurance products such as public health and free education, they stifle the business of insurance companies that provide products for such needs. This will make insurance companies in this line of business less competitive, and they may go bankrupt. Also, if the government unilaterally pays for damages of people who have suffered a disaster like flood or fire to gain political support, it will make people less inclined to go for insurance knowing the government can intervene.

Political Interference

Change in governments can lead to changes in board of directors of regulating bodies of insurance or even the insurance commissioner. The new regulating body might set rules that favour insurers on the side of the ruling government. Government insurance contracts that ordinarily should be competitive for every insurance company will be ceded with insurance companies on its side contributing to the imperfect nature of the market.

Regulation

The scope of regulation can stifle competition at the insurance market. When regulatory bodies in their bid to clean bad practices among insurers pass regulations or restrict a particular behaviour but turn a blind eye to another insurer that violates these restrictions, competition at the market is stifled. Also, regulation is meant to provide a level playing field for all insurers. However, when a regulation meant to hinder an undesirable act in the industry affords large insurers the chance to achieve or violate the rule using alternative means, smaller sized companies are disadvantaged. This does not create a level ground for competition.

One-Sided Price Determination

Insurance prices are largely determined by insurers making the insurance market imperfect. In a highly competitive market, prices are determined by the interaction of demand and supply. Though competition can play a role, consumers generally do not have a vital say in this matter. Insurers set prices that cover their expected claim cost, profit loading and expenses. The contract between the insurer and the insured is described as one of adhesion (i.e., the terms and conditions are fixed by one party (insurer), and with minor exceptions, must be accepted *en totale* by the other party (the prospective policyowner) (Black & Skipper, 2000, p. 191).

Capital Shocks and Underwriting Cycles

Capital shocks can deplete capital available in the insurance industry making it difficult for insurers to offer every product sought by consumers. Even when these products are available, consumers will have to pay a high price for them. In the process, some policyholders will be lost until the industry regains its needed capital.

Underwriting cycles is mostly prevalent in many lines of property-liability and business insurance where premiums have exhibited a cycle around the fair premium. They are described as hard and soft market times. In the hard market, coverage is restricted and the price of insurance products are high. In the soft market, coverage is available and the prices are stable or may even fall (Harrington & Niehaus, 2004, pp. 148–149).

When these conditions hit the industry, they make the market imperfect.

Factors Limiting the Patronage of Insurance Products

There are many factors that hamper the patronage of insurance products. In this section we will discuss some of these.

Level of Education

Having a low level of education or literacy obviously serves as a hindrance to the purchasing of insurance policies as potential buyers do not have adequate knowledge to read and understand the policy documents. This is a pronounced problem in the rural areas of developing economies. Adequate education and properly targeted publicity materials can increase the demand for insurance.

Poor Marketing Strategy

Marketing strategies must make insurance attractive to the target market to increase the pool of participants. Most insurance companies restrict their advertising to traditional target groups, thereby reducing patronage in the process. Most people in the informal sector perceive insurance products as designed to syphon monies from the public. There should be intensive marketing to people in the informal sector, such as those employed in hawking, as they constitute most of the workforce in a developing economy.

Local Languages

The insurance companies find it difficult to reach the people living outside the big cities. Extra expenses are incurred in recruiting sales personnel who can speak native languages and translating insurance policies. Many insurance companies in developing economies do not attempt to do this.

Lack of Technical Expertise

The industry lacks the necessary technical expertise, especially in life insurance, and is therefore not able to carry out its operations efficiently to meet customer expectations. Such inefficient service delivery disappoints existing customers and the repercussions of this on the company make it more difficult to attract new ones. Some insurance agents have inadequate technical know-how of the products that they sell. Hence, they are not able to explain or sell the benefits of their products to prospective buyers leading to poor take-up.

Payment of Claims

Prompt payment of claims constitutes one of the most important factors that prospective buyers of insurance products and claimants use to determine whether a particular insurance company can be relied upon. Some insurance companies either renege on their promises to pay claims or take very long periods of time to settle claims. This has led to a low level of confidence among potential customers in the services offered by insurers.

Compulsory Insurance

The requirement for the compulsory purchase of motor insurance has in a way encouraged insurance companies to develop their expertise in that area while neglecting other areas of insurance vital for developing nations. The consequence is that a large proportion of the population, who do not possess vehicles, do not have insurance products available to meet their needs. For those that do have vehicles, the cost of compulsory motor insurance makes other products prohibitive.

Because the regulators of insurance have made certain insurance policies compulsory, it is difficult to market those that are not mandatory. For example, it is far easier to sell motor, health and pension products than convince a person to take out a funeral plan.

The Slow Pay-Out Processes

Many insurance companies take too long for claims to be settled. Very often this is due to the centralised nature of the claim management function of the insurance companies. Also, the policy language can be so technical that the public find it difficult to understand which risks are covered in the contract. Hence, when insurers fail to pay out for risks that are not covered, bad will is created. An example is when a policyholder's claim is not settled after a car accident caused by the policyholder because the policyholder holds an expired driving licence. Strictly speaking, the insurance company should not pay such a claim, but on occasion, to safeguard the reputation of the company, some claims to third parties are settled.

Structure and Size of the Population

The structure (i.e., the composition and the belief and customary systems) and the size of the population also limit insurance patronage.

Due to the high dependency ratio in certain economies, there is little or no disposable income to fund insurance. An ageing population may also not be interested in insurance, unlike a more youthful demographic who may want to mitigate losses that they may occur. Unfortunately, in Ghana, most of the youth demographic are either unemployed or at school. Also, in countries with a large informal sector of the economy the value of insurance is not appreciated.

The more people in an economy that patronise insurance, the more predictable are the expected claim costs for the insurance sector. This is then reflected by low premium charges that, in turn, induce more people to patronise insurance. The reverse is true for economies with a low patronage of insurance.

Socio-Cultural Practices

There are people in developing countries that believe that they are protected by God and that insurance is only meant for unbelievers. They trust in the efficacy of their faith and do not believe that any loss can happen to them. Any misfortune is considered the will of God and consequently there is no need for insurance. For some Muslims, it is believed that whatever calamity befalls a person is the will of Allah and they are therefore reluctant to take up insurance policies.

Low Propensity to Save

If a person decides to put aside some amount of money to cater for future needs, the patronage of insurance will invariably be high. In many developing countries however, either low salaries do not allow this luxury or people tend to spend money on immediate needs. This low propensity or likelihood to save drains people of any income that could have been used to purchase insurance products, some of which have investment packages that could improve lives. In addition, income distribution is skewed towards the rich of the population making it virtually impossible for the majority to have the ability to save.

Low Growth of National Income

It is assumed that the higher the growth in one's income, the more willing one is to buy insurance products. Hence the low rate of growth of a nation's national income is a determinant of the low patronage of insurance products. For economies with higher standards of living it is more likely that people will be able to afford insurance.

Bad Actors in the Insurance Sector

Some insurance companies could swindle their customers with fraudulent policies. When this happens, it breeds a distrust of insurance in the general population that would be difficult to overcome.

Document Requirements

Some insurance companies require so many documents to take out an insurance product that it puts some potential customers off.

Other Means of Financing Losses

Individuals might have other sources of funding losses. If an individual is certain of getting support from friends, family members or employers who can help in times of financial distress or catastrophic events, they do not worry about purchasing insurance. Funds from government intervention and aid from NGOs and other benevolent bodies may give an individual a sense of security that can limit or prevent them from purchasing insurance.

Non-Monetary Losses

Certain losses cannot be quantified financially, hence the absence of a demand for their insurance. For example, many people may not want to have insurance for the pain they go through for receiving a slap from someone.

Premium Loadings

Premium loadings determine the price of insurance. If loadings were high, only high-risk individuals would purchase insurance whereas low-risk individuals would desist. The high premiums may be due to high administrative or capital costs and this is a disincentive for prospective purchasers.

Individual Perceptions About Risk

If an individual overestimates their risk, then higher coverage will be bought. For example, the degree of uncertainty about an individual's retirement can influence their demand for insurance. Most employees are uncertain about their retirement because they could be fired or made redundant at any time. Because of this and other uncertainties about retirement benefits, individuals will be influenced to purchase insurance.

On the other hand, if a person underestimates their risk exposure, then less insurance will be bought.

Government Regulation

If insurance is mandatory by law, individuals will be compelled to purchase insurance and consequently, the demand of insurance will be high.

Emphasising the Importance of Insurance

Insurance is very important to every economy of the world. Many industrialists and investors will not invest if they are not assured of protection of their investments. Insurance provides policies that will cover such investments when an appropriate transaction has taken place.

Although the benefits of insurance products are enormous, many people still do not insure their assets. Many houses and businesses have been destroyed by fire whose owners have no insurance cover. Others have also incurred liabilities to their employees, customers or other third parties for which no insurance cover was taken out and have had to pay such claims themselves. Thus, all stakeholders have a collective responsibility to ensure that the importance of insurance is emphasised.

One major criticism levelled against key stakeholders in the insurance industry in sub-Saharan Africa is that they have not done enough to sensitise people about the importance of insurance. Among other things, this has led to the low take up of insurance products. Several things can be done by these key stakeholders to change this situation. This section discusses actionable points that can be implemented.

Education

As insurance is not a tangible product, a lot of education must be done by industry stakeholders to increase the population's knowledge of insurance products. The number of academic institutions that teach insurance is low in sub-Saharan Africa; therefore, more of such institutions should be set up. Besides, insurance products can be explained at venues where people congregate such as churches, mosques, funerals and durbar grounds. Insurance companies can organise talk shows on both radio and television to educate the populace on the essence of insurance. There should be collaboration between the driving schools and insurers so that insurance awareness programmes can be added to the programme of study. In addition, insurance companies should make it a priority to ensure that their agents and other employees are given periodic training about the products that they offer, so these can be properly communicated to prospective customers. Open air events and workshops, etc., on the importance of insurance can be organised for relevant people in society such as car and business owners. The use of radio and television stations that make use of the local dialect is an effective way of educating the public in rural areas. Stakeholders could also push the case for the introduction of insurance education not only at the tertiary level but also at the secondary level. Within schools, insurance representatives could speak at parent/teacher association events. As insurance is a financial product, the use of banks as agents through bancassurance is increasingly important. The banks have a large clientele base and can be a good source of educating the public about the benefits of insurance and selling policies as agents of the insurance companies.

Prompt Payment of Claims

The prompt payment of claims for losses will go a long way to help communicate to the public the main benefits of insurance. Many people are of the view that insurers do nothing other than collect premiums and offer no compensation when a loss occurs. By making the process for policyholders that suffer a loss as fast and pain-free as possible can allay these preconceptions.

Proper Explanation of Products

Products and policies offered for sale by insurance companies to both existing and potential clients should be properly explained. Often, buyers of insurance products do not have adequate knowledge about the policies they purchase. Some may have incorrect ideas about the amount to be received in the event of a loss. In the event of an insured loss, the policyholder may receive a shock. Such misunderstandings result in the insured not realising the importance of the type of insurance purchased. However, if the insurance company fully explains both the benefits of a policy—and what is excluded from it—the customer will be satisfied with the importance of the service the insurance company is offering.

Insurance Companies Working Closely with Intermediaries

Insurance companies can also communicate the importance of insurance to the public by working closely with intermediaries such as customer-facing agents and brokers. People's concerns are shared with these intermediaries and when there is effective coordination between them and insurers, the needs of the public become clear. Insurers then can fashion the necessary products and policies that address the important needs of society. Society will then realise the importance of insurance.

Effective Regulation and Monitoring of Insurers

The solvency level of insurance companies is critical since an insurer cannot be in business without being able to fulfil its obligations to policyholders. Regulators must therefore ensure that all insurance companies meet the minimum capital requirements necessary to underwrite their business. Regulators must also regulate the asset worth of insurance companies as this will offset their liabilities. Insurance companies are required to file reports related to their asset management, investments and capital surplus positions to the regulator at the end of every year. This enhances the continuity of the insurance business by ensuring that companies are solvent. In addition, regulators must assure the professional capacity of insurers to underwrite certain complex high value risks such as oil and gas operations. This is because an inexperienced underwriter may insure a business to a value that may be beyond a company's retention limit or underwriting capacity and this might result in the collapse of an insurance company. The pricing system for insurance also needs to be regulated to avoid unscrupulous operators exploiting innocent policyholders in a situation where there is no standardised price for insurance products. Bad sales practice should also be monitored by regulators and fines imposed on individuals who engage in them. Thus, the effective regulation and monitoring of insurers can restore the confidence of the public that promises made by insurance companies, if not fulfilled, can be reported to the appropriate authorities for redress. When people know such a regulatory regime exists and is enforced, they will have more confidence that the promises made by insurers will be fulfilled.

There should also be strict enforcement of compulsory insurance products such as motor and fire (for commercial buildings) for government assets. If the assets of the government are insured, individuals and private companies will be motivated to do the same.

Corporate Social Responsibility

Insurance companies can also incorporate social responsibilities in their activities. By incorporating development projects such as constructing schools or hospitals and other philanthropic activities into their way of doing business, insurance companies will let people know that premiums collected are put to good use. As a result, the patronage of the services that they offer will increase.

Government Legislation

The government can legislate to increase the compulsory insurance the public must buy. The government could, for example, require all mining companies or other companies whose activities pollute the environment to take out public liability policy. In Ghana, the Motor Vehicle and Third-Party Act of 1958 made it compulsory for any motor vehicle to have at least third-party insurance cover (to cover injury, death, vehicle or property damage to a third party when there is an accident). Without this undertaking there would have been greater likelihood of 'judgement proof' holding sway (Harrington & Niehaus, 2004, pp. 228). This allows someone who causes damage to another to go free once if they have limited worth. Hence, through the enactment of laws, government agencies require entities to comply with requirements for insurance and the benefits of such policies are clear. The introduction of flexible payment plans can be arranged for people who cannot pay the full premium at once.

Enhance the Availability of Certain Types of Insurance

Governments can enhance the availability of niche insurance products by assisting insurance companies to obtain the relevant information and expertise necessary to underwrite such complex risks typical in sectors such as oil and gas. The curriculum of courses on insurance studies should be reviewed from time to time so that it conforms to current trends and new risks.

Good Marketing Strategies

The sector should adopt proven marketing strategies to convince more of the public about the benefits of insurance. The use of public figures and celebrity endorsements can be effective in emphasising the importance of insurance. Insurance sales outlets should be set up close to business centres and in the heart of communities just as is the case for banks. This will make it much easier for people needing information to obtain it quickly instead of having to travel long distances to acquire it.

Publication in the Newspaper of Huge Losses by Insurers

The publication of payment of huge losses by the insurers will signal people that truly insurance restores and gives peace of mind to people that partake in it.

Well-Motivated Staff

A well-motivated workforce is beneficial to any employer. For an insurer, staff should be well motivated to know the products that they are offering extremely well and achieve sales targets. Apart from core salary, staff should also be given bonuses, performance-related benefits and other fringe benefits such as scholarships for their children.

Distributing Insurance to the Market

Insurance Intermediaries

Insurance can be distributed through intermediaries such as agents and brokers. Agents sell policies to clients on behalf of the insurance company. Brokers arrange policies with insurers on behalf of their clients. Both act as a link between insurers and customers, provide personal assistance to the insured and educate the public about insurance products by having strong technical knowledge of what each policy offers and expertise in the sales and marketing of insurance products. Agents and brokers are good avenues for distributing insurance products since they are in frequent touch with their clients and the public. Insurance consultants also offer expert counsel and advice on the best policy options to prospective clients.

Company Employees

The employees of an insurance company can help distribute insurance products since they have friends and relatives who have insurance needs. This method is used by Enterprise Insurance Company in Ghana who reward employees for each customer they bring to the company.

The Media

The media can also serve as a major way through which insurance can be advertised or distributed. This can be done through the banks and media outlets such as newspapers, television, radio stations and magazines.

Bancassurance is a term used to describe the collaboration between banks and insurance companies to distribute insurance products. This is another avenue for distributing insurance as the banking sector in Ghana is more developed than the insurance industry and many people have bank accounts. In addition, bank employees serve as indirect agents for insurers.

Direct Marketing

This method includes methods such as telemarketing, online marketing, SMS marketing and direct mail. With telemarketing, insurers obtain the telephone numbers of prospective clients from companies and make calls explaining the products available for sale. With online marketing, customers are contacted by email or through marketing on social media. This medium is becoming increasingly important as smart phone network coverage and the amount of time people spend online continues to grow. Insurance companies can also consider partnerships with telecommunications companies through which they could market products via text messages to all potential clients.

Through Groups, Associations and Institutions

By collaborating with institutions like schools, churches and trade unions, insurers can form alliances to supply insurance policies to their members. Insurance products can be designed to address the specific needs of these groups. For example, during the announcements after a church service or prayer meeting, an insurance agent can explain the availability of insurance products. Educational institutions are also great places to distribute insurance products as some products are tailored specifically to the needs of students.

Through Tribal Elders and Other Renowned Persons in Society

Elders and other nationally known personalities are very much respected and listened to in society and so can serve as a potential avenue through which insurance products can be endorsed. When they endorse insurance products, they increase public confidence in the products and hence aid in its distribution. Chiefs can announce insurance products at durbars or invite insurance companies to come and market their products at such functions.

Transportation Systems

Transportation systems can be a good form of distributing insurance products especially for long distance travellers. An alliance with various transport associations such as Ghana Private Road Transport Union (GPRTU) can work effectively for the distribution of insurance products.

Through Post Offices

The use of the post offices has declined as more people communicate online. However, as with banks, it is still a good avenue for distributing insurance products as people continue to visit post offices and patronise their services. Publicity materials for insurance products can be prominently displayed to inform people about available products.

Community Centres and Hospitals

In the rural parts of sub-Saharan Africa, the best place to meet people is in community centres. There, people gather to socialise and talk about what might be new in town.

Insurers can benefit by doing some outreach to such centres. Hospitals can also serve as major channels for distributing insurance products, especially those that offer health coverage.

Funerals, Festivals and Ceremonies

Funerals present an opportunity to get access to many people. Refreshment times can be taken advantage of to distribute information on the availability of insurance products through agents or insurance company employees. Agents can talk to people, alluding to how the funeral has gone smoothly because of the funds provided through the insurance of the deceased and drawing attention to how insurance will provide care for the dependants. Products could also be effectively marketed at festivals and ceremonies such as engagement and wedding ceremonies where people gather to celebrate as part of every activity at the festival ground.

Sports Stadiums

This is another place where large numbers of people converge. With a public address system, effective advertising of insurance products can be undertaken.

Markets

A market is also a place where many people gather. They can serve as a good venue for providing information and raising awareness about insurance products.

Policyholders/Existing Clients

Existing policyholders can also serve as a means of distributing insurance. If they are satisfied with the services of an insurer, they are likely to recommend that insurer to their friends. It is therefore paramount that an insurer provides an excellent customer service to its clients to tap into this mode of distribution.

Competition in the Insurance Industry

Competition is healthy in every field of endeavour and the insurance industry is no exception. When there are a number of insurance companies and potential buyers have full knowledge about the products available, the liberty to choose who to deal with and the possibility to switch providers at low cost, everyone benefits. There are a number of reasons why competition is healthy for the insurance industry, and these are discussed below.

Benefits of Healthy Competition

Healthy competition allows the free entry and exit of providers. This ensures that at any given time, new companies can enter the market if they have the appropriate resources to redress a situation where existing companies may be making unfairly high profits. With the entry of new firms, given that demand remains constant, existing companies will be forced to reduce their premiums and offer greater transparency to show to policyholders that there is fair play in the market to ensure customer confidence and loyalty.

Maximising Stakeholder Value

Permitting competition also forces managers to maximise stakeholder value. The demand for hardworking and innovative managers increases. Big and reputable insurance companies need managers with excellent track records, but they must also prove themselves to the talent pool available by being seen to have a good reputation.

Allowing competition results in various companies offering similar products to the market. This prevents a situation whereby a single company could have a monopoly over any product and use this to exploit consumers. It is therefore to the benefit of consumers. In addition, as information comes to the players in a competitive market from diverse sources and at different times, no single insurer can monopolise or profit unduly.

Competition leads to economic progress through the provision of quality products and services that enhance the lives of consumers and improve the standard of living. It motivates innovation and creativity that is essential in designing insurance products. Some companies will invest in research and enter new areas establishing niche products and services. More creative products will be designed to satisfy the needs of customers.

Competition also ensures zero transaction costs to the consumer. In the absence of competition, companies can easily transfer such costs to the customer. However, because of competition this tendency is checked.

When there is competition, it helps to minimise the cost of risk. This is because all insurance companies will do their best to include educational materials and advice in their policies to assist the insured in managing risk. As the insured learn more about loss control measures and take them seriously the cost of risk in society will be minimised.

Competition brings about the development and improvement of technology by linking all branches of a company to better serve the public in the most cost-effective and efficient way. By endeavouring to outperform a competitor, a company may need to go the extra mile in convincing clients that it is the best option. This may involve an upgrade in technology.

Competition minimises adverse selection and enhances risk classification (see the discussion in Harrington & Niehaus[, 2004, pp. 136–138]). Since the aim of every firm is to maximise profit, competition requires firms to classify the type of risk they insure to avoid being adversely selected.

Competition also helps to check weak performers. Because of the nature of free entry and exit in a competitive market, weak performers are quickly found out and removed from the market. This, however, does not offset the equilibrium since other insurance companies can absorb customers that they have failed.

Intensive competition among insurers means that every insurer must struggle for survival and therefore there will be the need for comprehensive marketing and education drives. As a result, potential customers are provided with key information on the various products offered by insurance companies, raising awareness in the market.

Competition also encourages insurers to differentiate themselves from competitors by investing in corporate social responsibility projects such as housing projects and creating funds to support the needy. As a result of this, insurers can create a positive public image of their brand in the eyes of customers, who are more likely to purchase their products.

Governments benefit from healthy competition and the existence of many firms in the insurance sector as it reduces unemployment and increases the number of people insured, potentially reducing losses that could otherwise have been left for the government to cover.

Underwriting cycles describe the fluctuation of premiums charged over a period. This happens when insurers incorrectly predict future losses and either charge premiums that are too low because they anticipate low losses or too high because they anticipate high losses. The premium charged could be based on experience. Competition minimises underwriting cycles because prices are decided by market forces.

Competition minimises the dual asymmetry of information because it is easily available to both the insured and the insurer.

Underpricing

Underpricing is the deliberate act of charging below the market rate premium that an insurer underwrites. It is the practice of some insurance companies to underprice their products in a bid to win customers from other insurance companies. Established companies may do this to eliminate the threat from new market entrants, or new entrants may underprice to persuade the customers of established companies to switch their allegiance to them. The lack of adequate regulation by the supervisory authorities contributes to this problem. The next section discusses the reasons for underpricing, its effects and the methods that can be employed to mitigate this menace.

Reasons for Underpricing

There are a number of reasons why insurance companies sell some products below the fair premium. These include the following:

Favourable Investment

Investment is one of the key components of insurance business and this is considered in the pricing of insurance products. An insurer who obtains favourable investment returns can afford to sell some products below the fair premium and still be able to operate.

Increase Market Share

The insurance market is a very competitive one, and with quite a number of sellers, it has its own strategy for attracting customers. Customers, on their part, base their selection of a product primarily on the price offered by the insurer. As with any product, the lower the price, the higher the quantity demanded and vice versa. Thus, an insurer would sell some products below the fair premium as part of a strategy to win customers. This can result in greater market share for an insurer and trigger competition among insurers.

Regulation

When the regulator of insurance companies imposes restrictions on insurance classification, an insurer may be forced to charge a price for everyone including those with high risk. Because of this restriction, high-risk policyholders end up paying below the fair premium. Another factor is when the regulator compels insurance companies to reduce the prices of some products they sell. This may be because of customer complaints about the excessive pricing of those products. In addition, regulation may compel insurers to sell insurance to certain groups of people who ordinary cannot obtain insurance at the voluntary market (i.e., residual market participants). Premiums charged at the residual market are generally lower than the expected claim cost of participants at these markets. By selling insurance below their standard rates, insurance is made affordable to people who ordinarily will not be able to afford insurance at the voluntary market. A typical example is health insurance where regulation may compel insurers to provide cover for the poor at a price below the fair premium.

Price Discrimination

An insurer may decide to charge a low price (below the fair premium) for one segment of a market and recover that loss from another segment of the market even though the risk exposures are the same. For example, an insurer may charge GH¢140 for one segment of the market and charge GH¢200 for another segment when the fair premium is GH¢150. It does this through strategies like prompt payment of claims which gives them a favourable market outlook. On the strength of this, they charge below the fair premium to one group of customers and retrieve the deficit from another group by charging high for this group.

Technical Nature of Insurance Pricing and Lack of Technical Expertise

Many consumers of insurance products do not understand the pricing of insurance products. Holding the benefit constant, many consumers will elect the insurer that offers the lowest price, even though such an insurer may be unable to honour its side of the insurance contract. If they understood how the pricing were done, they would have chosen wisely.

Also, lack of technical expertise or in-house actuaries to compute the risks in an environment could lead to pricing below the fair premium. For example, some insurance companies in some jurisdictions use mortality tables of other countries in the computation of the life insurance products and this could possibly lead to underpricing.

Administrative Expenses

Some insurers sell below the fair premium model to increase revenue emanating from administrative income. For the portion of the administrative expenses which are fixed such as setting up records for a new contract, more revenue can be realised as the number of consumers increase, and this can allow an insurer to stay in business even if prices are lower than what the fair premium model will predict.

Less Demand for Insurance Products

Low income of employees and credibility of some insurers do not encourage people to purchase insurance products. This affects insurers and consequently causes some to sell below the fair premium to attract buyers and/or maintain existing clients.

Economies of Scale or Scope

When the average cost of production declines when production increases, an insurer can afford to sell products below the fair premium. Thus, an insurer enjoying economies of scale by its sheer size and the quality of human resource it possesses can reduce administrative and other fixed costs and consequently can afford to sell some products below the fair premium and still make some profits.

Also, an insurance company enjoying economies of scope offers more than one product on the market. Economies of scope arises when the joint production cost of two or more products are lesser than the separate production cost of two or more products. Here, an insurer can afford to sell its products below the fair premium offered on the market and yet not lose or pack out of business.

Information Problems

Information is not evenly distributed among insurers and policyholders. When the insurer does not have the relevant information needed for pricing of the risk being sought, an insurer might price a product below the fair premium.

Liquidity Challenges

An insurer might sell products below fair premium because of liquidity or solvency challenges. When an insurance company is cash strapped, it might consider selling some products below the fair premium to gain cash in the short run to meet claims.

Entry Strategy and Entry Barrier

The insurance market is a competitive one. As a result, new entrants may sell below the fair premium to gain a large market share. Some insurers also sell products below the fair premium to prevent new entrants from surviving in the market. This causes the new entrants to operate at a loss and eventually leave the market. It also takes away the lucrativeness of the insurance business so that prospective insurance companies are kept at bay.

Less Patronised Products

An insurer may sell products below the fair premium for products that are less patronised in a bid to entice customers to purchase such products.

Loyal Customers

An insurer may charge below the fair premium model for its loyal customers as a means of reward for staying with them for long.

Insured with Large Stake

When the insured is a large institution or entity with its risk exposure consisting of a greater proportion of the business an insurance company underwrites, it gives the insured a high bargaining power. This power allows the insured to bargain the cost of insurance charged by the insurer to an amount that may be lower than the fair premium will dictate. Failure to comply will mean losing the biggest customer.

Effects of Underpricing

When some insurers decide to sell products or some products below the fair premium, then the following can arise.

Competition

Insurance companies pricing behaviour affects their performance in the market as the insurance industry is not monopolised. Companies, therefore, with better offers in the market gain competitive advantage over others and because every insurer wants to retain their market share, they would also offer lower prices to compete and attract consumers from their competitors. Prospective insurance companies may find the market unprofitable and may decide not to risk their capital and join the market.

Early Exit

Due to competition in the market, underpricing can trigger some insurance companies to exit the market or a line of business where serious underpricing exists. This may compel an insurer to develop new products so that they can stay in business.

Lowering prices of products increases the risks of potential losses and as a result, insurers who are unable to cover their operating costs would have to exit the market. This could have a direct effect on the economy by increasing the unemployment rate.

Adverse Selection

People with higher-than-average risk exposure will be buying insurance policies at lower costs. Also, classification restriction will also cause high-risk policyholders and low-risk persons to be charged the same rate thus causing the high-risk policyholder to adversely select the insurer. Consequently, high-risk persons will obtain insurance at low rates despite their loss exposure.

Moral Hazard

This behaviour encourages moral hazard as buyers of insurance policies may be lax in adhering to conditions outlined in the insurance contract due to cost of premium being low. Also, some individuals who pay less than their true cost of insurance may intentionally inflict losses so that they benefit since it costs them less.

Lock up Investible Funds of the Insurer

Investment is an integral part of the insurance business and investment income forms an important part of the pricing. If an insurer underprices its products, investible funds are locked up which could have an adverse effect on the payment of claims when they fall due and the insurer may also be unable to meet its other financial commitments.

Sanctions from Regulator

An insurer that underprices its products can be sanctioned by the regulator. Severe violations of pricing set by the regulator can result in the revoking of licence of an insurer.

Curbing Underpricing

Even though there should be competition in the insurance industry, the firms in the industry must not engage in unfair and destructive practices. Charging an artificially lower rate to win another firm's customer is greatly unfair and since the insurance industry does not readily adjust to market conditions, a reduction in the price of a policy does not necessarily increase demand but rather can lead to collapse of some weaker firms. To reduce the possibility of underpricing, the following measures should be taken.

Risk Classification

Insurers should wherever possible classify similar risks and charge a rate commensurate with the risk members of the group bring. A smart insurer, who identifies discrepancies in pricing, could offer a lower rate for a certain group of people to attract them to its policies causing adverse selection to a competitor who fails to classify appropriately.

Restrict Incorporation

Restrictions can be placed on the number of companies that can enter the insurance market. This may be through regulations raising the minimum capital requirement or having high registration and administrative fees. If there are no barriers to entry, some new entrants (in order to survive) may be tempted to underprice in order to attract clients from competitors. High registration and administrative fees will serve as a disincentive for insurers entering the insurance market and charging low premiums. A percentage of these fees could be returned to well-behaved insurers on a yearly basis. Companies that follow the rules could also be publicised by the regulator for being credible.

Regulation

Insurance companies and the regulators must come together to develop a fair premium model for all risk classes. Legislation can then be passed which will forbid insurance companies from charging below a certain amount for certain classes of risk. Thus, there should be laws to set floor prices (i.e., prices below which no insurance company can charge). These floor prices must, however, vary with the risk level of each class. As a result, insurance companies will desist from underpricing their products. Instead, they will look for other innovative ways of attracting customers (e.g., excellent customer service, speedy claim settlements, prime location, etc.).

There should also be regulation on the policy language presented to the insured. Insurers should be compelled to write the contract terms in language understandable by all without any opaque or confusing clauses. There should also be regulation on the sales practices of insurers. Personnel recruited for such jobs should have appropriate educational qualifications in insurance or undertake some form of training.

Financial Reports

Insurance companies should be required to issue reports on their assets, liabilities and investments. Regulators should then examine these financial reports to check for irregularities.

Education

Regulators should bring all stakeholders together in the form of educational seminars and highlight the dangers of underpricing, especially to new insurance companies. Also, periodic public education should be organised to sensitise the public about their rights and that they should pay the right premium commensurate with the risk they insure. It must be emphasised to the public that insurance thrives on its ability to pay genuine claims and that underpricing adversely affects this requirement. The public should also be encouraged to question insurers if there are disparities in the prices of insurance products in the same risk groups offered by different insurance companies. Prospective buyers must be educated to evaluate the benefits or compensation packages offered by various insurance companies before deciding on where to buy their policy.

Insurance companies should be required to publish a comprehensive listing of their premium charges under various conditions.

Experts

There should be training of more experts in the business of insurance. In this way an expert who knows the effects of underpricing will not sit back and watch it happen.

Supervision

There should be a regulatory unit solely in charge of the pricing of insurance products. Their responsibility would be to monitor insurance companies so that they do not charge below or above a certain price range. These regulatory units must be equipped to carry out their functions effectively. Companies who are experiencing large decreases in customer numbers should notify the unit who should check whether pricing was a motivation for the change. In this way, insurers engaging in underpricing can be identified and sanctioned accordingly. The regulatory unit should also ensure that the solvency of insurance companies is periodically ascertained as a way of determining whether they are financially stable.

Imposition of Sanctions

Punitive measures must be implemented after the regulatory bodies have adopted rules for: (i) rate setting; (ii) policy language; and (iii) sales practices, and insurers found flouting regulations should be sanctioned. Measures such as a revocation or suspension of a licence, the imposition of fines, etc., can deter insurance companies from underpricing to the detriment of other firms. It should be made illegal to price a product below the floor price set by regulators.

Reward Schemes

Reward schemes should be initiated for any member of the public who informs regulators about the underpricing of products by an insurance company.

Examination of Expenditure

An insurer should carefully examine its administrative expenses and rid-off any unnecessary expenditure. This will give it the freedom to charge lower prices for its products as expected claim cost cannot be reduced (see Chapter 8 of Harrington and Niehaus [2004], for the determinant of fair premium).

Exercises

1. Identify and explain three reasons why the insurance market is imperfect.
2. What is market power? Discuss how an insurance company can exercise market power in each of the following cases:

   (i) Price discrimination
   (ii) Product differentiation
   (iii) Economies of scale/scope

3. Asymmetric problems can occur in four ways. Name and explain these.
4. What is a principal-agent problem? Discuss four techniques that can be employed by an insurer to mitigate the principal-agent problem.
5. How do you understand the term externalities in insurance? Give 2 examples in each case for a positive and negative externality.
6. Explain the following terms as applied to insurance:

   (i) Agent
   (ii) Broker
   (iii) Non-existent information

(iv) Lemon problem

7. Explain the concept of underpricing and discuss its effects.
8. Discuss five ways in which people can be sensitised to insurance.
9. What methods can be employed to distribute insurance products in the insurance market?
10. Discuss two reasons why it is difficult for an insurer to exit the insurance market.
11. Outline and explain some benefits of healthy competition.
12. Discuss three conditions under which an insurance company can afford to reduce its premiums for its customers.
13. Some insurance companies sell some products below the fair premium.
    (i) Discuss three reasons why they do this in the absence of soft and hard market times.
    (ii) Discuss 2 effects of this behaviour on the insurance market.
    (iii) As the CEO of an insurance company, you may not be privy to the pricing of products. Explain 2 things you will do so that underpricing is curtailed.
14. Explain five ways to curb underpricing.
15. Discuss the importance of competition in the insurance market and in doing so highlight the following concepts:

(i) Stakeholder maximisation
(ii) Adverse selection
(iii) Information asymmetry
(iv) Promoting CSR

References

Black, K. J., & Skipper, H. D. J. (2000). *Life and Health Insurance* (13th ed.). Prentice Hall.
Harrington, S. E., & Niehaus, G. R. (2004). *Risk Management and Insurance.* McGraw-Hill.

Further Reading

Black, K. J., & Skipper, H. D. J. (2000). *Life and Health Insurance* (13th ed.). Prentice Hall. Chapter 10, 24.

Kimball, S. L., Bartlett, A., & Jackson, B. A. (1961). The Regulation of Insurance Marketing. *Columbia Law Review, 61*(2), 141–200.

Redja, G. E., McNamara, J., & Rabel, W. H. (2022). *Principles of Risk Management and Insurance.* Pearson Addison Wesley. Chapter 5.

Ungern-Sternberg, T. V. (1996). The Limits of Competition: Housing Insurance in Switzerland. *European Economic Review, 40*, 1111–1121.

Chapter 9
Regulation in the Insurance Industry

Abstract The regulation of insurance companies by governmental and other regulatory bodies is essential for ensuring the orderly functioning of the insurance sector and for mitigating the market imperfections inherent in the industry. In the absence of such regulations, insurers may exploit policyholders, and conversely, policyholders may engage in practices detrimental to insurers. This chapter provides a comprehensive analysis of insurance regulation, including the rationale for regulatory oversight, the entities responsible for enforcing regulations, and the justification for compulsory insurance, highlighting why certain insurance products must be mandated. The chapter further examines strategies for aligning the objectives of regulators with the interests of policyholders and explores mechanisms for ensuring accountability and oversight of regulatory authorities themselves.

Keywords Compulsory insurance · Compulsory insurance products · Policyholder · Regulation · Regulator

Introduction

The regulation of insurance companies by governments and other oversight bodies is vital to maintaining the stability, fairness, and integrity of the sector. Regulation addresses imperfections in the insurance market, ensuring that both insurers and policyholders are protected from exploitation and that the system operates efficiently. In the absence of effective oversight, insurance companies may take undue advantage of policyholders, while policyholders themselves may engage in practices that compromise the fairness of the market. This chapter is organised around six central themes. First, it explores the reasons for regulation, outlining why oversight is indispensable in correcting market failures, promoting transparency, and safeguarding consumer interests. Second, it examines the bodies responsible for regulation, including governmental agencies and other institutions tasked with enforcing standards and maintaining accountability. Third, the chapter makes the case for compulsory insurance, explaining why certain forms of coverage must be mandated to protect individuals and

C. Andoh, *Fundamentals of Managing Risk and Insurance*,
https://doi.org/10.1007/978-981-95-4581-0_9

society at large. Fourth, it considers the case for making specific products compulsory, highlighting the rationale for requiring coverage in areas such as motor insurance or health insurance where risks are widespread and significant consequences. Beyond these foundations, the discussion turns to the human dimension of oversight. Fifth, it emphasises the importance of motivating regulators to act in the interest of policyholders, ensuring that regulatory bodies remain committed to fairness, consumer protection, and public trust. Finally, the chapter addresses the challenge of regulating the regulator, presenting mechanisms to ensure that oversight itself is transparent, accountable, and aligned with the broader public interest. Together, these themes provide a comprehensive framework for understanding the role of regulation in the insurance industry.

Reasons for Regulation

Industry Protection

Insurance companies are regulated to protect both the industry itself and consumers.

Regulators ensure that insurance companies have a high level of financial stability so that they will be able to meet their obligations to customers. Regulatory bodies make sure that an insurance company has adequate capital before issuing insurance policies. Even before a licence is issued to commence operations, regulators require proof of a certain minimum amount of capital from insurers. This minimum capital requirement (GH¢50 million in the case of Ghana) weeds out charlatans and ensures that only financially credible insurance companies are allowed into the market. Regulators also check the investment portfolios of an insurer, its sufficient surplus position, admitted assets, dividend policy and reserves to confirm that a company has sufficient assets to pay for claims from policyholders. Some insurers may undertake very risky investments with the premiums collected from policyholders that can result in high losses or even bankruptcy. Regulators monitor such investment decisions. Regulators also prevent insurance companies from issuing policies that go above their retention limit or undertake activities that may lead to bankruptcy or liquidation.

Regulators must check the competency and expertise of personnel that work in specialised areas of insurance companies. This ensures that insurance companies employ people that are highly professional, capable and effective to avoid the provision of sub-standard products in the insurance market.

Consumer Protection

Consumer protection is another important reason why insurance companies are regulated. Because many consumers may have little or no knowledge of insurance products, an insurance company may decide to exclude vital information or cloak vital information on the proposal in ambiguity or opacity thereby misleading the insured or consumers. Regulations on the activities of insurance companies ensure that consumers have adequate information and knowledge of insurance policies and are not misled. Consequently, there are regulations on sales practices with appropriate sanctions, such as the loss of a licence, to deter an insurance company from mis-selling. Regulations also stipulate that the insurance company's agents and brokers are properly licensed to prevent unscrupulous behaviour.

Regulations also tackle pricing issues and ensure that these are fair for consumers. This stabilises the insurance market by weeding out bad actors that either overcharge or underprice for market advantage.

Regulation also protects the consumer against the refusal of claims by an insurer. Thus, insurance companies are legally required to honour their part of the contract when justified claims are made, or face sanctions. In addition, regulation ensures that fake insurance companies do not simply enter the insurance market, collect premiums and bolt with it. Regulators ensure that companies with the requisite capital are allowed entry so that they will be able to honour the contract they have with policy-holders. Regulators approve all products sold on the insurance market to ensure that consumers are not disadvantaged. Regulators also oversee mechanisms for resolving complaints brought against insurers. They also play a role in educating consumers on insurance products and enforce information disclosures by insurers.

Provision of Certain Types of Insurance

If insurers were not regulated, some insurance policies or products would never reach the market because of the nature of the cost involved in offering them. High claim costs, high administrative and risk load can deter an insurer from offering certain types of policies. Alternatively, insurers might charge exorbitant fees to deter consumers from patronising these products. Regulation ensures that such products are available at a reasonable rate so that the consuming public have access to them. For example, regulation has made certain types of insurance such as vehicle cover, retirement plans and worker compensation schemes compulsory so that these products will always be available. Without the availability of such products, consumers may have taken other risk reduction techniques to protect their properties or businesses that would have been more expensive.

Insurable Interest

Insurable interest means that insurance purchasers must have a financial stake in the destruction or loss of the asset they are seeking cover for. Without regulation, people could insure the properties of others and either trigger their destruction or hope for an early loss. Regulation ensures that individuals do not use insurance as a platform for gambling.

Tax Purposes

Insurance companies are regulated to ensure their proper accountability in terms of the payment of taxes. Insurance companies must present a true and fair annual financial statement devoid of any material misstatement. Auditors must validate these financial statements. This ensures that the right amount of tax is charged at the end of every accounting period.

Third-Party Protection

Regulation helps to protect third parties who are victims of an insured loss. For example, when an accident occurs and innocent third parties are hurt or injured, regulation ensures that these people are protected and compensated.

Public Policy

Insurance companies are regulated to ensure that their activities are in line with public policy. This might not necessarily be the case without regulation. For example, providing insurance cover for illegal activities such as cover for the sale of illegal drugs is against the interest of the public and insurance companies should not be allowed to provide cover for this.

Competition

A well-regulated insurance market creates healthy competition. If the market is unregulated, destructive competition can ensue as a market player might take aggressive or fraudulent measures to make profits, hence inflicting losses on other insurers. Regulation assists in the creation of a level playing field for all qualified insurers, preventing large international companies from sabotaging (by underpricing) or having undue advantage over local, smaller companies by virtue of their size.

Bodies Responsible for Regulating Insurance

Three main bodies for regulating insurance can be identified in Ghana: The National Insurance Commission, Parliament and the Courts.

The National Insurance Commission

The National Insurance Commission is the regulatory body (in the case of Ghana) that guarantees the proper implementation of laws relating to insurance companies. It issues licences to companies, brokers and agents to operate in the insurance market and ensures that the laws governing the insurance companies are adhered to. It also monitors the activities of insurance companies and regulates the prices of insurance products sold on the insurance market. The Commission is responsible for revoking the licence of insurance companies, agents and brokers if the laws are not adhered to. The Commission is also responsible for maintaining contacts and developing relations with foreign insurance regulators and maintaining international regulation standards.

Parliament

Parliament is the state body that enacts and amends all laws and other regulations in democratic countries. In Ghana, the state constitution mandates the legislature to enact business laws that are binding for all sectors, including insurance. Parliament formulates laws for insurance companies in consultation with the National Insurance Commission. It decides which insurance products should be compulsory.

Courts

The courts are the legal custodians of laws. They arbitrate any claim settlement issues, cases of fraud and other unlawful acts committed by insurance companies, their clients and other players in the insurance market. They interpret insurance policies and conditions when disputes arise and settle claim disputes between insurers and the insured. They also decide who the right beneficiary is when there is some ambiguity in the beneficiary assignment made by the policyholder (for example, in the case of a life insurance policy). In addition, they settle disputes that may arise between actors in the insurance market and third parties and punish transgressors of the law.

The Department of the Registrar General

This is a body that sets the general requirements for businesses in Ghana. It stipulates the minimum number of shareholders required and the maximum number (where necessary) and whether directors need to be resident and/or non-resident in Ghana among other things.

The Case for Compulsory Insurance

Insurance is very important in every society. When an employee suffers a serious injury at work, the burden for compensation falls on the company owners. When the company is not able to pay adequate compensation to such workers, they become a liability to their family, to society and to the nation at large. Insurance alleviates the consequences of such suffering when a covered loss occurs. In developing countries where the concept of insurance is not fully understood by most people, compulsory insurance for certain risks ensures that there are adequate funds to meet the needs of those who suffer a loss and reduces the burden on government. In addition, making insurance compulsory for certain risks creates awareness and educates the public about its importance, makes funds available for the capital market and positively changes behaviour. Mandatory insurance frees up government funds for national development. The following section expands on these points.

Reducing the Burden on Government

When losses that occur affect many people without insurance, the burden for compensating the affected victims usually falls on the already overburdened shoulders of the government. Government has a role as the protector of the vulnerable in society. However, this need not always be the case, and when insurance is made compulsory for certain types of exposures, in the event of a loss, it is the insurance companies that indemnify the victims. Compulsory insurance also compels insurers to provide cover for certain types of risk they would perhaps prefer not to because of the financial impact that claims can have when a major loss occurs. However, mandatory insurance also increases the size of the insurance pool, moderates the financial exposure of insurance companies and improves the predictability of expected losses.

Guaranteeing Compensation for Innocent Third Parties

In the event of any loss, innocent third parties can be affected. If the guilty party does not have insurance cover it is very likely that the affected third party will go uncompensated, which should not be the case. Making insurance compulsory solves this problem. This was exactly the rationale for making third-party motor vehicle insurance compulsory in Ghana. All employers are also required to have employee liability cover to pay claims to or on behalf of their employees when they suffer injuries or even death in the course of their employment. Despite these advances in Ghana, other types of insurance should also be made compulsory since protecting innocent third parties is always a laudable idea. Most property insurers are reluctant to provide homeowner policies; hence there is a need for the government to force their hand.

Mobilising Capital

The ability to mobilise and channel capital into productive ventures is a hallmark of any serious economy. Through compulsory insurance, companies collect money in the form of premiums and in turn invest this to create a favourable multiplier effect in the economy. This often leads to the creation of more jobs and ultimately strengthens economic growth.

Checking Moral Hazard

Compulsory insurance has the tendency to reduce moral hazard. As people pay premiums for compulsory insurance, more care is taken in one's daily activities not to cause damage that may result in an increase in these premiums in subsequent years. This is common practice in motor insurance where adjustments are made to premiums depending on whether the insured had an accident or not. The insurance company often offers an incentive in the form of a discount or no claim bonus for those that do not make a claim on their policy each year. Most drivers in Ghana are therefore cautious when driving because they know that their involvement in an accident no matter how minor will lead to an increase in their premiums, thereby reducing moral hazard. Thus, compulsory insurance can also alter the behaviour of society in a positive way. These benefits can be extended to other areas where insurance is made compulsory.

Increasing the Predictability of Expected Losses

Compulsory insurance radically increases the pool which in turn improves the predictability of the expected losses of participants in the pool. The consequence is that insurance companies can better plan revenues collected from premiums.

Promoting Awareness of Insurance

Compulsory insurance promotes the awareness of insurance in a country. Since people are forced to purchase specific insurance products, they become better informed about the basic underlying principles of insurance and its benefits to society. For example, people become aware of how insurance can positively impact on behaviour.

Judgement Proof

Judgement proof, in the context of contract law, debt collection or civil liability, happens when a tortfeasor (a person who commits a tort, or civil wrong either intentionally or through negligence) is released of all liability due to being financially insolvent, or a person whose income or assets cannot be obtained in satisfaction of a judgement. In such a case, the plaintiff goes uncompensated. If this becomes common in a society, there are potentially serious economic ramifications. The problem is curbed by making insurance mandatory as if the tortfeasor is incapable of paying compensation, an insurance company will take responsibility for the loss.

Retirement Plans

Compulsory insurance for retirement will help reduce the burden of old age on families and help improve the living standard of retired people. The informal sector is generally averse to insurance of any kind and as so many people rely on it for a livelihood, action is required to force such individuals to purchase insurance for their retirement.

Safe Products

Insurance must be compulsory in certain exposures such as product liability to ensure or provide incentives for manufacturers to exercise care and caution during their production activities. When consumers of defective products are not compensated, it serves as a disincentive to consumers to buy and use the products, thereby affecting national productivity.

Growing the Insurance Sector

Because of the existence of compulsory insurance more people are beginning to see the sense and logic of insurance in other aspects of their lives. Thus, the requirements for compulsory insurance serve as a source of increased business for the insurance industry.

The Case for Making Certain Insurance Products Compulsory

Many people have little or no knowledge of insurance and the benefits it offers individuals, businesses and organisations. By making certain insurance products compulsory it becomes imperative for everyone to know more about the potential benefits. This will encourage people to purchase insurance cover for themselves to safeguard against losses. In addition, it will reduce the financial burden on the government thereby increasing resources available for economic development projects.

Employee Liability Policies

Workers who suffer work-related injuries must have a guaranteed income to live on and this should be through mandatory employer liability policies. This is especially important for high-risk jobs such as those involving the use of heavy machinery, mining, construction workers and those that work with hazardous chemicals, etc. Without compulsory insurance for workers, the burden falls on the government.

Retirement Plans

Private pensions or retirement plans provide the insured with funds when their working life is over. Most people in developing countries, especially in the informal sector, do not have such insurance and therefore rely on their families and loved ones when they retire. Insurance for retirement should be made compulsory so that every worker will have a source of funding upon retirement to reduce or eliminate the burden they currently impose on the active workforce. Having security for retirement can act as a motivating factor for workers who do not have the stress of worrying how they will survive when they can no longer work. This will also ease the burden on the government for retired workers and satisfy public concern for helping those of pensionable age.

Property Insurance

The houses and premises that people and business buy, or build are essential assets. For businesses, such assets act as major sources of finance. When a company loses an asset like its place of business, and this asset is not insured, the business will likely fail with consequences for both the owners and their employees. For this reason, all businesses must be compelled to have property insurance policies so that in the event of a loss, they can be restored to their previous position and continue business operations. Such insurance will also protect third parties who might be inside a building when a fire or other catastrophic event occurs. Individuals should also have property insurance.

Child Education Policies

This is a policy that provides financial protection for the education of a dependent of the insured up to a certain level. For any nation to develop, it needs a well-educated population. Making child education policies compulsory up to the secondary level will help the child further their education to the tertiary level.

Also, when people drop out of school, they engage in all sorts of social vices. This may be because of lack of finance because their parents died. Child education policy when made compulsory will secure the child's education. The skills and the knowledge acquired will be useful in the productivity of the economy. In addition, since education equips a person with the requisite knowledge and skills to ensure positive transformational change and development in society, making educational policy compulsory will bring about development. This is because more people will be educated in the society.

Education policy will ease government burden. Governments support education from the basic level to the tertiary level. If the policy is made compulsory, every student at some point in his/her education will have insurance coverage paying his/her fees. Governments can then channel educational subsidies to other productive ventures.

Health Insurance

Everyone is bound to be sick at some point in their life. Many people die yearly by not having access to proper medical attention. If health insurance is made compulsory, it will reduce the burden on families, society and the government. This is because it will allow easy access to health care for all: the poor, the elderly, pregnant women, etc., who may not be able to afford health care costs. In developing countries where poverty is high, there is the need for a good health insurance scheme to cover health costs. This will greatly reduce the mortality rate and reduce the financial burden on families. People will be able to visit the hospital frequently for medical check-ups. It will also reduce cases where people resort to social media, radio or TV to appeal for funds to cover the costs of an illness they cannot afford to treat.

Life Insurance

Life insurance provides financial protection for beneficiaries when the policyholder dies. When life insurance is made compulsory, it will reduce or prevent the financial hardships dependents suffer when a breadwinner passes on. If dependents are assured of having financial support through the realisation of a life insurance policy, economic hardships and their social consequences will be reduced. The burden on the government will also decrease as the requirement for life insurance will reduce funds needed for social care.

Life insurance also reduces the burden on family members in the case of a policyholder dying, as funds will be available for the funeral.

In a case where the deceased had a mortgaged loan, the proceeds from the insurance policy can be used to pay this off. This allows creditors to retrieve their money when debtors die.

When life insurance is made compulsory, the level of potential investment capital in an economy increases leading to a wealthier society.

Liability Insurance

Liability insurance should be made compulsory for government institutions. With high incidents of judgement debts against government institutions, liability insurance will reduce losses to the state in the case when these events occur. For limited liability companies and small- and medium-sized enterprises, liability insurance can allow managers the freedom to explore new business opportunities and be innovative. It also ensures that in the case of insolvency any creditors they may have will be paid. Such third parties will therefore still be able to continue their business and may even aid the insolvent business to start up again.

A third party may be at risk when visiting the premises of a business. For example, a customer at a shopping centre may fall and get injured. If the shopping centre has liability insurance the insurer will take care of the loss instead of the individual needing to cover it.

There are many types of liability insurance available on the market including public liability, employer's liability, product liability, directors' and officers' liability and professional indemnity. *Product liability* insurance provides protection for a business for losses or damages a third party suffers (or claims to have suffered) because of using a product a business manufactures. It covers legal and court costs if someone is hurt or suffers damage to their property because of a product or service provided by a business. *Employers' liability* insurance provides protection for employers if a worker sustains a work-related injury not covered by workers compensation insurance (see Evans, 2000, chapter 8). *Directors' and officers' liability insurance* provides cover for key company personnel culpable for management errors and omissions while serving on a board of directors and/or as a company officer. Directors' and officers' insurance has two parts. The first provides coverage for directors and officers for losses that are not indemnified by the corporation. The second provides coverage to the corporation for indemnification costs (see Harrington & Niehaus, 2004, p. 620). Finally, *Professional indemnity liability insurance* protects a business or an organisation against professional indemnity claims.

Professional Negligence Insurance

While discharging their duties, professionals such as doctors, architects, auditors, insurance brokers and consultants can commit negligent acts that affect innocent third parties. All should be required to take out compulsory professional insurance to cover such eventualities. This should ensure that all professionals take extreme care in their work to avoid any claim arising that could affect their reputation and increase the premiums that they would have to pay.

International Sales Transactions

By virtue of the risk exposure involved in the shipment of goods, there is the need to have compulsory insurance for goods to ensure that corporations and individuals have peace of mind when a loss occurs. It will also help businesses to easily raise funds for new investments.

Fire Insurance

When there is an outbreak of fire properties may be destroyed disrupting the lives of those affected. Making fire insurance compulsory will positively influence property owners to adopt fire control measures such as the installation of fire extinguishers or water sprinklers in their homes or premises to mitigate the damage that fire can cause. People who lose their assets through fire can also be indemnified with such policies.

Motivating Regulators to Work in the Interest of Policyholders

Regulators of the insurance market are agents of the public (i.e., they protect the interests of the insured). One of their key responsibilities is to minimise information asymmetry problems that can put policyholders at a disadvantage. However, regulators can also be beneficiaries of regulation. To ensure that the regulator acts in the interest of the insuring public, the following measures should be put in place so that the regulator maximises value for policyholders.

Election and regulation of regulators

Regulators should be elected to office. Individuals, businesses or entities with large insurance coverage should have greater voting rights in such elections. Because regulators possess insurance products themselves, not acting in the public interest would be counterproductive. Regulators will be affected by the decisions that they make and will therefore defend the interests of the insuring public.

Public Education on Insurance

If the regulator knows that most of the insuring public are well informed about insurance, they are more likely to be good advocates for them. Educating the public through public awareness campaigns, and in schools, universities and the national media can help stop the exploitation of policyholders. Public debate on the work of the regulator will assist in creating a healthy regulatory environment. By welcoming suggestions and criticisms, the regulator is exposed to checks and balances.

The Legal Liability System

Laws and the legal liability system impose fiduciary duties on regulators. Failing to act in the interest of the insuring public could attract lawsuits against the regulator. Thus, fear of possible lawsuits acts as a check on the regulator to act in the interest of policyholders.

Working Environment

If the regulator is highly paid by the government and has good working conditions and benefits, he or she will not favour an insurance company at the expense of policyholders. The regulator must be above suspicion and not tempted to take bribes from insurance companies in return for measures that favour them over policyholders. Periodic incentives and rewards, state-of-the-art technological resources can also be motivating influence for a regulator.

State Institutions

State institutions that work closely with the regulator in executing its mandate must support the achievement of the core functions. The Ministry of Justice and the Attorney General must act proactively when any legal issues are brought before them concerning the misconduct of any insurance company.

Financial Rewards for Other Regulatory Staff

Financial rewards can be instituted for any employee of the regulatory office who diligently works to unravel any dubious activity of an insurance company. This will motivate other employees of the regulatory office to follow suit.

Benefits of Insurance

The societal benefits of insurance should motivate regulators to maximise value for policyholders. If regulators recognise that insurance provides peace of mind and reduces worry and fear in society, then they should support this cause. Also, insurance serves as a key aid for small businesses and as a financial shock absorber when a covered loss materialises. Insurance also makes funds available for investment that creates jobs.

Workshops and Other Training Programmes

Regulators should have the very best information available to them in working for the benefit of the insured. Training sessions and workshops for regulators should be held regularly to provide the latest international thinking on insurance and maximising value for policyholders.

Alternatively, a professional institute can be set up to train and equip the regulator for its role. A heavy emphasis should be placed on the use of technology, analysing information and formulating strategies.

Work Specialists

Staff working in a regulatory capacity should develop their own specialist interests and skill sets. Consequently, the government must ensure that the work of the regulator is divided in such a way that its staff have correctly assigned duties and have the possibility to develop professionally.

Regulating the Regulator

There is the possibility that regulators of the insurance market will act in the interest of insurers at the expense of policyholders. This section considers measures that can be put in place to regulate the regulators.

Employment Contracts

Employment contracts should clearly state that regulators will act in the interest of the public, and that a breach of this maxim will lead to termination.

Prohibition of Having Financial Interest in the Insurance Industry

There should be a regulation that prohibits a regulator from having any financial connection to any insurance business in terms of ownership, employment or consultancy or during or after having a regulatory position. This prevents any conflict of interest and hence ensures that the regulator will work on behalf of the public rather than for themselves. This will also help regulators focus on dealing with cases of bribery and corruption by insurance companies.

Sanctions

If regulators act in their own interest or that of insurers to the detriment of the public, insurance companies should be severely sanctioned. The government must make insurance companies aware of the repercussions of conniving with or bribing a regulator. If, for example, an audit shows that an insurance company has conspired with a regulator, the company's licence should be revoked. The regulator should, of course, be fired.

Grievances

There should be a mechanism through which policyholders can address their grievances directly to the regulator. The work of the regulator should also be subject to review by the public. By developing such a culture, the government will be able to ascertain information concerning regulators who indulge in fraudulent acts so that further investigations can be pursued and appropriate sanctions taken. In addition, insurance companies should be given the opportunity to seek redress. In situations where decisions were not properly handled, insurers should be given the opportunity to appeal and argue their case out. This will help the regulator address all grievances equally and make regulations that will generally protect everyone.

Legal Empowerment

Regulators should be given legal backing by governments to operate and sanction any insurance company that is caught flouting the rules. Regulators should work together with the law enforcement agencies such as the police.

Gifts

There should be a regulation that prohibits a regulator from accepting any material gifts in any form, whether cash or in kind from any insurance company. This will prevent a regulator from being bribed or biased and will maintain objectivity.

Monitoring

The activities of regulators should be monitored both internally and externally. Internally, an official should be appointed to oversee the activities of the regulator. An external body or watchdog should also be put in place to monitor regulators by requiring periodic reports to ensure transparency. Such reports should be thoroughly analysed to detect any discrepancies. External monitors can pay unannounced visits to see first-hand how work is being performed. By doing so, governments will come to know the strengths and weaknesses of the regulator and determine whether the regulator is diligently performing their duty.

Exercises

1. Discuss five reasons why the insurance market must be regulated.
2. State the bodies responsible for regulating insurers and briefly explain their responsibilities.
3. Regulators of the insurance market are agents of the insuring public. However, regulators can also be beneficiaries of regulation (i.e., they may seek their own interest at the expense of the insuring public). Explain four motivating influences that can help the regulator maximise value for policyholders.
4. State four insurance products that in your view must be made compulsory. Your answer should not include products that are already compulsory.
5. Discuss the reasons underlying the regulation of insurance products sold in the Ghanaian insurance market.
6. Some people purchase life insurance without notifying beneficiaries or contingent beneficiaries. Do you think there should be a law by parliament that compels insurers to notify beneficiaries upon the death of the insured? Discuss each point you provide.
7. Given the free Senior High School policy by the government of Ghana, would you recommend that parents or guardian purchase compulsory education policy for their wards? Provide 3 convincing arguments for your choice.
8. Consider the following insurance products sold on the Ghanaian insurance market:

   (i) Life insurance
   (ii) Educational policies
   (iii) Health insurance

   In each case provide two reasons why the product should be made compulsory.

References

Evans, A. (2000). *Liability, Risk and the Law* (1st ed.). The Institute of Risk Management, Witherby.
Harrington, S. E., & Niehaus, G. R. (2004). *Risk Management and Insurance*. McGraw-Hill.

Further Reading

Alemanno, R. (2015). *How Much Better Is Better Regulation?* Assessing the Impact of the Better Regulation Package on the European Union—A Research Agenda (HEC Paris Research Paper No. Law-2015-1119).

Black, K. J., & Skipper, H. D. J. (2000). *Life and Health Insurance* (13th ed., Chapter 35). Prentice Hall.

Brown, E. F. (2009). The Development of International Norms for Insurance Regulation. *Brooklyn Journal of International Law, 34*, 3.

Gupta, P. K. (2016). *Essentials of Insurance and Risk Management* (1st ed., Part IV: Chapter 16). Himalaya Publishing House Pvt Ltd., Mumbai.

Gupta, P. K. (2008). *Fundamental of Insurance* (1st ed., Unit 2: Chapter 4). Himalaya Publishing House, Mumbai.

Harrington, S. E., & Niehaus, G. R. (2004). *Risk Management and Insurance* (Chapter 6). McGraw-Hill.

Holyoake, J., & Weiper, W. (2002). *Insurance* (4th ed., Chapter 4), AITBS Education Books.

Brady, J. L. (1995). *The Regulation of Insurance* (1st ed.), Insurance Institute of America.

Lowry, J., & Rawlings, P. (2005). *Insurance Law. Doctrine and Principles* (2nd ed., p. 15f). Hart Publishing.

Redja, G. E., McNamara, J., & Rabel, W. H. (2022). *Principles of Risk Management and Insurance* (Chapter 8). Pearson Addison Wesley.

Vaughan, E. J., & Vaughan, T. M. (2008). *Fundamentals of Risk Management and Insurance* (10th ed., Chapter 6). Wiley.

Chapter 10
Premium and Claim Management

Abstract Effective management of premiums collected by insurers is critical to ensure that promised benefits are duly paid to policyholders. Claims management represents a central component of the insurance business, as the sustainability and reputation of an insurance company are closely linked to the efficiency and accuracy of its claims handling processes. This chapter examines the various avenues available to insurers for investing collected premiums and provides a detailed analysis of claims management. It explores the causes of delays in claim settlements, considering the roles of the insured, the insurer, and third-party actors, and identifies the factors that hinder third parties from performing their functions efficiently. The chapter further introduces the processes of liability determination and claims procedure. Finally, it outlines practical measures insurers can adopt to minimise delays, strategies to motivate third parties to expedite their responsibilities, and approaches for delivering high-quality service to policyholders.

Keywords and Phrases Claim · Claim delay · General insurance products · Life insurance products · Premium

Premium Management

One of the most critical decisions insurers must make on a regular basis is how to invest the premiums collected that are not immediately required for day-to-day operations. Since the pricing of insurance products incorporates the time value of money, insurers are obliged to invest these funds prudently to ensure they can meet future claims. Inflation further complicates this responsibility, as money collected today will inevitably lose value over time, making strategic investment essential. To maximise returns while safeguarding liquidity, insurers must carefully select investment avenues that align with the nature of the insurance products offered. For general insurance products, premiums are typically invested in short-term, easily redeemable instruments such as treasury bills, commercial paper, time-deposit accounts, and mutual funds. These options ensure that funds remain accessible to meet claims

C. Andoh, *Fundamentals of Managing Risk and Insurance*,
https://doi.org/10.1007/978-981-95-4581-0_10

that may arise in the near future. In contrast, life insurance products provide insurers with the opportunity to pursue long-term investments, given the extended duration of policyholder commitments. Such investments may include stocks, real estate, business financing, and venture capital, which offer the potential for higher returns over time. This section expands on the investment strategies available to insurers, beginning with options suited to general insurance products and then examining those appropriate for life insurance products. By exploring these avenues, the discussion highlights how insurers balance profitability, liquidity, and long-term sustainability in managing premium funds.

General Insurance Products

General insurance products offer policies that are usually short term or require the impromptu payment of claims. They include property, liability, marine and motor insurance. Because these contracts have a relatively short lifespan it is prudent to invest premiums in money market instruments or other investments that are easy to convert into cash at short notice to meet claims brought against the insurer. Some of these investment avenues include:

Treasury bills: These are short-term securities with no risk attached and are provided by governments either to raise funds or to reduce the amount of money in circulation. Since the government issues these securities, there is no default risk.

Commercial paper: These are short-term debt securities issued by financial companies or large corporations. The issuer promises the buyer a return, or profit, for making the loan. The return is stated as an interest rate or percentage of the loan, such as 5%. Companies sell commercial paper when they need a short-term loan to pay for such things as accounts payable and inventories. Insurers can choose this type of investment by buying commercial paper from organisations and earning profit in the form of interest on their loan usually redeemable within 6–9 months.

Certificate of deposit: A certificate of deposit (CD) is a savings certificate with a fixed maturity rate and specified fixed interest rate. A CD restricts access to the funds until the maturity date of the investment. After maturity the insurer will take back the money with interest any time it needs it.

Mutual funds: A mutual fund is an investment programme funded by a pool of investors who come together to trade in diversified holdings and is professionally managed. Profit or interest that might accrue is shared or distributed based on how much each investor has contributed. This investment option might run for a long period of time, but it is also appropriate for the investment of general insurance products premiums because the investor is free to withdraw their investment any time.

Savings accounts: Premiums can be put into a savings account to earn interest. The insurer will be able to withdraw funds any time claims are brought against it.

Time-deposit accounts: Some banks offer market-linked time-deposit accounts which offer potentially higher returns than savings accounts. A time deposit is an interest-bearing bank deposit that has a specified date of maturity. The insurer may, therefore, invest premiums in a time deposit for a specific amount of time.

Term deposits: A term deposit is a fixed-term deposit held at a financial institution. They are generally short-term deposits with maturities ranging anywhere from a month to a few years. When a term deposit is purchased, the client understands that the money can only be accessed after the term has ended or by giving a predetermined number of days' notice. Generally, term deposits are difficult to realise before they reach maturity and early withdrawal may come with higher costs.

Short-term loans: Insurers can advance loans with interest to individuals on short-term basis. When properly managed, the insurer should be able to ensure that it has adequate funds to meet its financial obligations.

Inventory loans: These are short-term loans made to businesses that are secured with the borrower's goods. The lender may take temporary custody of the borrower's goods and have the option to sell them if the borrower defaults. The lender may also keep the inventory at the borrower's premises or residence and hire someone to monitor the goods on their behalf. Due to the high liquidity of goods, such investments are ideal for short term.

Promissory note: These are signed legal documents that promise the holder that they will be paid a specified sum at a specified time. The notes are short-term debt instruments that vest in the holder the right to receive a cash payment at a specified time or on demand. An insurer can issue these notes to companies and call them when the need arises.

Forex market: An insurer can enter the foreign currency exchange business by using capital to purchase currencies that are relatively stable. This market is highly risky but with the requisite knowledge and experience, the funds invested can yield large returns. Currencies can be traded on an Electronic Communication Network (ECN) that matches buy and sell orders for securities without the need for a middleman.

Reinsurance: Reinsurance is also a form of investment for an insurance company. The primary insurer cedes the part of its risk that exceeds its retention limit to a reinsurance company based on an agreed format of premium and risk sharing. When a loss occurs, the reinsurance company reimburses its portion of the loss. Other benefits, such as availability of technical expertise, are made available to the primary insurer. This ensures that the primary insurer will have the funds available to cater for losses that exceed its retention limit.

Other business ventures: Insurers can invest in other business ventures that may not be capital intensive in nature, such as the distribution of goods internally or for exports. Trading in activities such as the sale of consumables such as rice, maize, wheat, etc., is one option for an insurance company. These goods are generally in high demand and consequently there should be funds available year-round to pay for claims.

Life Insurance Products

Life insurance products provide coverage for the life of an individual by paying a claim upon his or her death to the named beneficiaries. People buy such policies to provide for uncertainties that their dependants would experience on their demise. Premiums for such policies are paid monthly or yearly, usually for long periods of time before claims are realised. Due to the length of the claim tail, it makes sense for insurance companies to invest premiums in long-term products. Such avenues include shares, bonds, debentures, real estate and mortgages.

Shares: A share is a part ownership of a corporation. The owners of shares in a corporation are known as shareholders and they are entitled to periodic payments from the earnings of the share known as dividend. Shares do not have a maturity period and the insurer can sell shares to others whenever it wishes. Shares can be extremely rewarding if held over a long period of time. They can be acquired through private brokers or on the stock exchange. The insurer can either buy common stock that entitles the investor to a share in the company's profit through dividends and/or capital appreciation or preferred stock, which is less risky and typically has less potential for profit, offering a fixed dividend over a period.

Bonds: A bond is a long-term debt security offered by both governments and corporations to generate funds. The bond entitles the bondholder to periodic interest payments called coupons and the payment of the face amount upon maturity. Bonds are usually long-term investments and very often they are negotiable, that is, the ownership of the instrument can be transferred in the secondary market. A floating rate bond is a type of bond that ties coupon payments to economic factors such as inflation. It should be noted, however, that government bonds are risk free and so payment is assured. Corporate bonds, on the other hand, are subject to default risk and there is therefore the need to check the corporation's credit rating to assess its repayment capabilities.

Real estate: Investment in real estate is an important vehicle for life insurance product premiums. Real estate investment requires huge funds and can yield equally high returns with proper management. It involves the purchase or construction of buildings for rental to individuals and businesses. A typical example is the massive real estate development in Ghana by the Social Security and National Insurance Trust (SSNIT).

Mortgages: This is when properties such as buildings, machines and other valuables attached to land are given on a long-term loan and holders pay instalments for such properties as an annuity. That is, it is amortised for a period. This form of investment increases the cashflow for insurers availing insurers' liquid capital and increasing their working capital to finance claims.

Long-term loans: The insurer can utilise the premiums that it receives as long-term loans and earn interest on these. The insurer can lend money to banks, other financial institutions and reputable companies. The insurer can demand collateral so that if the borrower defaults, the insurer can sell the collateral to recover its capital.

Policy loans: These are loans, an insurance company provides to its policyholders using proceeds from their life insurance cover as collateral. The policyholder is expected to pay interest on the loan and the principal sum over the agreed period. These interest payments are investment income for the insurance company. Policy loans are usually given to life insurance holders.

Fixed-time savings accounts: Premiums collected can be invested in fixed-time savings accounts with commercial banks. The capital in an account can be withdrawn after a specified period and is a suitable investment for premiums from life insurance products.

Debentures: These are legislative instruments that show that an individual or entity is a creditor of a business. Since debenture (also called loan notes) holders are creditors of a firm, once a profit is declared, they are paid their share of the profit before any dividend is paid to shareholders. In fact, even when the firm makes a loss, debenture holders are paid. Debenture holders may sometimes be converted into shareholders of the borrowing company.

Venture capital: Life insurance companies can act as angel investors or set up a venture capital firm to assist promising businesses to get on their feet. There is a profit and cost sharing agreement between the venture capital company and the start-up business, and the investor will have a percentage stake in the new business. This can be a viable, though sometimes risky investment instrument for generating investment income for the life insurer.

Acquisitions and mergers: Life insurance companies by virtue of the large funds available to them can either acquire new companies or merge with other life insurance companies. The aim is to expand the scope and strength of the insurance company and solidify its dominance within the market.

General services: Insurers can use funds to build schools, hotels, restaurants, supermarkets and offer consultancy services from the premiums collected. The revenue generated from these activities can be very substantial.

Treasury notes: These are long-term investment instruments issued by governments that entitle the buyer to receive certain payments over a long period of time. It is a risk-free investment, just like treasury bills, but long-term.

Financial sector investment: Premiums collected can be invested in financial institutions, micro-lending institutions and even banks. Insurance companies have the skills to manage such investments.

Health facilities: Insurers can use the premiums collected to build and manage health facilities such as hospitals, clinics, pharmacies, gyms and other recreational centres that promote health. Such projects can help generate greater profits for life and health insurers as they promote healthier living and consequently reduce the long-term exposure of the insurer to claims.

Purchase and sale of precious stones: Premiums can be used to purchase precious stones such as gold and diamonds since these generally increase in value.

Leasing: An insurer can set up a subsidiary to engage in the leasing of assets to businesses or the public to generate income.

Transport sector: One lucrative venture for insurers, at least in some developing countries, is the transport sector. An insurer can set up a subsidiary to handle its transport business, which might involve moving freight, people or selling cars. Although, such an investment is capital intensive, it provides a regular flow of income.

Highway construction: In countries where there is a significant infrastructure deficit, this is another opportunity for investment. A subsidiary could be created that enters a partnership with a government to construct highways and install toll booths to recoup the investment.

Funeral homes: A subsidiary can also be created to set up and manage a funeral home. Funeral homes can be built to take care of the needs of the funeral activities of people. The home will provide all the things needed for funerals from casket, food, hearse and so on. This will provide the insurer with a regular source of income.

Subsidiary insurance companies: An insurance company can invest in the opening of a subsidiary company that trades in other profitable insurance ventures. New insurance products that have been neglected by the market can be introduced once approval from the appropriate authorities has been received.

Claim Management

Claim management is a critical pillar of the insurance business, as the long-term survival of any insurer depends largely on how effectively claims are handled. Prompt settlement of claims not only fulfills the insurer's contractual obligations but also serves as a powerful marketing tool. Policyholders often judge the true value of their insurance coverage by the speed and fairness with which their claims are processed. For major clients, particularly corporate entities, the claim payment history of an insurer is a decisive factor in awarding large contracts or placing substantial business. A claim delay refers to the period between the notification of a claim and its eventual settlement. Such delays typically arise from verification procedures designed to confirm the authenticity of the claim. Responsibility for delays may rest with the insurer, the insured, or third parties who are indirectly involved in the claims process. These third parties may include vehicle testing officers, police, medical practitioners, courts, reinsurers, claim adjustors, or fire service personnel, whose investigations and reports are often necessary before a claim can be finalised. It is therefore important for clients to appreciate that delays are not always attributable to the insurer alone. No insurer deliberately postpones the payment of a valid claim, as doing so would undermine the fundamental social and contractual purpose of insurance, protecting the insured against loss. Moreover, prolonged delays generally increase the overall cost of claims for the insurer, creating a strong incentive to settle valid claims efficiently. Ultimately, claims can only be honoured when the loss or damage sustained falls within the scope of coverage defined by the policy.

Insurers, the Insured and Claim Delays

Although most companies may wish to pay claims as fast as possible to prevent increased costs there are reasons why delays take place in the settlement of losses. These include:

Late Notification of the Loss by the Insured

When a loss occurs but the insured fails to notify the insurer quickly, there will be a delay because the evidence or necessary information needed for claim processing may not be readily available. Early notification allows the insurer to investigate the loss while it is still fresh and to suggest measures that will prevent future losses.

Disputes About the Amount Recoverable Under the Policy

In a case where there is a dispute about the amount to be paid to the insured, there will be a delay. Such a disagreement might occur when the terms of the contract may not have been fully understood by the insured because of the technical nature in which it was written. Both parties will need an appraiser who will decide on how much should be paid after inspecting the loss. If no agreement is reached, an umpire will be invited to take a final decision. Delays can also occur when there is a dispute about whether the policy purchased covers the loss.

Financial Constraints on the Part of the Insurer

The insurer may not have sufficient funds to cover a large loss because of recent large payments to other claimants. Most insurance companies are not able to cover unexpected large losses that they do not expect. Thus, when such losses occur, they have to seek support from their reinsurance company or other sources of funding and this may affect the speed of claim payments. This situation usually arises when the insurance company takes out either facultative reinsurance or facultative treaty reinsurance to cover the risk with a reinsurer (see Redja (2008), pp. 118). Improper financial management on the part of the insurer can also cause temporary liquidity problems hampering its ability to settle claims quickly. For example, if an insurer invests in long-term securities and needs to realise those investments to settle claims, delays can arise. This situation can also come about when there is a major natural disaster or systemic loss and the insurer has to honour many claims within a relatively short time horizon.

Delays in Investigating Claims

Major claims by customers need careful investigation before payments are made and this can take a considerable amount of time. This slows down the claim settlement process and causes delay. Some insured entities conceal the true events that led to a loss, and if the insurance company suspects this to be the case they may hold back until the full facts are known before further action is taken. If an insured entity was negligent or the insurer believes that a claim may be fraudulent, there will be delays as investigations ensue. If, for example, notification of a loss by the insured was deliberately delayed eliminating evidence indicating negligence or fraud, long investigations are likely.

Delays in Accessing Relevant Documents or Information

To pay claims the insurer must have access to the relevant documents to validate the occurrence of a loss. For instance, under a life insurance policy, a police report, post-mortem or death certificate would be needed. In the case of a motor insurance claim, depending on the type of cover provided, a police accident report form, the driving licence of the insured person, a repair estimate, a medical report, photographic evidence of the accident or the damaged vehicle and an assessment of damage report from the insurer may be needed. For a fire claim, a fire officer's report will be needed. Delays in acquiring this documentation could culminate in delays to claim settlements. Also, when the insured fails to give all the material facts concerning a loss, the insurer will investigate to discover the true value of the loss. In the case of a serious incident or accident where the insured is the victim of a loss and the person may not be in the right state of mind to give accurate information on what transpired to the insurer, causing eventual delays in the payment of a claim.

Centralisation

Some insurance companies are centralised in nature. Thus, claims made at branch offices must be forwarded to the head office for processing. This could be time consuming leading to delays in claim settlements.

Legal Requirements

In some cases, before a claim can be finalised a pending court case must first be settled. In other cases, there are disputes about who should receive the benefits of a claim. This might, for example, be in the case of a life insurance policy where the will of the deceased person is disputed. In such cases, the claim is paid to the court to make the final decision, but such procedures can take a long time.

Technological Deficiencies

If the insurer does not have an adequate system to store and retrieve the information of its customers via a database, then the claim settlement process can be very slow. Lack of requisite technologies such as drones for collecting information quickly from an accident scene can result in delays in claim settlement.

Lack of Knowledge on Claim Procedures

If the claimant does not have a clear idea about how to make a claim, problems arise. The tendency of some insurers to focus solely on the selling of a policy and not on offering full and clear information on how to proceed should a loss occur, may result in an insured person not using the right channels, forms or procedures when making a claim, causing delay.

Inadequacy of Claim Inspectors

When an insurance company does not have sufficient qualified surveyors to investigate a loss (particularly a very large loss), it may need to bring in personnel from other cities or even abroad, resulting in a slow process.

Discrimination on the Part of the Insurer

Some insurers prioritise the claims of important clients to the detriment of others at times when there are issues with their capacity to deal with multiple claims.

Long-Tailed Liabilities

Insurers that offer liability insurance may see claims come in a long time after a claim event occurs. For example, a patient may sue a doctor months after a surgery if he or she thinks that medical malpractice has been involved. The long settlement period associated with liability insurance is the result of a variety of factors. Liability insurance claims can be for larger sums of money than other insurance claims and may result in settlement offers as well as court cases. The insurance company will also want to examine the claim thoroughly to ensure that it is being made in good faith and is not fraudulent.

Lack of Cooperation from the Insured

Sometimes, the insured may be reluctant to provide answers to important questions from third parties such as the police, fire officers, etc., to enable the quick processing of reports needed by insurers. This attitude obviously affects the speed of claim settlement.

Insurance companies need to know that the slow payment of claims creates unsatisfied customers who are likely to share their experiences with friends and family and potentially the media. This creates reputational damage for insurers. On the other hand, a satisfied customer can create good publicity for an insurer. Mechanisms must be put in place to ensure that claims do not take more time than necessary to be processed. The fair and prompt payment of claims promotes the fundamental social and contractual purpose of protecting the insured and maintains the reputation of an insurance company.

Third Party's Contributions to Claim Delays

Before an insurer decides to pay a claim, it must verify that the covered loss has happened. Investigations must be conducted into what caused the loss and whether this cause is specified in the insurance contract. These investigations are carried out by investigators such as police, medical and fire officers and other third parties not directly involved in the contract. The insurer will want to know if there was any kind of moral hazard or whether the loss was intentionally caused. Moral hazard can increase the frequency and/or the severity of loss. For instance, a person may insure a family member's life as the beneficiary and murder him/her to collect the policy proceeds. An insured person with property insurance may burn down his/her house to benefit from the insurance policy. Such attempts to defraud the insurance company require investigation by the insurer as the insurer has to wait for reports from investigators and this could lead to delays. In the following section, we discuss how third parties can contribute to delays in claim payments.

Medical Officers

Doctors can delay claim payments through the late delivery of autopsy reports. As life insurance policies contain exclusions explicitly stating that certain conditions or types of death (such as suicide) are not covered, autopsy reports are often required. In addition, there are instances where the insured person may conspire with the beneficiary to fake their own death to get access to the sum assured. Therefore, the insurer will need to determine, possibly through an autopsy report to ensure that the deceased person really is the insured. If a medical officer has difficulty in determining the cause of death after the autopsy is performed this can cause the claim to be delayed.

In the case of health insurance, the drugs prescribed to the insured (or medical procedures undertaken) need to be verified by a doctor to ensure that the expenses incurred to treat a determined illness are correctly accounted for. The insurer will also want proof from a medical practitioner that any claim made is not for a pre-existing condition, as this would be excluded from the health insurance policy. In addition, the insurer will require the medical officer to verify that the insured event occurred as proclaimed by the insured. All these examinations and reports take time to complete. Medical reports are also sometimes not conclusive and a second or third opinion may be needed which will evidently lengthen the whole claim process.

Police Officers

Claim payments can be delayed if the police do not conduct speedy investigations in the case of theft and burglary. With property insurance, for example, people sometimes make false claims by deliberately arranging for valuables to be stolen to claim from the insurer.

Fire Officers

If fire service reports do not provide the definitive cause of a fire at an insured property or when their investigations into the cause are inconclusive, insurance companies can delay the payment of claims as policies stipulate that a fire should not be caused by the negligence of the insured. In the case of major or catastrophic fires, fire insurance personnel are mandated to make appropriate suggestions to avoid a reoccurrence. When the cause of the fire outbreak remains unclear, claims will be delayed and only settled when the report issued by the fire service has been received.

Delayed Court Proceedings

Some losses may require court involvement to verify the payment of claims. If a liability claim is made against an insured person or entity and this involves legal matters, the outcome of the claim will be based on the verdict of the judge. This can be a very lengthy process. In cases where there is a dispute between the insurer and the insured on the value of the insurance policy, arbitration may be required. In the worst-case scenario, such disputes need to be resolved by the courts. In many countries this is a slow process.

Other third parties could also be involved in the resolution of a claim in the courts. For example, witnesses to events related to the loss. In the case of someone with life insurance being murdered, a court case would ensue with witnesses called. No claim resolution would be possible until the court case was concluded.

Members of the Public

The public can interfere in the investigations of authorities when losses occur and hamper their rapid conclusion. For example, in the event of a fire, people may enter the area to collect remains, salvage property or loot. This can slow down investigations concerning the cause of the accident and subsequently delay claim payments.

Investments

Insurers invest the premiums they receive in line with the time value of money incorporated in the pricing of their products. When huge claims are made, there might be the need to convert some investments into cash to pay claimants. Delays caused by converting investments into cash or by slow functioning of the banking system can have an impact on the speed in which claims are settled.

Government Restrictions

In certain situations, when a loss occurs, government regulations may not grant third parties, including the representatives of insurance companies, access to the most affected areas so that any evidence is not disturbed. It may also be the case that third parties, when granted access, are compelled by law to keep some details secret. All of this put obstacles in the path of a smooth and timely investigation of a claim.

Reinsurers

When a large loss occurs and exceeds the retention limit of the insurer, the insurer may need its reinsurers to assist in the payment of claims. This may take some time especially if the reinsurer is incapable of paying the entire loss. When this happens, the insured must wait till the insurer has access to the needed capital to pay out.

Property Valuations

If an insured property is destroyed or damaged by fire or some other calamity, a valuation must establish its worth at the time of the loss. Valuation experts are third parties entrusted with this task. This process can be complex and may result in delays to the claim especially when there is partial destruction of the property.

Creditors

When the policyholder is in debt complications can arise that delay the settlement of claims. For example, if the policyholder is operating under bankruptcy law, creditors may be entitled to the proceeds of insurance policies at maturity rather than the stated beneficiary. Tax officials might also make claims against a person's estate including the value of a realised insurance policy in the case of unpaid taxes.

Disputed Beneficiaries

When there are disputes over the beneficiaries of an insurance policy, delays are almost certain. This may happen because of a contested will. The insurer will have to investigate the matter and if no easy resolution is possible pay the proceeds to a court for a decision on the rightful recipient.

Costs of Third Parties

Claim payments can be delayed because of exorbitant fees charged by third parties. Most third parties think that insurers have very deep pockets and so they charge high fees for the services they render. If there is also the possibility that a third party can be held liable for carrying out their role negligently under the principle of subrogation, they will conduct their investigations in a stringent and time-consuming manner. It may also transpire that because of confidentiality rules, third parties withhold information that is critical to the insurer in deciding whether to pay a claim or not. Lack of logistics or skilled personnel for investigations can hamper the work of third parties. In other cases, conflicting reports provided by different third parties mean that the insurer must withhold claim payments until all discrepancies are ironed out. When third parties are direct beneficiaries of insurance policies, the insurance company will likely investigate any conflict of interest before paying claims. In addition, if third parties are involved in the cause of a loss, they might be reluctant to issue a report that would implicate them. Third parties might also become involved in court proceedings. For example, the survivor of a motor accident could issue a court order challenging the settlement made to them by the insured's insurers. An attempt to deal with this by the insurer can delay the insured's claim settlement.

There can be disagreements between third parties and the insurer about the cause of a loss. Such disagreements can arise when the findings of a third-party point to a cause that is different from what the insurers own investigation reveals. Also, unforeseen circumstances such as strike action or natural disasters can prevent third parties from providing the insurer with needed information in a timely fashion.

Problems may also occur when a beneficiary is mentally unfit. Such a beneficiary may need to have to prove their mental fitness through treatment with a doctor or psychiatrist.

Fraudulent Reports

In some cases, the insurer will have to employ the services of private investigators, agents and medical officers to verify the findings of the original reports. This is because there are numerous cases where third parties conspire with policyholders to inflate or make fraudulent claims. This is a time-consuming process, in effect duplicating the original work, and evidently causing delays to claim payments even if the original reports are proven to be correct. Contradictory reports produced by third parties will also lead to further investigations. A third-party report may also flag up a potential issue pointing to the culpability of the insured for a loss. Again, such a report will require additional investigation.

Bribery and Corruption

When an insured entity bribes a third party to produce an inaccurate report of an investigation to boost the value of the claim and this is discovered by the insurance company, the process will be delayed. Insurers expecting a high claim cost can also bribe third parties to conduct a shoddy investigation to minimise their loss exposure.

Delays in Allowing the Insurer to Inspect Damaged Items or Access the Accident Scene

If the police, for example, fail to allow the insurer to inspect a damaged vehicle quickly, a claim for the damage to the vehicle will be delayed. Also, when the police prevent loss adjustors from accessing or visiting the scene of an accident to ascertain its cause, there are delays.

In conclusion, third parties, though not directly involved in the insurance contract can cause, for a myriad of reasons, delays in the payment of claims.

Problems Encountered by Third Parties

As we have seen when a loss occurs, third parties investigate to ascertain the cause. However, many factors make it difficult to undertake this work. In this section, we examine some of the issues and reasons that hamper their work.

Logistics, Equipment and Funds

When third parties lack the state-of-the-art technology, adequate funds or logistics required to complete complicated investigations, then their work will be hindered. For example, police officers may not have the devices needed to ascertain the cause of a car accident. Technology is needed to determine the speed that a vehicle was travelling at the time of the accident. They may also need fast communication and access to a rapid internet network and this may not be possible at the accident scene. In the case of a stolen car, the police may not have the human resources, time or available vehicles to track it down. The availability of funds is also important. For example, if a substantial amount of money is needed for a test to be conducted so that a credible report can be obtained on a person's health status and there are no funds for it, no reported can be provided.

Lack of Cooperation from Related Parties

When involved parties in a loss, such as witnesses, are reluctant to provide material information to third parties, investigations can be compromised. In a road accident, this may be because the driver at fault does not wish to admit to culpability and provides a false account to investigators. Anyone who is potentially negatively affected by an investigation, such as someone who has conspired in an incident to create a loss, will attempt to sabotage the work of third parties.

Poor Coordination Between Third Parties

Various third parties may be involved in the investigation of a covered loss and problems will occur if there is not good coordination between them. For example, the death of someone with a life insurance policy may need an autopsy to be performed and a medical report issued before the police can commence their investigations. Similarly, in the case of a fire, the report from fire officers will be needed to inform the police whether further action is needed.

Court Injunctions

A court injunction can also hinder the investigations by third parties. In situations where the insured is involved in a court case that freezes his or her assets, investigations will need to wait until the case is settled. There may also be a situation where a court believes that an investigation may reveal sensitive information to the security of a country and therefore prevents third parties from proceeding.

Lack of Skilled Personnel

If third parties such as the police lack the needed experts, skills or manpower, investigations into a covered loss will be compromised. For example, if evidence is damaged because of the incompetency of an investigator, the process will be compromised.

Scope of Loss

When the type of loss reported has rarely happened in the past or is completely new, an investigation is likely to be slow because there are few if any precedents for investigators to follow.

Record Keeping

The lack of proper record keeping can mean that investigators do not have the necessary information to proceed. For example, an inventory of items at a business facility can help determine the number of items lost in the case of a robbery or a fire. If the inventory does not exist, the investigation will likely take more time.

Complexity of the Loss

When a very large loss occurs and has other consequential losses, investigations can be impeded because investigators or other third parties need time to discover and verify the true cause.

Late Notification of Loss by the Insured

It is the responsibility of the insured to advise the insurer that a loss has occurred and make a claim. When the covered loss is reported long after the event (for example, the consequences of a botched medical procedure), it will hamper third parties from gathering enough evidence for their report to be sent to the insurer.

Reluctance of a Beneficiary or an Insured Entity to Cooperate

A beneficiary may be unwilling to provide information about a covered loss. For example, the beneficiary to a life insurance policy may have been involved in the death of the insured and will therefore provide false information. Investigations can also be hampered by an insured person's unwillingness to provide—or deliberate attempt to conceal—evidence that may prove their culpability for a loss. False or incomplete information provided by the insured or beneficiary will greatly mar the success of an investigation. Some policyholders also conspire with third parties such as police officers to alter evidence found at the scene of an incident in order to defraud the insurer.

Interference from the Public

Sometimes, when an accident occurs, people gather at the scene to look at what is happening. These people may simply be a nuisance to first responders, but they may also disturb the scene, remove evidence or loot which will create problems for investigators.

Contradictory Reports from Witnesses

When eyewitnesses provide contradictory versions of an incident, the job of the investigator is complicated.

Accessibility

Difficulties in accessing an accident scene can hamper the efforts of investigators. Bad or non-existent road or other transport networks mean that investigators cannot do their work easily. When the people who matter to the investigation are unwilling to make themselves available to the third party, it hampers investigations. For example, if a doctor asks the insured person to report to the hospital on an agreed day and time for a blood test and the insured does not come, this will slow the doctor's investigation. Investigative work can involve locating key witnesses to talk to. If such people are not easily accessible to investigators, they will need to spend time trying to find them.

Religious Beliefs

Medical officers face many challenges in determining the cause of death due to religious beliefs. For example, the dead body of a Muslim is not supposed to undergo an autopsy. As this may be the only way of determining the cause of death, the medical officer may not be able to offer a definitive conclusion.

Knowledge of Insurance Business

Some third parties lack knowledge about the insurance market and may not know how essential their investigation is to the claimer and the insurance company. For this reason, they may not attach any sense of urgency or importance to the function.

Workload

In many cases, a heavy workload is a delaying factor for third parties. Completing the paperwork on an insurance claim may not be high on their list of everyday priorities. For example, a court may have many cases to settle and hence keep adjourning a suit related to verifying the events that led to a loss and a subsequent insurance claim.

Poor Remuneration

When third parties are not well motivated in terms of having a good salary and incentives to do their job well, they may not be enthused to carry out investigations adequately. At times, some third parties intentionally delay investigations to prompt parties to pay bribes to facilitate the investigation process.

Complications in Determining Medical Conditions

Determining whether a medical condition is valid under the terms of a particular insurance policy could pose a challenge to a medical officer. For example, if the insured claims against a pre-existing condition, the doctor would need to be aware of this. Some claimants may try to make false claims, for example, by stating that they have a disability when none exists.

Incapacity of Key Witnesses

A key witness may be seriously injured in an accident that leads to an insurance claim and may therefore not be able to give an account of what happened.

The Liability Determination Process

An insurer when handling claims must establish whether a legal liability has arisen and whether or not the loss that has taken place is in breach of any policy conditions. Before claims are paid, it is imperative that a claims adjustor conducts thorough investigations to determine the extent of liability of the insurer. Firstly, the claim must be verified. In claim verification, it is of great importance to have proof of a loss—a statement made and signed by the claimant confirming the loss occurrence. The insurer must then ask questions that it has about the circumstances of the loss to prevent fraudulent or excessive claims that will invariably raise premium rates for the insured—and potentially, in the case of a large claim, the whole insured pool. Some of the important questions that a claim adjustor needs to ask include the following:

Is What Caused the Accident the Insured Peril?

This question is important because the insured can only recover a loss under their policy if a named peril in the policy is the cause of loss. Some perils are not covered, and the insurer would not settle a claim in such a case.

Was the Policy in Force When the Accident Occurred?

If a loss occurred either before a policy came into force or after it expired, the insurer will not be liable to a claim. Thus, if the client's policy ended a day before an accident occurred, the insurer will not be liable. A common example is motor insurance that is usually renewed annually. Some policyholders may overlook the renewal process and be uninsured when a loss take place.

Is the Loss Covered Under the Policy?

Every insurance policy contains an operative clause that specifies exactly what is covered under the policy. Thus, if the loss sustained by the policyholder is not specified, the insurer cannot be held liable.

Did the Loss Occur Within the Insured Territory?

If the policy was restricted to the country in which the policyholder is resident, then the insured cannot file for a loss that occurred in another country.

Was There Compliance with All the Terms and Conditions of the Contract?

Every insurance contract has conditions that, if violated, will make the policy void. For a motor insurance policy for example, the claim adjuster must establish whether the car was being driven by the insured person, was speeding, was overloaded or if the driver was intoxicated, among other things.

Was the Accident Reported to the Police or Was There Any Negligence?

An insured person must report any loss to the police. In the case of a motor accident, the police will investigate, and their report will determine the cause. If it is discovered that a negligent third party caused the accident, then the subrogation right will exist for the insurer to recover the loss of the policyholder from them. On the other hand, if it is found that the claimant was negligent, then the insurer does not owe its client anything. For example, if the claimant was drunk while driving or failed to wear a seatbelt then this negligence makes the contract void.

Has the Premium Been Paid in Full?

An individual only has full insurance coverage once the premium has been paid in full (unless an easy payment scheme has been enacted). If full payment has not been made the loss may not be covered under the policy.

Is the Claim Fraudulent?

One objective of the claim settlement process is to establish that there is no intent to defraud the insurer with a false claim. The loss adjustor must be satisfied that the claimant did not intentionally cause an accident or loss to defraud the insurer. This is to prevent moral hazard.

Should the Claim Be Negotiated?

The loss adjuster must ensure that they provide the optimum compensation to the insured and nothing above it. This is in line with the principle of indemnity where the insured should be returned to a financial state prior to the loss but should not make a profit on a claim. Thus, the loss adjuster must determine the extent of the damage and negotiate with the insured so that the correct amount of compensation is paid out.

Was the Insurer Notified Within the Stipulated Time as Specified in the Policy?

If there is a clause in the policy that requires policyholders to notify the insurer within a stipulated time limit after the occurrence of a loss and the insured fails to abide by this condition, then the insurer cannot be held liable.

Is the Extent of Loss Within the Policy Limit?

Here the loss adjustor will verify whether the loss that occurred is within the financial limits stipulated in the policy. If the loss incurred exceeds the limit, the insurer cannot be held liable for the excess.

In the case of motor insurance additional questions that need to be asked include:

Was the Driver Physically Impaired at the Time of the Accident?

People with conditions such as epilepsy and other types of afflictions that can cause physical impairment are generally not permitted to drive. Should a loss occur because of a fit, for example, the insurer cannot be held liable.

How Many Passengers Were in the Vehicle at the Time of the Accident?

Every insured vehicle has a stipulated use: either for private or commercial purposes. If a privately insured vehicle is used for commercial purposes and an accident occurs, third-party injuries will not be covered by the insurer.

The Claim Procedure

In administering a claim, there are a number of steps in the process. We discuss these below.

Claim Notification

The first step is for the insured person or entity to inform the insurer about an event which will lead to a claim. Normally, this must be done using an official claim form and be signed and dated by the insured.

Initial Response

After the insurer has been notified of the claim, they should respond to the claimant in writing or acknowledge receipt of the claim by telephone or email.

Investigation

The third step is the investigation into the circumstances that led to the loss. The insurer has the responsibility of visiting the site of the incident or accident so that it can confirm that its policy covers the event that led to the loss and that the claim is valid. The insurer will ask a number of questions (as discussed above) in response to the explanation of the loss outlined on the claim form. Reports may be requested from third parties such as medics or the police.

Final Response

Once the investigation has been completed, the insurer will notify the insured person or entity of the outcome and whether the loss is covered. If there are third parties involved and threatening court action, this decision process may be lengthier.

Settlement of the Amount

Once an insurer determines that it is liable for the loss, a settlement offer will be made. If this is unacceptable to the insured, a period of negotiation may commence.

Practical Steps for Insurers to Avoid Delays in Dealing with Claims

The efficiency of the claim process largely determines how customers value the services of insurers. A slow or inefficient claim settlement process sends bad signals to the insuring public and can be costly to everyone involved in an insurance contract. Therefore, it is very important for an insurer to know how to handle claims efficiently. Some of the practical steps that can be undertaken by an insurer to ensure good practice that avoids unnecessary delays are enumerated below.

Despatch Team

A despatch or claim response team should be established by the claim department and charged with the responsibility for visiting accident scenes, organising documentation, obtaining evidence and verifying or asking for further investigation on claims that have been reported. If such a team is in place, when a claim is submitted for which the insurance company is liable; the necessary information will be ready allowing for a speedy settlement.

Claim Monitoring

The loss adjustor of the claim department should monitor the progress of claim files as they move from desk to desk so that there are no undue delays. A computerised claim monitoring system should be set up if not already in existence to ensure that this process runs smoothly.

Good Relationships with Agencies Involved in Claim Settlements

An insurance company should have cordial relationships with agencies such as the police, fire service and professionals in the medical field whose reports may be needed for claim settlements to proceed smoothly. When this is the case, third-party reports are likely to be submitted in a timely manner, allowing for the fast resolution of the claims process.

Speeding up the Claim Notification Process

Claim request forms should be made available online for policyholders. If internet access is a problem (for example, in rural areas) the company can despatch claim forms to policyholders using a courier firm. In addition, an insurance company can educate its policyholders through the media or via publicity materials or workshops about the need to notify the company as fast as possible when a covered loss occurs.

Naming of Beneficiaries in Life Insurance Products

Delays in the settlement of claims sometimes arise because policyholders who purchase life insurance products do not name their beneficiaries properly. Therefore, it is important that policyholders are educated to name their beneficiaries specifically during the underwriting process. The underwriting department of the insurer should ensure that all clients name their beneficiaries (including contingent beneficiaries) before a policy is executed.

Local Branches

An insurance company should equip its local branches or outlets to handle claim settlements so that customers, especially those with small claims, do not necessarily have to visit the headquarters for their claims to be paid. Empowering local branches is also an effective way of combatting over-centralisation in the insurance industry.

Good Working Conditions for Members of the Claim Department

To ensure that claims are dealt with efficiently and effectively it is important that the management of an insurance company reward their employees competitively. Consequently, good working conditions, good salaries and bonuses and good retirement packages all contribute to a well-motivated workforce.

Triggers for Third Parties to Deal with Claims Faster

Third parties such as police, medical and fire officers, the courts and witnesses, among others, all affect the timing of claim settlements. Their reports and judgements are needed to complete the claim process. Certain conditions can motivate third parties to carry out their investigations speedily in the occurrence of a covered loss. We discuss some of these conditions below.

Good Remuneration

A third party will carry out investigations speedily if they are well remunerated by their employers. Other incentives such as bonuses will also help to encourage third parties to work speedily.

Fast Notification of Loss by the Insured

Fast notification of a loss by the insured person or entity will allow the insurance company to notify the appropriate third parties so that investigations can be carried out immediately. This will likely mean that a claim is settled earlier. For example, in the case of a burglary, the police should investigate the scene of the crime for evidence as soon as possible to avoid contamination. In the case of a fire, the faster that the fire service investigates, the more likely they are to determine the cause of the fire.

Availability of Expertise, Resources and Logistics for Third Parties

Some investigations can be extremely complex. If a third party has the requisite expertise in the type of work to be executed, it will carry out investigations quickly. A medical officer, for example may need the services of a specialist to ensure that a report is sufficiently factual. If the investigators do not have the right personnel on their team, the process will stall. Resources are also important. The same medical officer may need to use an expensive piece of technology to ascertain the cause of death. Insurance companies can assist in providing resources as part of their corporate social responsibility programme.

Pressure from Other Third Parties

Investigations can be accelerated by the influence of another third party. For example, if the judge in a court case requests that evidence be provided by third parties such as medics or fire officers, they will be under pressure to deliver their reports quickly for the trial case to continue. The court can also give an order to a hospital for certain findings to assist in the verification of a claim.

Legal Requirements

It is a legal obligation for third parties in certain fields such as the police, fire and medical profession to investigate the cause of loss. Failure to discharge that duty diligently can result in dismissal.

Accountability

Third parties are accountable to their superiors. The presence of a supervisor will ensure that investigations are carried smoothly and quickly. Accountability should also ensure transparency and therefore efficiency in the investigative process.

Public Interest in a Loss

If a claim is of public interest or the loss is widely publicised it will likely compel third parties to reach speedy conclusions to their investigations; for example, a bombing carried out by terrorists that takes lives and destroys property. In this case, investigations must be carried out quickly to discover if there is a threat to other buildings.

Working Environment

The working environment plays a crucial role in the performance of any worker. A third party will work quickly on an investigation if the working environment is calm and friendly and there is a good working relationship between members of the various units in an organisation. A bad working environment will stifle the work of investigators because they need the cooperation of others for their work to be successful.

Contractual Basis

When a third party is engaged on a strict contractual basis to investigate a covered loss, the likelihood that they will deliver a report on time is higher.

Information

High quality and reliable information about a loss will ensure that investigations can be conducted without too many complications. In a case where a witness or the insured is reluctant to provide reliable information, investigations will stall. Third parties may require information from the insurer, the insured and/or eyewitnesses to gain a full picture of an incident.

Cumbersome Nature of Investigations

Third parties will be willing to cooperate with investigations if the process is not too cumbersome. Sometimes eyewitnesses to a crime fail to come forward because of the stress in making a police statement and having to later testify in court.

Providing Great Service to the Insured

The insurer should ensure that claims are promptly investigated and settled as quickly as possible. Insurance companies should make its existing policyholders aware of the challenges they face while trying to settle a claim. Claimants get frustrated when they perceive that the insurer is doing nothing after their initial notification of a claim. Providing such information to clients can alleviate their concerns and avoid bad word of mouth for the insurance company.

An insurer can also provide personal assistance to its clients who have reported losses. For example, in the case of a fire, the claim adjustor can suggest loss reduction measures and loss control measures to prevent a reoccurrence of the loss and/or minimise the impact of a future loss should it occur. This will boost the image of the insurer as a trusted partner of its clients and as a provider of good customer service. Companies that provide such value-added services are likely to be successful in the market as their clients recommend them to peers.

An insurer should be completely transparent about its processes for claim handling in all interactions with its clients, whether these are in person or online. This will help to inform clients and prospective customers that the insurer is not out to simply collect premiums but to effectively settle legitimate claims. The company should also make clear in its policy proposals, its offices and on its website, all activities on the part of the insured that will prevent the settlement of a claim such as a misrepresentation, concealment of material facts and false warranties.

Insurers should create proposal forms and policy documents that are easily understood and interpretable. The conditions and the exclusions of the policy should be clearly stated so that customers have no doubts about what is permissible. As more policyholders comply with the terms of the contract, an insurer will experience less court cases.

An insurer can organise events and programmes to inform people on the basic tenets of insurance—both the advantages and potential disadvantages. Customers should be encouraged to ask questions, to learn and to leave events better informed.

The standard time for the payment of claims should be communicated to the insured. If the insurer, then does not pay a legitimate claim within this period compensation should be paid to the client. That is, an amount should be paid to the policyholder to compensate them for any inconvenience that may have been caused because of the delay in processing their claim, in addition to the actual claim cost. This will reassure policyholders and send good signals to prospective clients.

Exercises

1. To ensure that an insurer meets its obligations under an insurance contract, premiums collected must be prudently invested. Explain four productive investment options for the premiums collected by an insurer in each of the following:

    a. General insurance products
    b. Life insurance products

2. Discuss how each of the following third parties can contribute to delays in settling claims.

    a. Fire officers
    b. Police officers
    c. Bankers
    d. Law courts
    e. Beneficiaries

3. Discuss five factors that hamper third parties (i.e., police officers, medical officers, fire officers, etc.) from carrying out their investigations into claims.
4. Discuss three instances where the following third party's actions can be costly to an insurance company.

    a. Fire officers
    b. Medical officers
    c. Police officers

5. Explain how the actions of the insured can be costly to the insurer in the process of a claim.
6. You are the loss adjustor of a large insurance company. What practical steps would you undertake to ensure that claims are speedily settled?
7. Explain under what conditions a third party (i.e., police officer, medical officer, fire officer, etc.) will carry out investigations into a loss speedily.
8. Discuss four ways by which insurance companies can provide good service to their clients.
9. One of the major concerns of purchasers of insurance products is the willingness or ability of an insurer to honour its side of the contract without lengthy court wrangling when a loss occurs. Discuss three strategies that can be employed by an insurance company to reassure prospective policyholders.

Reference

Redja, G. E. (2008). Principles of risk management and insurance, (10th ed.). Boston, MA: Pearson Addison Wesley.

Further Reading

Black, K. J., & Skipper, H. D. J. (2000). *Life and Health Insurance* (13th ed.), Upper Saddle River, NJ: Prentice Hall. *Chapter 10, 24.*

Redja, G. E., McNamara, J. & Rabel, W. H. (2022). *Principles of Risk Management and Insurance.* Boston, MA: Pearson Addison Wesley. *Chapter 5.*

Index

C. Andoh, *Fundamentals of Managing Risk and Insurance*,
https://doi.org/10.1007/978-981-95-4581-0

T

U

V

MIX
Papier aus verantwortungsvollen Quellen
Paper from responsible sources
FSC® C105338

If you have any concerns about our products,
you can contact us on
ProductSafety@springernature.com

In case Publisher is established outside the EU,
the EU authorized representative is:
Springer Nature Customer Service Center GmbH
Europaplatz 3, 69115 Heidelberg, Germany

Printed by Libri Plureos GmbH
in Hamburg, Germany